KOREATOWN, NYC

ASIAN AMERICAN SOCIOLOGY SERIES
General Editor: Anthony Christian Ocampo

Japanese Americans and the Racial Uniform: Citizenship, Belonging, and the Limits of Assimilation
Dana Y. Nakano

Brown and Gay in LA: The Lives of Immigrant Sons
Anthony Christian Ocampo

Out of Place: The Lives of Korean Adoptee Immigrants
SunAh M Laybourn

Koreatown, NYC: The Consumption of a Transnational Brand
Jinwon Kim

Koreatown, NYC

The Consumption of a Transnational Brand

Jinwon Kim

New York University Press

New York

NEW YORK UNIVERSITY PRESS
New York
www.nyupress.org

© 2026 by New York University
All rights reserved

Please contact the Library of Congress for Cataloging-in-Publication data.

ISBN: 9781479833627 (hardback)
ISBN: 9781479833634 (paperback)
ISBN: 9781479833665 (library ebook)
ISBN: 9781479833658 (consumer ebook)

This book is printed on acid-free paper, and its binding materials are chosen for strength and durability. We strive to use environmentally responsible suppliers and materials to the greatest extent possible in publishing our books.

The manufacturer's authorized representative in the EU for product safety is Mare Nostrum Group B.V., Mauritskade 21D, 1091 GC Amsterdam, The Netherlands. Email: gpsr@mare-nostrum.co.uk.

Manufactured in the United States of America

10 9 8 7 6 5 4 3 2 1

Also available as an ebook

CONTENTS

Introduction: Theorizing the Transclave ... 1

PART I: BRANDING KOREA

1. Nation Branding: Economic Restructuring and the Cultural Industry in Korea ... 41
2. Transclave: Selling Korea in a Global City ... 68

PART II: CONSUMING ETHNICITY

3. (Re)Making Koreatown: Nostalgia and Collective Memories ... 103
4. "It Is My Street": Symbolic Struggle over Koreatown ... 121
5. Hallyu in Koreatown: Disneyland or Imagined Community? ... 146
6. Korean Food: Authenticity, Exoticism, and Cultural Omnivorousness ... 166

Conclusion: See You in Koreatown ... 191

Acknowledgments ... 201
Appendix: Methodological Notes ... 207
Notes ... 215
Bibliography ... 239
Index ... 269
About the Author ... 287

Introduction

Theorizing the Transclave

Take a trip to Seoul without leaving Manhattan.
—*Thrillist*, October 23, 2018

NYC's K-Town isn't what it used to be: Most mom-and-pops are gone, and 32nd Street is now dominated by chains.
—Sam Kim, July 31, 2018, *Eater New York*

"Tourists are coming because it's a hot spot in New York City. It's not just Herald Square. It is Herald Square and K-town," said Jessica.[1]

On an early evening in February of 2018, I was talking via Facebook video chat to Jessica, a then-twenty-six-year-old Black American and native New Yorker who was born and raised in Harlem. Jessica was a former student of mine who took a Korean class with me at a local community college in New York City back in 2011. She was one of those dedicated students who did not mind attending a three-and-half-hour-long 10:30 a.m. Saturday class and one of the early non-Korean fans of K-pop who has been exposed to Korean pop culture since 2006, when K-pop was a very niche genre in the US music market. We had not seen each other for about six years after our first interview in 2012 in New York City, and we were having our follow-up interview about 280 miles apart—Jessica in New York, and me in Geneva in upstate New York. When I asked Jessica if she was still interested in Korean popular culture and consumption in Koreatown in Manhattan and speaking with me once again, she pleasantly agreed.[2]

However, in the past decades, Jessica had observed ample changes in the landscape of Koreatown—mainly its people. For Jessica, until 2011, Manhattan's Koreatown was a place that she had walked past "without even realizing it was K-town." At that time, Koreatown was a "hidden world"³ and "best-kept secret"⁴ for non-Korean New Yorkers, mainly serving Korean nationals and Korean Americans for decades. Brianna, a twenty-two-year-old Black American, echoes Jessica and says that Koreatown was something that many non-Asian New Yorkers might have slowly and unintentionally encountered. Brianna reminisces that it was a "funny" moment discovering Koreatown, and that she had basically stumbled upon it accidentally. She recalls that she "kind of got lost" while walking to Grand Central Terminal on 42nd Street and Park Avenue. She wondered, "Where am I? And like, why do I see signs in Korean?" Yet, in the past few years, both Jessica and Brianna have seen a big change in Koreatown, mainly in the number of non-Koreans—particularly non-Asian New Yorkers and tourists—and mainstream media attention to the space. Jessica felt that "they're little bit less surprised when they see people of color walking through [Koreatown]."

Over the past decade, Koreatown in Midtown Manhattan has drawn Koreans and non-Koreans, tourists, and locals seeking everything Korean, from day spas to nightlife. Koreatown was once "hidden" or "shadowed" by adjacent New York icons such as the Empire State Building, Herald Square, Penn Station, and the flagship Macy's. But today, it is known as the home for a taste of Korea for both ethnic Koreans and non-Korean New Yorkers, where restaurants, bars, noraebang (karaoke bars), internet cafés, and all-night spas offer "Seoul-style" consumption, as Deborah Baldwin described in a 2008 *New York Times* piece.⁵ This visibility comes with the growing popularity of breakout stars like the K-pop group BTS as well as Korean pop culture products such as Korean dramas and Korean movies, such as *Squid Game* and *Parasite*, respectively. International social media has played a significant role in the popularity and increased visibility of the aforementioned Korean cultural content. However, while Koreatown is newly visible to non-Korean New Yorkers, the Korean government and corporations' transnational strategy of engagement beginning in the early 2000s through Koreatown has yet to be explored. Yes, Jessica is right. It is no longer just about Herald Square. As Madison, a twenty-three-year-old Black American from Brooklyn, echoes, "People are starting to realize this more than just 34th Street and Macy's." Indeed, as Jessica told me in 2024, "It [Koreatown] is a tourist trap."

One solitary block of Manhattan's West 32nd Street between Broadway and Fifth Avenue is officially called Korea Way, but it is usually referred

Figure I.1. A Scene of Koreatown from Broadway, 2016. Photo by the author.

to by its nickname, Koreatown or K-town. Extending to some parts of 35th Street, Sixth Avenue, and Park Avenue, at first glance this space appears to be an ethnic enclave, where members of an ethnic group share their unique culture, values, beliefs, and lifestyles. The area once offered food and services for Koreans who had immigrated after the liberalized Immigration and Nationality Act of 1965. During the 1970s, the majority of these Korean immigrants owned or worked in the nearby Korean Business District, a rectangular area from 24th to 34th Streets between Fifth and Sixth Avenues, home to Korean wholesalers. At the time, very few non-Koreans could be seen in the area. But things have changed drastically. Koreatown now contains a cluster of homeland-style businesses such as Korean restaurants, bars with Korean-style food, a food court, Korean franchise bakery-cafés, Korean brand cosmetic stores, Korean hair salons, and noraebang, representing Korean ethnic identity via shared lifestyle and consumer culture.

Using in-depth interviews with 135 producers and consumers of Koreatown in Manhattan, archival research, and participant observation, I examine how Korea's nation branding strategy, new patterns in Korean migration, changes in the sociocultural and urban landscape both in South Korea (hereafter Korea unless specified) and in the United States, and shifts in tourism and urban policies in New York City have shaped the development of Manhattan's Koreatown into a new type of ethnic enclave, which I call a *transclave*. I define transclave as a commercialized ethnic space that exists exclusively for consumption, leisure, and entertainment. It is a space where transnational consumer culture from a sending country is embedded within a physical space in a receiving society, reflecting the landscape of the sending country's consumer culture through the physical appearance of buildings and stores and the inclusion of franchise brands. This particular transclave—Manhattan's Koreatown—becomes a cultural platform for the Korean government and relatively small-to-medium-sized Korean corporations to market the nation and its brands for both economic and political benefit, cultivating it as an entertainment space with the intention of nation branding and promoting Korean culture and products overseas in order to bolster the economy after the 1997 financial crisis.

Korea's cultural policies demonstrate the growing importance of nations' "soft power" and "cultural wealth" in the current era of global

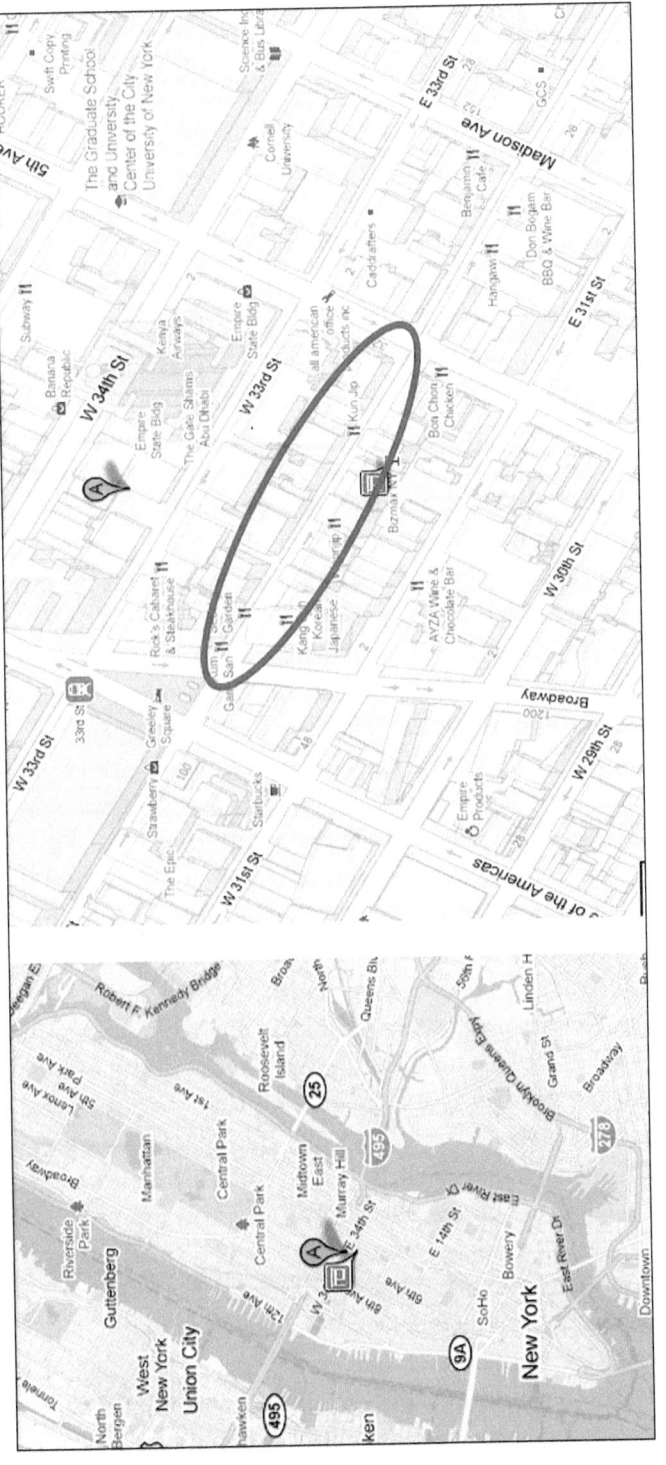

Figure 1.2. The location of Koreatown in Manhattan. Map by Google Maps.

competition.[6] Korea has actively participated in new global trends by adapting national cultural products for overseas consumers and consumer culture. The financial crisis of 1997 was a critical moment for the Korean government, as new economic and sociocultural policies and strategies were introduced to overcome financial uncertainties. I argue that the government, rather than stepping in as the main actor, took the role of facilitator for the new global order in implementing International Monetary Fund policies. In addition, the Korean government actively collaborated with various economic actors—in this case Korean corporations—in order to bring new revenues and to overcome the financial crisis through business strategies as part of its broader nation branding plan. I contextualize the nation's strategy of promoting certain industries within global economic restructuring and political changes. Soft power becomes a marketing tool for the nation and reinforces the idea that the nation can be a brand that targets a wider audience.

New York City is one of the most critical global markets in nation branding projects, and the landscape of Koreatown in Manhattan reflects the flow of new cultural and economic investment. Because cultural products from a sending country are often placed in traditional ethnic enclaves, the new branding policies mobilize different types of business owners to create a new type of ethnic space. As a transclave, Koreatown serves as an intersection at which Korea's political, economic, social, and cultural influences meet New York City's diverse cultural mosaic. As with a traditional ethnic enclave, ethnicity enters the marketplace to become commodified in a small section of New York City. Koreatown consists primarily of small- and medium-sized commercial and office buildings, as well as a handful of manufacturing buildings left over from the area's history as a garment district. This small block, however, has unique traits that differentiate it from other ethnic enclaves, particularly the typical Chinatown model. First and foremost, Koreatown exists only for consumption and has rarely served any residential purpose. Koreatown is zoned as a commercial district by the New York City Department of City Planning,[7] which allows Koreatown to be open for business at all hours. Furthermore, investors in Koreatown tend to open restaurants and bars not only on the first floor of buildings, but also on the second, third, and fourth floors; this is a common practice in Seoul, but atypical of New York

City business spaces. As such, Manhattan's Koreatown has a higher concentration of stores than do other consumption spaces in New York City, which endows the space with a plethora of shopping, eating, and entertainment opportunities.

I emphasize two dimensions of Koreatown as a transclave. First, Koreatown offers a space for "branding Korea." New York City is one of the most critical global markets in Korea's nation branding projects in North America, and Manhattan's Koreatown landscape reflects the flow of branding strategies and cultural policies that stem from the Korean government's cultural and economic investments in the aftermath of the financial crisis of 1997. Since the crisis, the Korean government has invested in the so-called new economy, including games (such as PC, online, mobile, and video games), information technology, popular culture (such as K-pop music, movies, dramas, and related products), tourism, and food, in order to promote the nation as a fun and interesting country and to bolster and grow the economy. While cultural products from sending countries are often placed in traditional ethnic enclaves, Korea's branding policies mobilize different types of business owners to create a new type of ethnic space.

Prior research on nation branding has focused mainly on top-down policies and the roles of government agencies, branding professionals, and consultants who design, develop, and engage in decision-making processes.[8] However, this book takes a different approach and highlights the role of local actors outside the territorial boundary of the state, such as businesspeople, the media, the diaspora, and non-coethnic consumers, and emphasizes the voices of bottom-up participants who "live the brand" from a lens of national (or collective) identity.[9] As a transclave, Manhattan's Koreatown is also a space of cultural significance constructed by both consumers and producers, including temporary Korean migrants, Korean Americans, non-Koreans, Korean entrepreneurs, Korean corporations, and the Korean government.

Second, Koreatown in Manhattan is a space for "consuming ethnicity." Americans expect Koreatown to be like other ethnic enclaves, such as various Chinatowns, Little Italys, and Little Indias in New York and in other metropolitan areas. Koreatown shares common elements with these other ethnic enclaves but is also unique. I locate Koreatown in the rise and fall of ethnic enclaves in urban America and their transition from a space of isolation to a space for residence or work,[10] and, finally, to a new iteration of a space for entertainment, leisure, and consumption.[11] This shift coincides with increased consumer demand for authenticity, diversification of ethnicity, and the rise of the "omnivore society" in some pockets of the United States. Indulging in and having knowledge about ethnic foods is one of the most common and popular ways for city dwellers to demonstrate their understanding and appreciation of diversity and multiculturalism; in addition, it is also important in establishing a cosmopolitan identity.[12] Rather than focus solely on the role of government and corporations in nation branding projects, I pay attention to various consumer groups: Korean nationals, Korean Americans, and non-Koreans. For many consumers—particularly non-Koreans—Koreatown is a commercialized space where one can seek out and be immersed in an authentic experience: a transnational culture embedded in New York City's diverse racial and ethnic mosaic. In fact, Koreatown in Manhattan is a space where a sending state's socioeconomic strategies and policies are negotiated with the ethnic community and shape the cityscape in urban America.

Nation Branding in the Postindustrial World

Nation branding is a significant twenty-first century economic strategy that nation-states develop to improve their competitive position in a global economy. "Brand" generally refers to the "name, term, sign, symbol or design or a combination of them intended to identify the goods and services of one seller or group of sellers and to differentiate them from those of competition," as defined by the American Marketing Association.[13] Brands thus initially represent the producers' perspective rather than the consumers.[14] But a brand is not static and evolves through the stories it generates. Consumers value some products more than others because they help them construct distinctive identities. This is an economically based method of self-identification. In this process, successful brands become iconic through interaction with their consumers and environments.[15]

In the past few decades, this sort of branding, along with related business strategies such as risk-taking, inventiveness, promotion, and profit motivation,[16] has been adopted and promoted by various political entities such as city governments and nation-states to reinforce nations and cities as tourist destinations and opportunities for capital investment.[17] Such public-private partnerships increasingly play a significant role in the realms of public policy and legislation as "place branding."[18] For instance, New York State's "I ♥ New York" campaign was part of a marketing-driven recovery effort to transform New York City's negative post–white flight and 1970s fiscal crisis image; after 9/11, the Bloomberg administration's economic policies and urban branding strategies followed the same path.[19]

Likewise, some experts have convinced national governments that they too can develop a brand. A national brand, "the reputation of countries and cities like the brand images of companies," as defined by marketing guru Simon Anholt, has financial impact when it leads to the rest of the world contributing to the nation's revenue.[20] Place branding and place marketing go back to the early 1990s. Anholt argues that in a globalized world, countries try to attract tourists, business investors, students, academics, and entrepreneurs and simultaneously export policies, services, products, culture and ideas. Clichés and stereotypes of countries' or cities' qualities (e.g., Parisian stylishness, Swiss wealth and precision, Japanese technological expertise) fundamentally affect people's opinions and behavior toward these places, people, and products. Brands build on the nation's image, such as in consumer association of France with fashion, Switzerland with watches, and Japan with electronics. Some transnational megacorporations maintain their brand by reinforcing connotations with their countries of origin: Mercedes Benz from Germany; Sony and Toyota from Japan; Apple, Starbucks, and McDonalds from the United States.[21]

Nation branding can regenerate a nation's image through such marketing and branding devices as logos and slogans. For example, Estonia was the first former Soviet state to launch a branding campaign in an effort to change its image from "post-Soviet" to "pre-EU"; this self-redefinition, reflecting radical economic and political reform, repositioned the national identity in part through association with the global economy.[22] Other nations, such as Belgium, Bulgaria, Canada, China, Croatia, Finland, Germany, India, Japan, Latvia, Poland, Portugal, Romania, Singapore, South Africa, South Korea, Spain, and New Zealand have also participated in this trend.[23]

While marketing gurus and scholars are pioneers in the field, political scientists have also paid attention to the emergence of new players in public diplomacy, such as new global media, global culture, nation branding, and soft power.[24] Unlike nation branding, which is a relatively new term for image management, public diplomacy dates back to the 1960s and was mainly used for US propaganda promoting military expansion during the Cold War by conveying positive American values to foreigners.[25] Public diplomacy, thus, should be understood as a form of "soft power" that co-opts and attracts people through the nation's cultural assets rather than threatening them with "hard" military power.[26] With the emergence of nonstate actors and two-way communication between states,[27] states and nonstate actors, such as NGOs, interact with one another to enact soft power,[28] exerted through cultural industries such as film and television that allow a nation to express and promote itself and its self-image targeting foreign citizens.[29]

More recently, scholars in media, communications, and cultural studies have increasingly paid attention to nation branding by analyzing the role of identity politics, national identity, culture, and nationhood in nation branding.[30] Nation branding, as marketing strategies or marketizing politics, targets external markets in order to construct and manage specific and positive images of the nation and national identity. These nation branding strategies are increasingly enacted through government councils and committees,[31] and they often collaborate with marketing firms. For example, Brand Estonia hired a British communication firm called Interbrand to efficiently promote positive images of the nation with the goal of attracting financial investment, increasing exports, and attracting tourists.[32] This redefinition, reflecting radical economic and political reform, repositioned national identity in part through association with the global economy and global consumerism.[33]

In this process, through marketing and commodification of popular culture, the creative industry aimed not only to bring economic gain based on the government's registration and policy-making but also to politicize consumer habits and to generate domestic consumerism.[34] For instance, "Cool Britannia," a slogan adopted by Britain's Labour Party in 1997, was designed to promote London's cultural renaissance as a fashion hub,[35] albeit with some sarcastic criticism of the concept as superficial.[36] Another example is "Cool Japan." As suggested by Douglas McGray as

"Japan's Gross National Cool" and borrowed from Cool Britannia,[37] the Japanese government has embarked on its own nation branding project by using cultural content industries, such as anime and manga, to reimagine their nation with a fresh approach after an economic bubble collapse and prolonged recession. More importantly, their new nation branding strategies are rooted in "geopolitical anxiety," which can be attributed to Japan's declining global economic power in manufacturing and the rise of China as a new economic power.[38]

Likewise, food is often used to promote culture and positive national associations and to attract noncitizens who seek authentic experiences, or simply participate in the experience economy,[39] to particular destinations (e.g., gastro or culinary tourism). It is also used to increase awareness of the nation's culture and historical roots,[40] often called culinary diplomacy or gastrodiplomacy. For example, the Thai government launched "Global Thai" in order to help open Thai restaurants overseas in 2002, followed by "Thailand: Kitchen of the World" to educate overseas consumers on the history and practice of Thai cuisine. The government encouraged Thai chefs to open restaurants overseas, granting the "Thai Select" label to restaurants that met and maintained a certain level of quality set by the Ministry of Commerce in Thailand.[41] The Ministry for Europe and Foreign Affairs in France and Chef Alain Ducasse also launched Goût de France/Good France in 2015, a nation branding project that recognized French cuisine as a diplomatic tool;[42] this is an example of gastrodiplomacy.[43] Likewise, Taiwan, Korea, Japan, Canada, and many others have followed this trend.

Through a combination of food and pop culture production and consumption and nationalist sentiment, governments generally aim to improve the nation's image and, thus, bring people together politically and promote a sense of nationhood, as well as economically enhance both production and industry.[44] In this context, nation branding is the connection between nationalism and marketing, or simply a manifestation of commercial nationalism, "which combines the exclusionary and totalizing force of ethnonationalism with the depoliticizing and individualizing impulses of global consumerism."[45]

However, more importantly, nation-states see food promotion as an economic opportunity. According to Statista Market Insights, revenue in the food industry amounts to $9.45 trillion in 2025 worldwide, and the industry is expected to grow by 6.34 percent annually.⁴⁶ The Fancy Food Shows by the Specialty Food Association (SFA) are good examples of the food and beverage industry collaborating with various government agencies to promote their foods to buyers, marketers, distributors, brokers, press, influencers, investors, and trendsetters. The SFA offers two major exhibitions: the Summer Fancy Food Shows in New York City and the Winter Fancy Food Shows in Las Vegas.⁴⁷ The 68th Summer Fancy Food Show took place at the Jacob Javits Center in New York City between June 23 and June 25, 2024, and I was able to observe the exhibition for two hours on June 24. More than 2,400 domestic and international companies and more than 29,000 professionals in the specialty food and beverage industry participated.⁴⁸

Though the Fancy Food Shows are designed to bring various business entities in the food and beverage industry together for the purpose of networking, I also saw various government agencies collaborating with private corporations. Italy actively participated in that year's event, as did Korea, Japan, France, China, Spain, Mexico, Poland, Indonesia, Thailand, India, Portugal, Georgia (country), and Egypt among many others. The Italian Pavilion showcased Italian agri-food products from

Figure 1.3. The Italian Pavilion at the Fancy Food Show, held at the Jacob Javits Convention Center in New York City, June 2024. Photo by the author.

Figure 1.4. The entrance of the K-Food (Korean Food) booth at the Fancy Food Show at the Jacob Javits Convention Center in New York City, June 2024. Photo by the author.

pastas to cheese under the umbrella banner of "The Extraordinary Italian Taste," an international campaign financed and sponsored by the Ministry of Foreign Affairs in Italy and in collaboration with the Italian Chambers of Commerce Abroad.[49] While emphasizing authentic flavors and heritage from various regions of Italy, the Italian Pavilion highlights Italianness through Italy's Tricolor—green, white, and red—allowing viewers to experience their celebration of Italian food as an intangible UNESCO heritage and Italian pride.

Yet this public-private partnership is not just designed to promote positive images of the nation and to celebrate their tradition and culture. Their efforts clearly aim to create opportunities to export Italian-made food and agriculture products to the United States, the biggest market outside of the European Union, as emphasized by Matteo Zoppas, the president of the Italian Trade Agency, by reaching $7.35 billion in product imports in the United States in 2023.[50]

This kind of nation branding is highly visible and rooted in mainstream media. Nation branders must prove and assure "domestic elites, stakeholders and the public that their government is acting in their best interests,"[51] through metrics such as export increases, foreign investments, and tourism growth. However, as noted earlier, the legacies and voices of citizens and their bottom-up participation in nation branding brings the branding to life.[52] In this process, nation branding is reconstructed and cocreated by both producers and consumers;[53] as "a form of communication, the media of the message are effectively the citizens themselves."[54] Citizens, as citizen-diplomats, brand ambassadors, or public ambassadors, are targeted to improve and promote positive images of the nation overseas.[55]

However, despite their emphasis on "living in the brand," much research on nation branding has paid attention to policy analysis and the role of marketing professionals, elites, and government officials.[56] For instance, drawing from Leslie Sklair's transnational capitalist class, Melissa Aronczyk develops the concept of "a transnational promotional class" by highlighting the role of elites or experts, such as consultants, scholars, and government officials, who create, legitimatize, and reproduce national symbolism.[57] However, researchers have paid less attention to the empirical analysis of the bottom-up participation of ordinary citizens.[58] In fact, even less attention has been paid to transnational migrants or the diaspora, who also actively engage in transnational activities between the homeland and receiving country. Here, I call for attention to the role of various actors—both producers and consumers of the transclave—from transnational entrepreneurs to temporary migrants (international students and employees at the US branches of Korean corporations), to immigrants and their children, to non-coethnic consumers, as actors of nation branding. By analyzing their voices, this book navigates how these groups' nostalgia, collective memories, and symbolic struggle over the space produce, translate, and deliver the nation's commercial culture to a multiethnic and multinational public, thus offering us an avenue to understand nation and nationhood through consumerism in a global economy.

The Transclave in a Global City

Historically, an immigrant or ethnic enclave has been thought of as a negative form of urban segregation of racial and ethnic minority groups in major US cities. In the 1920s and 1930s, sociologists at the University of Chicago studied immigrant and racial minority communities through the lens of urban ecology and residential segregation. A few decades later, with the rise of new immigrant populations, changes in US immigration policy—particularly the Immigration and Nationality Act of 1965—and broader socioeconomic changes, sociologists in immigration studies and urban sociologists began to debate the role of emerging ethnic spaces in gateway cities such as New York and Los Angeles during the 1980s and 1990s. However, these debates have largely faded in recent years, while cultural geographers and urban studies scholars continue to navigate new forms of ethnic enclaves. In this context, I trace the rise and decline of ethnic enclave discourse in American sociology over the past century and introduce a new concept I have developed—a transclave.

The Past: From Chicago School Scholars to the Ethnic Enclave Economy Debate

Chicago School ecologists of the 1920s and '30s, whose research was rooted in social relations and their correlations with spatial relations, analyzed population clusters—enclaves and ghettos, with these terms often being used interchangeably—as a kind of social disorganization.[59]

Robert E. Park argued that the process of segregation was inevitable due to the growth of cities and occurred among all racial minority groups, whether immigrant or not. Immigrant colonies and other so-called ghettos, such as Chinatowns, Little Sicilies, and the Black Belt, were considered inevitable outcomes produced by tendencies of city life and immigrants' dislodging of inhabitants to the next zone.[60] Yet, as analyzed in Park's "race relations cycle," through contact and interactions, "as the ties of race, of language, and of culture are weakened, successful individuals move out [from the ghettos and immigrant colonies] and eventually find their places in business and in the professions, among the older population group."[61] Likewise, by historically tracing the residential segregation of Jews from medieval Europe to the city of Chicago in the early twentieth century, Louis Wirth saw the modern ghetto as a sociopsychological and ecological phenomenon. The ghettos were the poorest spaces, where immigrants, particularly Jews, were isolated.[62] The modern ghetto of the early twentieth century is an outcome of ecological change, through the growth of the city and the invasion of the slums by new immigrant groups. Due to this invasion, the ghetto was converted from an overgrown village in the urban outskirts to the slum of Chicago by displacing, for example, Germans and Irish, and later by being displaced by Poles, Italians, and, finally, Black Americans.[63]

Chicago School scholars did not clearly distinguish between ghettos and immigrant colonies or ethnic enclaves. In Park's writing, although not clearly stated, "The Ghetto" seems to mean the Jewish ghetto exclusively, while "so-called ghettos" likely refer to areas of ethnic concentrations in general.[64] Wirth refers to "ghetto" as "the modern Jewish immigrant settlement in the Western World."[65] Yet the ghettos studied by Park and Wirth were similar to today's immigrant enclaves or immigrant colonies, whereas the current understanding of "ghetto" resonates negatively, with the rise of poor Black urban neighborhoods and a series of urban unrest therein.[66] "Enclave" has a much more positive connotation, as a "temporary residential way-station" before spatial assimilation.[67] Unlike urban ghettos, which imply involuntary segregation, enclaves are often considered voluntarily segregated, without stigmatization by the white majority. In these areas, members of a minority group share language, culture, ethnicity, or nationality as a means to strengthen economic, social, political, and cultural development within the community.[68] They provide affordable housing, family ties, and job opportunities that are not easily found outside of immigrant communities.

Despite a long debate among immigration scholars around the concept of the ethnic economy, the term immigrant or ethnic enclave had not been clearly conceptualized even as late as the early 1990s.[69] Massive waves of immigration from Asia, Africa, the Caribbean, and Latin America fueled by Immigration and Nationality Act of 1965 and the restructuring of the US economy have drawn scholars' attention to the new occupations that certain ethnic and immigrant groups hold and the geographical concentrations of both residence and work, particularly in gateway metropolitan cities for immigrants. Such concentration holds true despite new destinations for immigrants, such as the Midwest, the South, small towns, and rural areas,[70] and the spatial assimilation of ethnic groups into wealthier and more suburban neighborhoods, or what John R. Logan, Richard D. Alba, and Wenquan Zhang call "ethnic community," a place "selected as living environment by those who have wider options based on their market resources."[71]

A popular belief in the immigration literature is that most immigrants, despite host nations' recruitment of skilled immigrants, are relegated to low-status positions in various host societies and are able to achieve economic success, despite hostility and initial disadvantages. Contrary to this, the ethnic economy is based on the position that ethnic minority groups, who often occupy intermediate positions, are mostly self-employed and create entrepreneurial communities.[72] Immigrants with intermediate positions are concentrated in certain occupations— trade and commerce in particular, but also other "middleman" jobs such as labor contracting, rent collecting, money lending, and brokerage. These middleman minorities are often believed to be used as buffers by dominate elites to divert mass frustrations; they have included Jews in Europe and the United States, Chinese in Southeast Asia, East Asians in East Africa, and Japanese, Greeks, and later Koreans in the United States. Immigrant-owned family stores tend to rely on unpaid family labor or cheap labor from extended family members and coethnics, who work long hours in labor-intensive jobs.[73] These immigrants tend to generate ethnic resources, such as relative satisfaction, reactive solidarity, sojourning orientation, and cultural endowments, but also bring class resources, such as private property, human capital, money, and bourgeois values, attitude, knowledge, and skills.[74]

The concept of the ethnic economy, however, does not explain "the geographical clustering" or density of immigrant-owned firms.[75] These businesses are simply "ethnic" because the owners and the employees are coethnics, regardless of whether or not their customers are coethnics.[76] For instance, Koreans both in New York City and Los Angeles in the post-1965 era have been heavily concentrated in the wholesale of wigs, footwear, and clothes; retail of clothing and jewelry; greengrocery stores; and as operator-owners of laundromats, nail salons, liquor stores, and convenience stores. These stores are not necessarily concentrated in proximate areas of immigrant residence. In fact, they are commonly spread out across the city, particularly in minority neighborhoods where the consumers are not always coethnics. This has had, at times, adverse consequences, such as the series of Black-Korean conflicts in gateway cities, such as the unrest following the Rodney King verdict in Los Angeles in 1992 and the Red Apple Boycotts in Brooklyn in the early 1990s (Family Red Apple was a Korean-owned grocery store).

However, by evaluating and criticizing the dual market labor theory, consisting of the primary sector (center) and the secondary sector (periphery) of the market, where most immigrants fall into the secondary market because of less skills, Alejandro Portes and his colleagues shed light on spatial concentrations of immigrant enterprises—what they call the "ethnic enclave economy"—by paying attention to Cuban refugees in Miami.[77] They contend that immigrants can benefit by creating opportunities through ethnic solidarity in the ethnic enclave economy and rebut the traditional understanding of the ethnic economy and dual labor market theory involving exploitative sweatshop conditions. Immigrants in that enclave, like the Cuban enclave in Miami, are similar to those in the primary sector, rather than those in the secondary sector. Even low-wage immigrant workers in the ethnic enclave economy gain similar returns on human capital investment, like workers in the primary market; due to ethnic solidarity, the ethnic enclave economy thus creates new opportunities for economic incorporation.[78]

The analysis by Portes and his colleagues, however, raised controversy, which was presented in Jimy Sanders and Victor Nee's article on Cuban immigrants in Miami and Hialeah, Florida, and the Chinese enclave in San Francisco, California. Their arguments centered on two main points. First, Sanders and Nee found that Cuban enclave immigrants in Miami and Hialeah earned less and received lower returns on human capital compared to Cuban immigrants elsewhere, while earnings and returns of Cuban immigrants and non-Latinx white immigrants who lived outside an enclave were similar to each other's. Enclave dwellers were also culturally less assimilated than Cuban immigrants living outside of Miami and Hialeah. Likewise, Chinese immigrants in San Francisco were more disadvantaged than Chinese immigrants outside of San Francisco. In fact, Sanders and Nee show that the ethnic enclave benefits the self-employed but not the employees in the private sector; their argument is in line with previous research indicating that the spatial concentration of minority groups exhausts good job opportunities.[79]

Second, they dispute the definition of an ethnic enclave as a place of work and argue that it should instead be understood as a place of residence. Portes and his colleagues argue that an ethnic enclave should be understood as a place of work or the location of ethnic firms, consisting of "immigrant groups which concentrate in a distinct spatial location and organize a variety of enterprises serving their own ethnic market and/or the general population."[80] Alejandro Portes and Leif Jensen insist that sociological understandings of the ethnic enclave—"immigrant enclave" or "enclave," used interchangeably—differ from everyday use as simple residential agglomerations.[81] Alejandro Portes and Robert L. Bach suggest the term "immigrant neighborhoods" (or "ethnic neighborhoods" in Portes and Jensen's article) as something distinct from "enclave"; immigrant neighborhoods are where "immigrant groups initially resettle in ethnically concentrated communities and generate a few small business to serve immediate, specialized consumption needs,"[82] yet "lack the extensive division of labor of the enclave and, especially, its highly differentiated entrepreneurial class."[83] Portes and his colleagues' understanding of immigrant enclaves as being in geographical proximity with "a dense network of industrial, commercial and financial enterprises" is dependent on social and economic resources and solidarity among coethnics.[84] However, Sanders and Nee understand ethnic enclaves as places of residence rather than merely places for work, unlike Portes and his colleagues.[85]

Such ambiguity and inconsistency of the term's definition might be drawn from the limited availability of quantitative data, such as census data.[86] Units of analysis vary from individuals to firms in cities (e.g., Cubans in Miami and Chinese in San Francisco by Portes and his colleagues, and by Jimy Sanders and Victor Nee, respectively), in boroughs (e.g., Chinese living in Manhattan or other boroughs in New York by Min Zhou and John R. Logan), or in metropolitan areas (e.g., various ethnic enclaves in the New York and Los Angeles metropolitan regions by John R. Logan, Richard D. Alba, and Wenquan Zhang; Chinese enclaves in Toronto, Calgary, and Vancouver by Eric Fong and Jing Shen). Yet if the regions in these analyses are that much larger and businesses are spread out across the borough, city, and metropolitan area, can such spatial concentration really be significant?

There would not be many ethnic enclave economies that meet the three dimensions of the enclave suggested by Portes and his colleagues: (1) co-ethnicity of owners and coethnic employees, (2) spatial concentration, and (3) sectoral specialization. For example, Iranians in LA do not necessarily hire co-ethnics; most are self-employed, and do not have to return human capital, as a form of apprenticeship, to their employees. Koreatown in LA and Little Havana in Miami might be the only two enclaves to meet all the criteria.[87] But Korean business owners hire not only coethnic Koreans but also Latinx workers.[88] Recently, this trend is more frequently observed not only in ethnic firms but also shops, restaurants, and stores. At any kind of ethnic restaurants in large gateway cities, it is easy to find non-coethnic workers as bussers, dishwashers, or even cooks, although ethnic division of labor is frequently observed in these cases.

Given these circumstances, is spatial concentration significant in analyzing the ethnic enclave economy and its possible return on human capital? Should we drop the term ethnic enclave?[89]

The Present: The Transclave Beyond Traditional Ethnic Enclaves

Different understandings of the enclave, from everyday use as a residential and commercial agglomeration to the sociological understanding, are limited within the economic sector. Many researchers from various fields such as geography and urban studies understand enclaves as places for a mixture of work, living, and consumption and interchangeably refer to them as ethnic enclaves, ethnic communities, quarters, barrios, ethnic neighborhoods, or ethnic places.[90] Their understanding of the enclave, especially if ethnic economies are entirely based on trade and service, is closer to what Portes and his colleagues call an immigrant or ethnic neighborhood.[91]

Yet, informed by earlier definitions of the word, we often think of ethnic enclaves as limited to a small geographic area—whether it is a place of work or residence—where an ethnic group is marked through the use of distinctive symbols, often expressed in signs, language, art and architecture, retail stores, and offices, like those seen in Chinatown, Little Tokyo, Little Havana, or Little India.[92] As many sociologists have observed in the past, it is a place for work and residence with class divisions and conflicts in a concentrated geographic space.[93] It is also, whether or not it has negative connotations among outsiders as a dangerous or crime-ridden ghetto or barrio, a place where many members of the ethnic community—both immigrants and their descendants—still maintain their symbolic and emotional ties and their roots through consumer goods and services.[94] In fact, enclaves are often a second home for immigrants and their children, in many cases for many decades.

More recent scholarship explores new trends in ethnic enclaves beyond the traditional understanding of the enclave. To begin, immigrants' residential areas have diversified over time. Immigrants do not necessarily live or establish their businesses in the inner city of gateway cities. Instead, as wealthier or upwardly mobile immigrants settle down in suburbs, ethnic businesses follow them.[95] Wei Li calls these "ethnoburbs," defined as "suburban ethnic clusters of residential areas and business districts in large metropolitan areas," such as the San Gabriel Valley in Los Angeles.[96] Since the 1990s, in the New York metropolitan area, newer middle-class Koreans immigrants often move directly to suburbs in Nassau and Suffolk Counties in Long Island and Bergen County in New Jersey.[97] Their children also tend to move out of the traditional Koreatown in Queens as they achieve upward mobility.

Though ethnic enclaves are considered stepping stones before moving up the social ladder, in the gateway cities of the United States and other receiving societies, some ethnic enclaves have lost their original residents, but conversely are experiencing a revival, attracting outsiders' attention and luring more locals and tourists to the space for consumption, entertainment, and leisure.[98] This trend traces back to the 1960s and '70s, when the United States began observing the rapid transformation of the American racial and ethnic mosaic. Coinciding with demographic changes driven by Immigration and Nationality Act of 1965, the new cultural politics of difference emerged as part of an effort to diffuse WASP male cultural hegemony.[99] Learning ancestral languages, embracing a hyphenated identity, eating ethnic foods, reversing the Anglicization of names, enjoying pop culture from the country of origin, and taking homeland trips became part of the new American way,[100] though ethnic identification does not always involve choices among racial and ethnic minority groups, unlike white Americans who choose to be ethnically identified.[101] Furthermore, the role of the marketplace in ethnic identification, which accompanied the initial ethnic revival and accelerated in the 1990s, has continued to intensify exponentially. In this neoliberal marketplace, consuming cultural products is a way to cultivate ethnic identity, but this has been profoundly enhanced in the past two to three decades. The mainstream marketplace has quickly responded to changes in the US racial composition by employing various "ethnic marketing" strategies; some of these are referred to as "differentiated marketing towards an ethnic group"[102] or "multicultural marketing" strategies, designed and promoted by mainstream marketers and practiced by both mainstream corporations and ethnic economic sectors.[103] In such a society, consumer culture has become symbolic, creating an economically based method of self-identification and reshaping the urban landscape. Ethnic consumer culture—commodified and commercialized—territorializes the urban landscape, making the nation's image more multicultural and socially diverse.[104]

This trend is, in fact, not a novel phenomenon but an ongoing process in gateway cities. For example, in New York since the early twentieth century, despite their spatial segregation due in part to Chinese Exclusion, Chinatowns across the city have seduced local New Yorkers and travelers in search of not only exotic food, but also gambling houses, brothels, and opium dens.[105] Chinatowns' ethnic themes and landscapes, from traditional entry gates to architectural styles, not only represent a sign of shared history and culture but also highlight their exoticism and market a sense of place to outsiders.[106] Likewise, by the

1980s, Little Italy, which was home to Italian immigrants and their descendants, experienced population loss due to a decrease in new Italian immigration coinciding with Italians' and Italian Americans' move to the suburbs.[107] Yet in the 1970s, with ethnic revival and a resurgence of ethnic pride, the preservation of New York City's Little Italy was organized by the Little Italy Restoration Association. This neighborhood on Mulberry Street transformed into a pedestrian mall on Sundays—*pedonalizzazione* (pedestrianization)—with the presence of red, white, and green flags, which symbolize Italian ethnic culture; it was claimed as New York's Historic Little Italy in the 1970s.[108]

While spatially concentrated ethnic enclaves are nothing new, public efforts to highlight diversity have intensified and become a part of urban policies fairly recently, from urban planning and (re)development to urban (or city) branding strategies.[109] In the postindustrial city, leisure, entertainment, and tourism industries are at the center of policy-making for municipal revenue.[110] This new tourism trend, often observed in historic preservation and heritage tourism, was enthusiastically upheld by urban policy makers, developers, entrepreneurs, and community leaders through various forms of public-private partnership and have been documented in recent literature. For example, the Explore Chinatown campaign, funded by the Lower Manhattan Development Corporation (LMDC) and the September 11th Fund, began to market Chinatown through advertisements about traditional events, such as the Lunar New Year and the Autumn Moon festival, in newspapers, magazines, and subway advertisements in order to encourage economic investment in the community, which was negatively impacted by the September 11 attack.[111] LMDC, the September 11th Fund and the New York Tourism Company sponsored a Chinatown Tourist Information kiosk where Canal, Baxter, and Walker Street meet.[112]

Tourism has extended its scope beyond traditional activities such as sightseeing, eating, or visiting museums and art galleries; ethnicity and diversity are now more attractive to tourists who seek "authentic" experiences.[113] There are many inconsistent and ambiguous definitions of authenticity, but it generally refers to things or ideas that are genuine, real, or true, capturing dimensions and assessment of truth or verification[114] and connoting "traditional culture and origin, a sense of the genuine, the real or the unique."[115] However, as many scholars have pointed out, tourists' desire for and value placed on authenticity is socially constructed, contextually determined, and ideological.[116]

Simply put, city governments spend significant money on advertisements in order to make their cities more marketable and interesting to outsiders. Yet, more fundamentally, by investing in ethnic enclaves and connecting ethnicity to tourism, and by collaborating with public and private stakeholders, city governments brand their image and reputation as "multicultural," whether or not this is true. As Kay Anderson shows, Melbourne's Chinatown, once an immigrant "ghetto," was selected as a symbol of cultural diversity and celebrated as a source of civic pride and tourist investment.[117] Similar patterns are documented in many enclaves of North American, Australian, and European cities, such as Vancouver, Sydney, and London.[118]

However, ethnic markers in an ethnic enclave's landscape are only quasi-authentic. For example, the preservation of historic Little Italy in the 1970s was typically understood as part of the ethnic preservation movement. However, it was in fact driven by restaurant owners who were eager to attract tourists.[119] Likewise, in Italian restaurants in Little Italy in Manhattan, although restaurant owners may still be of Italian descent, most of the staff and even many owners tend to be Albanian Kosovars, welcoming their patrons in limited Italian and posing as Italian ethnics.[120] In fact, their presence has nothing to do with their actual ethnicity and nativity, but rather how their ethnicity and ability to pass as Italian is perceived by and sold to outsiders. In such quasi-authentic places, ethnic enclaves might be turned into what Krase calls an "ethnic theme park," referring to "a place where the experience of the ethnic 'other' is for sale, particularly to tourists,"[121] offering pseudo-authentic and superficial experiences or "pseudo-events," due to the nature of mass tourism[122]—"the commoditization of culture and the associated homogenization and standardization of tourist experiences."[123] In such a commercialized space, tourists' experiences are often mystified[124] and "the real thing is as free as air,"[125] while ethnic diversity is fetishized by both tourists and locals.[126]

What is relatively new or intensified compared to the past is that the practice of ethnic identity through cultural consumption is becoming much more transnational, rather than embedded solely within the US territory, as discussed earlier in this chapter. It seems that ethnicity has been romanticized by consumers nostalgic for the homeland without requiring the intensive commitment of traditional and community-based ethnicity in the marketplace. Of course, these (quasi-)authentic products are more manageable and easily approachable.[127]

In order to analyze such "transnational changes" and increasing leisure, entertainment, and consumption opportunities in ethnic enclaves,[128] new concepts and terms have been introduced by scholars through case studies of various ethnic enclaves and neighborhoods. Michel S. Laguerre introduces the term "cosmonation" in order to analyze the global social formation of Chinatown in San Francisco, California, and the South Asian community in Sacramento, California. For Laguerre, an ethnic neighborhood should be understood as a local place as well as a transnational and global entity; each ethnic neighborhood across the globe is a node, a small part of a larger network, and is interconnected with each other as well as to the homeland.[129] Likewise, but with more solid empirical data, Tarry Hum uses the term "global neighborhood" to describe neighborhoods with more complex racial and ethnic dynamics—in most cases, neighborhoods with a mix of Asian and Latinx populations.[130] Based on her case study of Sunset Park, Brooklyn—a predominantly Chinese and Latinx neighborhood—Hum further explains that a "global neighborhood," transitioning from its industrial past to new postindustrial arenas, reflects flows of new migration and capital investments. In such areas, the neighborhood economy has evolved to focus on immigrant markets and international capital, including transnational real estate and ethnic banks for both Asians and Latinx; these capital-oriented institutions finance more affluent immigrants and investors for luxury condos and commercial developments, while working-class immigrants continue to suffer from low wages and sweatshop conditions.[131]

Moreover, Elizabeth Chacko and Stephen J. Shaw underline the "consumption" aspects of ethnic enclaves. Chacko introduces the concept of "ethnic place-making" and its four categories: (1) "ethnic institutional places," serving as connectors for community and helping immigrants to settle down in a new society (e.g., churches and secular associations and institutions); (2) "ethnic sociocommerscapes," areas with a concentration of ethnic businesses offering goods and services and community meeting places; (3) "arenas or transient ethnic places," which are neutral spaces for cultural and religious events (public spaces); and (4) "intangible ethnic places" (e.g., cyberspace).[132] Likewise, in his study on Banglatown—a London neighborhood with a large Bangladeshi population known as "The Curry Capital of the UK" from the mid-1990s—Shaw adopts the term "ethnoscape" from Appadurai, as landscapes of those who "constitute the shifting world in which we live."[133] By analyzing ethnoscapes as spaces of consumption, Shaw argues that Banglatown was promoted by local authorities under the New Labour Government, in collaboration with local businesspeople and nongovernmental agencies, as an "exotic [cityscape] that offer[s] possibilities for urban ethnic tourism."[134]

Koreatown: From Traditional Enclave to a Transclave

Manhattan's Koreatown is in line with such enclaves discussed in the previous section and has evolved from a traditional ethnic enclave into a transclave. The past of Koreatown dates back to the late 1960s, when the number of Korean immigrants quickly increased due to the Immigration and Nationality Act of 1965. Korean immigration in general is the result of a century-long relationship between the United States and Korea. Most Korean immigrants between 1950 and 1964 were young women who married American GIs in Korea or were adopted after the Korean War by Americans. The Immigration and Nationality Act of 1965 changed the socio-demographic composition of Korean immigrants considerably. Post-1965 Korean immigrants were highly selective and tended to show the following characteristics: they were well-educated, urban, middle-class individuals—mostly permanent immigrants—who arrived as nuclear families and presented a distinct sense of national identity.[135] Although many Korean immigrants were college-educated, they were not able to work at the level to which they were accustomed because of language barriers and racial discrimination against Asians in general. As a result, many Korean immigrants were self-employed in the grocery business, dry cleaning, and wholesale and retail sales of Korean-imported merchandise. They ran small businesses either in ethnic enclaves or in lower income neighborhoods serving racial minority groups.[136]

Koreatown as a Traditional Ethnic Enclave

Prior to the 1990s, Koreatown in Manhattan offered a space mostly for Korean wholesalers and their staff. The transnational character was limited to the usual model in which Korean immigrants imported goods from Korea and sold them on the American market. In New York City, Korean immigrants opened wig and garment wholesale businesses along Broadway between 24th and 34th Streets in Manhattan. The decline of the industrial sector in New York City in the 1960s and upward mobility among second- and third-generation Jewish and Italian wholesalers leaving the district led to cheap rents that allowed Korean businesspeople to successfully settle in this area.[137] The products sold by Korean businesses were mostly imported from Korea, under the military junta government policy of an export-oriented economy and labor-intensive manufacturing industries in the 1960s and '70s.[138] The increased demand for wigs among New Yorkers in particular as fashion items in the mid-1960s encouraged Korean immigrants to invest in wig industries through imported goods. As the wig industry faded in the early 1970s, Korean businesses expanded into garment manufacturing, such as jewelry and small bag production.[139] Furthermore, the Garment District in Midtown Manhattan, only a few blocks from 32nd Street, used to house many Korean factory owners and workers. Not surprisingly, the geographic proximity of these different sectors attracted coethnic owners and workers alike to Koreatown.

In response to these structural changes, restaurants opened to serve Korean immigrants and their children and students. Mi Cin at 130 West 45th Street was introduced by *The New York Times* on July 11, 1960, and is considered the first Korean restaurant in New York City;[140] Arirang House on 56th Street and Sambok on 43rd Street followed later in the decade.[141] Although the aforementioned restaurants tended to be more scattered across Midtown (between 27th Street and 56th Street), most Korean restaurants were clustered near the Korean Business District between 24th Street and 34th Street and Fifth and Seventh Avenues.[142] Seoul House, the first Korean restaurant on 32nd Street, opened in 1972. More restaurants and amenities began to aggregate in this very small section of Midtown in the 1980s, including New York Gomtang House (1982) and Kang Suh Heokwan (1984). Koryo Book Store (1980) was a pioneer business that brought another cultural component aside from food to the area, while the Hotel Stanford (1986), owned by Joong-Gap Kwon, optometrist offices, and beauty salons followed.[143]

However, Jinsook, an owner of one of the oldest restaurants in Koreatown (which is now closed) remembers that the space itself was not too attractive for non-Korean visitors, because "kids [from the Radisson Martinique Hotel] hung out and . . . came to my restaurant to use bathroom. Because too many kids came in, it was very hard to manage. They even threw out ketchup to pedestrians. People did not like to walk down here." The Radisson Martinique Hotel at Broadway and 32nd Street, previously called the Martinique, was one of the city's largest welfare hotels. Together with the Prince George Hotel at 28th Street between Fifth and Madison Avenues, it was considered the most notorious welfare hotel in the city, which served as an emergency shelter for homeless families between 1973 and 1988.[144]

The existence of the welfare hotels on 32nd Street reflects the role of local politics, urban planning, and federal government policies on shaping and reshaping Koreatown in Manhattan. The welfare hotels followed a significant increase in the homeless population in New York City due to the anti-urban sentiment of the Richard Nixon administration and the resulting cuts in federal assistance to cities, and the fiscal crisis of 1975 and its ensuing recession.[145] The situation continued to deteriorate during the Ronald Reagan administration, when the federal Housing and Urban Development budget was profoundly retrenched.[146] In American cities, rent had increased; families on public assistance and the working poor had to spend most of their wages on rent.[147] Across New York City, a half-million legal evictions were attempted in 1983 alone. In February 1987, 4,600 homeless families, with more than 10,000 children, were housed by New York City. Of these families, 75 percent were sheltered in the city's welfare hotels.[148]

These evictions were part of a rehabilitation plan that attempted to turn cheap housing for marginalized New Yorkers into high-end spaces. Mayor Ed Koch (1978–1989), who took office after the fiscal crisis, pursued a progrowth regime in which New York was reshaped as a market-oriented, finance-centric city that would take a prominent role in global capital flows.[149] With the ongoing decline of manufacturing in the 1970s and development of new service industries in global cities, city governments began to devise new strategies to counteract the economic downturn, encouraging leisure, shopping, tourism, and entertainment industries and developing infrastructure for these new industries.[150] Urban branding—for instance, New York City's "I ♥ NY" campaign—is one example of such strategies. The Martinique was closed in 1988.

Together with such changes in local politics and economic changes moving toward a postindustrial city, the landscape of Koreatown was also shaped by transnational factors—mainly political and economic changes, such as Korea's democratization and transition to heavy industry. New York City was trying to entice more visitors, and 32nd Street was no exception, despite the fact that the space itself had yet to be "discovered" by tourists and New Yorkers. Rather, Koreatown began to cater to a new group of consumers since the 1990s—Korean nationals, mostly temporary residents, such as international students enrolled at colleges or graduate schools, language students, or international tourists. During this shift, Koreatown became more of a cultural place for consumption and entertainment in line with the newly tourist-focused city economy.

This demographic change, in which more Korean nationals moved in and out of Koreatown, reflects structural changes both in Korea and in New York City. The Korean economy was growing more rapidly after the 1988 Olympics in Seoul. At the same time, several prodemocracy protests in Seoul in June 1987 drew international attention to Korea in terms of human rights issues and democratization, and direct elections followed shortly thereafter.[151] Pushed by such international variables, in the late 1980s, Korean society underwent a process of liberalization in terms of political and social policies, including the Foreign Travel Liberalization Act in 1989. At the same time, Korea began to move toward a consumer society, with a wage increase for the working and middle classes. It was a time when American consumer culture penetrated deeply into Korean daily lives. In the late 1980s, many American fast-food companies opened their first outlets in Seoul: Burger King (1984), KFC (1984), Pizza Hut (1985), Baskin-Robbins (1986), and finally McDonald's (1988). The American influence in Korea itself was thus combined with increased exposure of Koreans to Western culture through international study and travel. Younger generations thus began to take up such Western or American characteristics as valuing individualism, anti-authoritarianism, and consumption.

In parallel, 1.5- and second-generation children of immigrants in the United States became visible as a new consumer group. These young Korean Americans consist of working adults or college students; they are part of the US consumer generation, while actively engaging ethnic culture to develop their cultural identity and to feel a sense of belonging and home.[152] This will be discussed in chapters 3 and 4.

Koreatown as a Transclave

I have developed the concept of the transclave by locating Manhattan's Koreatown within the rise and fall of ethnic enclaves in US cities, and recent changes in academic and public understandings of such places. A transclave, in this context, refers to a hyperconsumption ethnic space lacking residences where people (entrepreneurs and consumers regardless of their race, ethnicity, gender, or sexual orientation), transnational corporations, and popular and consumer culture move back and forth between two nations and become embedded in a small section of a global city; a sending country's government and private corporations engages in the transnational process in order to (re)produce a nation's meaning and culture and to ultimately maximize its profits. Koreatown offers a unique but generalizable case study of an ethnic enclave in transition to a new type of transnational enclave for consumption and entertainment. Koreatown, as a transclave, is both "transnational" and an "enclave." It is not a singular case, as these traits are shared by new enclaves and traditional enclaves in transition. However, I argue that, despite its generalizability, Koreatown—and the transclave as a concept—also has unique traits differentiating it from other ethnic enclaves.

First, it is an enclave in a sociological sense, where Korean businesses such as restaurants, bars, cafés, local newspaper offices, language schools, lawyers' and doctors' offices, and wholesale stores are concentrated. The businesses mainly rely on coethnic laborers, but also non-coethnic workers, particularly Latinx workers. Their clients include both coethnics and non-coethnics. However, their target consumers, except for a few businesses such as lawyers and doctors, are non-Koreans. Although Korean restaurants, particularly high-end restaurants, exist throughout the city, as will be discussed in chapter 2, many are strategically aggregated within that block—32nd Street between Fifth Avenue and Broadway. However, unlike other enclaves, as pointed out earlier, Koreatown has rarely provided residence for newer immigrants, and is zoned as a commercial district by the New York City Department of City Planning. This has made Koreatown a unique district based on hyperconsumption, where restaurants and bars operate around the clock.

Second, Koreatown is not just ethnic but transnational in terms of its businesspeople and consumers and the characteristics of its businesses. Items and products imported directly from a sending country are common enough, of course. In this sense, every ethnic enclave has a degree of transnationality. However, in Koreatown, both entrepreneurs and consumers are transnational in terms of their movement between two nations as well as their unique form of engagement with the homeland, whether real or imagined. Most entrepreneurs go beyond selling "Korean" or "Korean-style" products, taking business trips to Korea in order to stay current with Seoul-style consumption trends and bring them back to New York. Moreover, unlike ethnic stores—mostly small mom-and-pop stores—in traditional ethnic neighborhoods, Koreatown businesses are not typically small businesses; in fact, many entrepreneurs have multiple stores across the city and New Jersey. Even many immigrant-owned stores have been replaced by Korean franchises and brands, a trend that has intensified since 2010 (see chapter 2). Various consumer groups—Korean nationals, Korean Americans, and non-Koreans in their twenties and thirties, the so-called consumer generation—also practice transnationalism by traveling between the two countries and consuming pop and consumer cultures in Koreatown and cyberspace. Their consumption has been (re)shaped by media outlets, such as YouTube, TikTok, Instagram, Twitter, and Netflix and various websites that offer English subtitles for newly released Korean media.

Most importantly, despite its similarities with other new enclaves, Koreatown, as a transclave, is unique in garnering investment from the Korean government and Korean corporations, including franchises (see chapters 1 and 2). Koreatown in Manhattan has been considered a platform to popularize and commercialize not only "ethnic culture" but more the "nation's culture" for the potential profit of both the Korean government and Korean corporations. Located in the heart of Manhattan and within walking distance of tourist attractions such as the Empire State Building, Herald Square, and Grand Central Terminal, Koreatown attracts many tourists. However, unlike Little Italy and Chinatown, which have longer histories and immigrant heritage, Koreatown had rarely been a target for "ethnic tourism" on the part of the local New York City government until recently. It has been only few years since the local media, both traditional and new media, began to pay attention to Koreatown, Korean pop culture (see chapter 5), and Korean food (see chapter 6). Instead, local entrepreneurs, mostly Korean immigrants, have been the main movers in boosting the enclave economy. More recently, in the past decade, the Korean government and Korean corporations have stepped in for nation branding projects, together creating positive images of the country through cultural content, leisure, entertainment, and consumer culture, aimed at maximizing profit returns not for coethnic employers, but for the nation's industry.

In this context, a transclave in a global city can play the role of a public advertisement within a nation branding effort, even if it does not make enough sales to make a profit. Manhattan's Koreatown is a unique case, but, in fact, not the only case studied. Ien Ang, albeit being very brief and lacking detail, has pointed to Thai Town on Campbell Street in Sydney, Australia, as separating itself from Chinatown in order to brand its own ethnic identity, with efforts by local Thai entrepreneurs and the support of the Thai consulate and Sydney City Council.[153] The concept of the transclave provides a new model for this form of enclave in a postindustrial society, as it best reflects how these global flows encourage cultural circulation and transmission, as well as economic benefit for the sending nation.

Qualitative Research in a Transclave

This book is based on qualitative research, consisting of in-depth interviews, archival research, and participant observation from 2008 to 2016, and again from winter 2017 to 2018 as a part of my follow-up research. I also did some participant observations and additional interviews from 2019 and 2024. I include 135 in-depth interviews with various Korean-cultural-product producers (thirty interviewees) and consumers (thirty-four Korean nationals, thirty Korean Americans, and forty-one non-Koreans) both in New York and Seoul. I also did participant observation during my time as a consumer, teacher, and employee in Koreatown from 2008 to 2016; and I did follow-up research both in Seoul and New York City between 2016 and 2018. While observing the landscape changes in Koreatown in 2019 and 2024, I completed two interviews with Koreans in the food and beverage industry who have engaged in the globalization of Korean food in New York City and two more interviews with a director and staff member of aT Center New York and a staff member at the Korean Cultural Center, all between 2022 and 2024. Additionally, I conducted an interview with a former employee in Koreatown in 2024.

My initial informal research began in February 2008, when I started to observe Koreatown as a transnational space for ethnic Koreans. At this point, my role was limited to passive participation; I did not seek out interaction until later in 2008 but observed the space as a consumer. In this role, I began to develop my research questions: Why does Koreatown lag behind Seoul in terms of physical appearance? Why do Korean nationals spend time in Koreatown even though they have other leisure spaces as alternative options? Why are these immigrant businesses able to open stores in the heart of Manhattan, where real estate is expensive?

One month later, I began working with a Korean American grassroots organization by teaching a Korean class and recruiting students. The classes were offered near Koreatown, and I taught there through 2008. Through this activity, I expanded my role to active participation as I interacted with my students and members at the organization, mostly 1.5- and second-generation Korean Americans who often expressed interest in their roots and ethnic culture. Having established rapport with some of my students and members at the organization, I later invited them for in-depth interviews during preliminary research from 2008 to summer 2010.

In January 2010, I was hired as an adjunct faculty member for the weekend language program at one of the community colleges in New York City that had not offered a Korean class in several years and were resuming them that semester. The first semester, I was the only Korean language instructor in the program. The class met on Saturday mornings for three hours. Based on my experience teaching Korean classes at the nonprofit organization, I expected to have more heritage learners. However, I only had three Korean American students, and eighteen were non-Koreans. I continued my participant observation as a teacher in the language programs until spring 2011; as with the Korean Americans in my earlier class, I invited some of these students for interviews during my official fieldwork between 2012 and 2016. In order to avoid ethical conflicts of interest in my role as an instructor, I invited them after classes ended or after I left the college in 2011.

In summer 2012, I began a new job at a small TOEFL prep school in Koreatown. My intent was to delve further into the field as an insider and employee in Koreatown. I was hired as a college application counselor, advising students on applying to college. In this position, I was able to observe how the system of enclave businesses worked, get inside information on Koreatown, and recruit some additional interviewees through the network I established at my work. I worked in this capacity for twenty hours per week in the fall of 2012.

Overlapping with this position, I taught Korean language at a second nonprofit organization, located on 32nd Street in Koreatown, between October 2012 and September 2013. While the first nonprofit was a grassroots political organization consisting of Korean American activists, the second organization was operated by a small Korean church in New York City. The first organization actively targeted students who identify as Korean; their purpose in offering Korean classes is to help shape and assert a Korean identity in an English-dominant society, and to bridge generational gaps between the first generation and the 1.5+ generations. The Korean classes at the second organization explicitly targeted non-Koreans who were interested in Korean culture, satisfying the growing desire for Korean language education among non-Koreans. This teaching experience at the second nonprofit was an opportunity to observe the logistics of the program and students' needs in terms of learning Korean. The number of students I taught in one term (ten weeks) was roughly ten. Most were non-Korean adults, except for a few Korean Americans.[154]

In spring 2013, while teaching at this organization, I also returned to the Korean language program at the community college to teach for another semester. While reaching out to consumers, I also conducted interviews with Koreatown businesspeople and staff at nonprofit organizations in New York, as well as a staff member at the Korean Food Foundation in Seoul. I completed my official fieldwork, both the in-depth interviews and participant observation in 2013, at which point

I left the second nonprofit organization. However, I have occasionally interviewed some people whom I have encountered since as well until 2015, and I continued participant observation until 2016 before I left New York City that summer.

In December 2016, I returned to Seoul to complete follow-up research for five weeks. In Seoul, I conducted interviews with a government employee of City Branding in the Seoul Metropolitan Government, staff members who worked at government-related agencies and research centers, and a staff member at one of the most prominent entertainment companies, which hosts the largest K-pop event in the United States. Between 2016 and 2019, while living in Ohio and upstate New York, I occasionally visited New York City and observed the changes in Koreatown. I also reached out to more consumers in New York for additional interviews in the winter and summer of 2017 and in winter 2018. In 2019, I returned to New York City for a new faculty position, and I have continued to observe changes in Koreatown while reaching out to producers in the space for final updates. After I returned to New York City, I began observing changes in Koreatown in 2019. In 2022 and 2023, I interviewed one of the major members of the Korean Cuisine Globalization Committee USA, who has had multiple businesses in Koreatown, and a Korean woman in the food and beverage industry who has been involved in the globalization of the Korean food project. In addition, I reached out to two Korean government agencies in New York City: aT Center New York and the Korean Cultural Center New York in 2024. I was able to speak with both a new director and a staff member at the aT Center New York—both of whom were dispatched from Korea—and a staff member at the Korean Cultural Center New York in order to learn more about the Korean government's approach and investments on food and nation branding strategies overseas.

Chapter Outline

The body of the book consists of two main parts. Part I, consisting of chapters 1 and 2, offers a historical analysis of nation branding in Korea, focusing on top-down policies that emerged after the 1997 financial crisis and the Korean government's collaboration with Korean corporations and Koreatown entrepreneurs. Chapter 1 analyzes how Korea has developed business strategies in the form of nation branding policies in response to the new global trend of nation-states promoting nations as tourist destinations and a form of capital investment in order to compete in a global market. I pay particular attention to how each administration since the financial crisis has implemented culture-based economic policies, focusing on Hallyu and food.[155] In chapter 2, I turn my attention to the Korean government's investment in New York City and its collaboration with transnational private sector entrepreneurs, including immigrants, Korea-based franchises, and nonprofit organizations. I explain how and why the Korean government and corporations consider New York City to be the cultural and economic center of the United States, making it one of the most critical overseas markets for Korea's nation branding projects. I also discuss how their approach often creates conflicts with local actors—mainly Korean entrepreneurs.

Part II, consisting of chapters 3, 4, 5, and 6, examines the stories of various transnational consumer groups—Korean nationals, Korean Americans, and non-Korean consumers—who participate in nation branding from the bottom up and their perceptions of, emotional attachments to, and struggles over the Koreatown space. Chapters 3 and 4 focus on intraethnic relations and conflicts between Korean nationals and Korean Americans—both immigrants and their children—and their symbolic struggle over the space. Chapter 3 underscores collective memories in the process of making and remaking Koreatown as a space for homemaking and nostalgia in a commercial neighborhood and navigates how nostalgia and collective memory have been transferred in Koreatown. Chapter 4 investigates how and why collective memories generate symbolic struggles and intraethnic conflicts over the street. I pay attention to how Korean nationals and Korean Americans develop "us" versus "them" distinctions and how these invisible or symbolic conflicts reconstruct a transclave as a symbolic space, based on collective memories. Chapters 5 and 6 explore more complicated intraethnic, interethnic, and interracial relations and conflicts over Koreatown. Chapter 5 explores how three consumer groups—particularly non-Korean Hallyu fans—practice Hallyu in Koreatown, changing the landscape into a more multiethnic and diverse space. Non-Korean Hallyu fans, largely based on online communities, extend their relationships with Korea by utilizing Koreatown. This "Korea" only exists or is imagined in the media, but it is also embedded in a transclave, a part of multicultural New York. Chapter 6 explores the popularity of Korean food in New York City by focusing on both transnational and domestic factors that have led to the new trend of commercialization of ethnic food, emphasis on authenticity, exoticness, and rise of the omnivore society in urban America. This chapter also analyzes how consumer groups navigate this new trend and how they (re)create Koreatown as a space for imagined Korean cuisine, though its authenticity is often contested by Korean nationals. Finally, it asks how we locate non-Koreans in Koreatown's map in the context of racial fetishization of Asian culture.

PART I

Branding Korea

1

Nation Branding

Economic Restructuring and the Cultural Industry in Korea

Korea is changing. Come and meet the new Korea.
—Kim Dae-Jung, then-president of Korea, in a public television advertisement, 1998

We never write to represent our countries, but this is the very first Oscar to South Korea.
—Bong Joon Ho, director of *Parasite*, at the onstage acceptance speech at the Academy Awards, 2020

Amid the COVID-19 pandemic in 2020, Korea was ecstatic to witness two achievements that no one would have expected a few years prior. It started with an Oscar-winning film, *Gisaengchung*, known in English as *Parasite*. In February, Koreans were ready to raise a toast to the most exciting news in Korea's film industry, while suffering from the COVID-19 pandemic that began earlier that year, when the Academy announced that Bong Joon Ho's film finally won four Oscars—Best Original Screenplay, Best International Feature Film, Best Director, and Best Picture. A couple of years back, it seemed like Bangtan Sonyeondan, better known as BTS outside Korea, was everywhere as they swept the world music scene from Asia to Europe to Latin America. The year 2020 was big for BTS and their dedicated fans, ARMY. BTS finally burst onto the US pop music scene, topping the Billboard music charts with "Dynamite" and "Life Goes On." In addition, they won two American Music Awards and were also nominated for a 2021 Grammy.

Koreans in Korea and overseas, from artists and filmmakers to politicians responded to such individual successes and achievements on a collective level and celebrated them with national pride. When Bong Joon Ho and Han Jin Won won the Best Original Screenplay at the Oscars, both Bong and Han acknowledged and highlighted the contributions of the Korean film industry and their nation. During the acceptance speech, Bong said, "Writing a script is such a lonely process. We never write to represent for our countries, but this is the very first Oscar to South Korea." Likewise, Han paid tribute to Korea's film industry and its members, saying, "I'd like to share this honor with all the storytellers and filmmakers at Chungmuro [Korea's Hollywood]."[1] In response to their individual triumphs at the Academy Awards, a congratulatory message arrived on February 10 from Cheongwadae, or the Blue House. Moon Jae-in, who was president of Korea at the time, wrote on Twitter and Facebook: "Taking home four Oscars, after winning the Palme d'Or at the Cannes Film Festival last year, can be attributed to the accumulated efforts of every Korean filmmaker over the past 100 years. I am very pleased to see a Korean film stand shoulder to shoulder with those of other countries and mark the beginning of another 100 years of Korean filmmaking."[2] Likewise, when BTS topped the Billboard music charts with the song "Dynamite," the president also sent a message to the members of the group on August 31, 2020. He wrote, "It will bring huge consolation to Koreans suffering from the national crisis caused by COVID-19. I offer my heartfelt congratulations." With another Billboard chart-topping song, "Life Goes On," sung in Korean, the National Assembly of the Republic of Korea revised the Military Service Act before the oldest member of BTS, Jin, turned twenty-eight years old. The act originally required Korean men to complete compulsory military service before age twenty-eight; exceptions included athletes who had won any kind of medal at the Olympic Games or gold medals at the Asian Games, and classical musicians and dancers who won recognized international and select domestic competitions.[3] Yet under the revised laws, some male K-pop entertainers who have received cultural medals from the government for their global and domestic contributions and have been recommended by the Minister of Culture, Sports, and Tourism (MCST)[4] are eligible to apply for the deferment.[5]

This national response reveals that their achievements are not recognized on a solely individual level; the nation has been collectively' ecstatic that the global audience, particularly Americans, finally developed an appetite for Korean pop music and movies. Why did individuals' successes become nationwide fever? Why did Koreans gather to celebrate their popularity in the US market? Why does the Korean government and the National Assembly care about an individual's accomplishments, going so far as to revise the military law in order to offer deferments for the two oldest members of BTS, Jin and Suga?

In this chapter, I argue that the collective response toward BTS's and Bong's success lies in how and why Korea has built and branded itself in the global neoliberal order, coinciding with the financial crisis of 1997–1998. Though I emphasize both top-down and bottom-up nation branding strategies, this chapter pays particular attention to the major top-down policies pushing to overcome economic hardship in the post-financial-crisis years by creating new national images to attract foreign investors and visitors. In the seventy years following the Korean War, Korea underwent massive, rapid changes—from several military dictatorships to a democratic government, and from being one of the world's poorest countries to establishing a leading and still rapidly growing economy—in a process termed "compressed modernity."[6] This chapter will pay special attention to nation branding to explore how the post-financial-crisis administrations (of Kim Dae-jung, Roh Moo-hyun, Lee Myung-bak, Park Geun-hye, and Moon Jae-in) devised cultural and economic policies to strategically overcome the economic uncertainty stemming from the 1997 financial crisis. These policies played a key role in leading Korea to become a postindustrial and consumer economy by emphasizing new and cultural industries, including the entertainment and food industries both in Korea and overseas.

Rebuilding a New Korea in a Neoliberal Order

As television news constantly showed Deputy Prime Minister for Economic Affairs Lim Chang-Yuel with Michel Camdessus, a managing director of the International Monetary Fund (IMF) signing the agreement on financial reform, Koreans—particularly those who experienced the economic boom of earlier years—mourned the country's failure. December 3, 1997, was declared the second national humiliation day, following the Japan-Korea Treaty of 1910.[7]

Koreans, who believed in a rosy promise that their nation was moving toward the economic forefront, after joining the OECD (Organisation for Economic Co-operation and Development) in 1996, suddenly had to confront economic uncertainty and crisis in the next year. Triggered by a series of financial crises in other Asian countries such as Thailand, Malaysia, Indonesia, and the Philippines, the economic situation in Korea was exacerbated by the newness of economic liberalization policies leading to the deregulation of finance and reduction of the state's economic role. Although there were earlier signs of the crisis—particularly the bankruptcies of Hanbo, Korea's fourteenth largest *chaebol* (family-owned conglomerate) in January and KIA, the eighth largest chaebol, in July—the Korean government was not prepared for the economic collapse that would occur within a year. With a $55 billion bailout—$35 billion from the IMF, the International Bank for Reconstruction and Development, and the Asian Development Bank, and $20 billion from the United States, Japan, Canada, Germany, France, the UK, and Australia—international pressure for market liberalization, privatization, and deregulation seemed to be inevitable. The long-standing alliance between the government and chaebol, and the ensuing corruption, highlighted the failure of the liberalized market mechanism. Such financial liberalization was a key cause of increasing foreign debt, particularly in the chaebol's short-term debt from foreign banks.[8]

The newly elected President Kim Dae-jung (1998–2003),[9] a political dissident, and his administration believed that Korea would achieve both economic liberalization and political democracy at the same time.[10] Not only did Korea follow the IMF reform policies, it also now had to seek alternatives for paying back the bailout from the IMF and revamping the economic downturn. Rather than stepping in as the main actor, the government took the role of facilitator for the new global order in implementing IMF policies.[11] New industries, such as information technology (IT) and cultural content industries, were targeted for national investment.[12]

While it may seem that national identity is blurred by the physical and cultural mobility of an economically liberalized global society, the nation and its meanings may also be reinforced. This is particularly true in the context of nation branding in a globalized world.[13] While the 1997 IMF bailout spurred the incorporation of the nation to a neoliberal global order, the nation itself remained an important social, political, and cultural rhetorical symbol for social integration, both within the nation and as a strategy to maintain global competitiveness through nation branding efforts. This new phenomenon, in fact, indicates the beginning of a new era in a neoliberal global order that Koreans did not anticipate in the past.

Korea under the IMF bailout program had to undergo radical economic restructuring. Many scholars perceived this as a sign of the demise of the East Asian development model.[14] According to Jang-Sup Shin and Ha-Joon Chang,[15] the IMF economic restructuring program for Korea had three broad components: (1) macroeconomic retrenchment through high interest rates and tight budgetary policy; (2) market opening, reinforcing the liberalization of products and finance and eradicating trade-related subsidies; and (3) structural reform of the financial, corporate, labor, and public sectors, to emphasize economic efficiency and market ability. This reflected the standard of the US system, embedding an American model in Korea.[16] The IMF was referred to as "I aM Fired" or "I aM Fined" by the local media, in response to the high unemployment rate and preponderance of fines for civil offenses. To boost domestic consumption, credit cards were issued indiscriminately, and Koreans who were already in debt became trapped in the cycle of credit card debt, leading massive credit card crisis in 2003.[17] Korea was, in fact, in serious crisis.

Collective Efforts and Public Advertisement

The media reported how the financial crisis would impact daily life, complete with images of crying and desperate Koreans. However, with the message that Koreans would survive this crisis as they had the Japan's Colonial Rule (1910–1945) and Korean War (1950–1953), Korean citizens collectively embraced the hope that "we" Koreans could overcome the nation's bankruptcy "together." This attitude was strongly supported by the state, businesses, and nonprofit organizations and promoted in a series of nationalistic and patriotic campaigns and a series of public advertisements.[18]

The "Gold Collection" campaign was one of the public advertisement efforts. Occurring sporadically among several groups, including grassroots organizations, after the government announced the bailout, this campaign caught national attention with an emotional news report by KBS (Korea Broadcasting System) in which citizens were urged to donate gold to the national treasury. The idea was simple: A lack of foreign currency could be paid off by purchasing gold from ordinary citizens at a cheaper price and subsequently exporting a large stock of gold. The official campaign kicked off on January 5, 1998; citizens waited for hours in lines at collection stations to donate wedding rings, medals, trophies, and good luck keys traditionally given for sixtieth birthdays. The campaign lasted for three months, netting 227 tons of gold; 3,510,000 citizens participated, including Koreans living in Korea and those living abroad.[19] Even then-president-elect, Kim Dae-jung, donated his personal gold, and he requested upper-middle-class and upper-class citizens to join him.[20]

Public advertisements sponsored by the government and private companies promoted similar attitudes toward overcoming the financial crisis. In 1998, the media regularly aired scenes of the golfer Pak Se-ri winning the US Women's Open with a memorable shot in her bare feet; after her ball landed in the sloped rough alongside the river, Pak took off her shoes and socks and went into the river to continue playing. The Office of Public Information used this image accompanied by a song with the lyrics "We will eventually win, although the journey is long and hard." Such nationalistic rhetoric was highly effective as political ideology, as was the imagery of a Korean overcoming racial barriers in a Western- and white-dominated sport.

Likewise, in 1998, President Kim Dae-jung, together with celebrities, including K-pop stars, actors, and actresses, made the first presidential appearance in a public television advertisement to attract foreign tourists. Holding a *cheongsachorong*, a traditional Korean lantern, the president stated that "Korea is changing. Come and meet the new Korea." The advertisement was made not only to entice foreign tourists but also to market the nation with a positive image and message: "Korea is evolving, so visit and invest in us."[21] This was a new moment for Korea's branding strategies. Though they did not call it "nation branding," it was clear that the Korean government began stepping into a new agenda to spread positive national images overseas and promote nationalist sentiment that emphasizes collective grief and hope at the same time.

New Korea: The Second Founding of the Nation

On August 15, 1998, the fifty-third anniversary of independence from Japan, President Kim announced "the Second Founding of the Nation" and the establishment of the National Commission for Rebuilding Korea for social and administrative reforms; six societal shifts were suggested: from (1) authoritarianism to participatory democracy; (2) strong state regulation to market autonomy; (3) exclusionary nationalism to public engagement and decentralization of power; (4) material-oriented growth to information-based society; (5) division and conflict to harmony and cooperation; and (6) North-South antagonism and confrontation to an emphasis on exchange between North Korea and South Korea.[22] The "New Korea" envisioned in this project emphasized the future economic importance of tourism, IT, and the cultural industry. While these had not yet brought much revenue for Korea, the government strategically invested in and promoted these industries to create more jobs and market itself in a different way.

Due to perceived political instability triggered by the North-South division and lack of tourism infrastructure, Korea did not consider tourism a viable source of revenue. Yet, new tourism policies were implemented in preparation for a series of national events: Asia-Europe Meeting in 2000, Visit Korea Year 2001, and the Korea-Japan World Cup in 2002. In addition, in order to create jobs and revenue, the government implemented Tourism Vision 21 (1999–2003) and the second Tourism Development Plan (2002–2011). Tourism Vision 21, a five-year plan, was devised in 1999 to develop Korea as a Northeast Asian tour hub, induce foreign and domestic investment, advance the information-based tourism industry, and promote domestic tourism among Koreans.[23] The Ministry of Culture, Sports, and Tourism (MCST),[24] Korea National Tourism Organization, Korea Tourism Research Institute, and local governments were involved in the tourism promotion; financial aid came from the national government, with a significant increase in the tourism budget between 1997 and 2002;[25] and tour infrastructure was built at a heavy rate.

The cultural industry was likewise promoted by the government, particularly targeting the Asian market. The cultural industry and foreign investment in the broadcasting industry in Korea had been strongly regulated by the government especially during the military dictatorships, while censorship prevailed in the national media. However, the popularity of Korean pop culture in Asia and the liberal administration of Kim Dae-jung (1998–2003) was a turning point, as the government shifted cultural policy from regulation to investment. This popularity of Hallyu is known for its market success and birth of new media.[26] Yet, it should be noted that the government was also involved in this process by creating "infrastructure" since the late 1990s and promoting Hallyu overseas, just like many other nation-states that began opening their eyes to such strategies. However, as discussed earlier, the role of the state government shifted from that of the main actor (as was the case in previous administrations) to more of a facilitator role, actively implementing neoliberal orders into the nation through new industries.

Hallyu, together with IT,[27] was promoted to export products with cultural content—music, drama, games, movies—but more importantly, to drive indirect benefits, such as sales on tie-in products and exposure of Korean brands to international consumers.[28] The promotion of the cultural industry was expected by the government to positively impact the nation's international image as a cultural frontier.[29] However, some criticism holds that the industry effects were often exaggerated and used for government PR.[30]

Dynamic Korea

The IMF bailout was repaid in three years and eight months on August 23, 2001. Although the newly elected president and his administration had not used the term "nation branding" until 2001, a year before the 2002 Korea-Japan World Cup, the administration often pointed out how Korean society should be positively depicted in other nations. In order to improve the nation's image and manage nation branding, several projects, such as Totally New Korea, were devised to promote Korea as a strong brand by 2010. The 2002 Korea-Japan World Cup offered momentum not only for the Korean government to actively engage in branding efforts but also for Koreans to participate in nation branding efforts from the bottom up. During the 2002 World Cup preparation, there was an increasing discussion on how Korea could shed its image of financial crisis through sporting events. The main concern was how to portray Korea as a young and dynamic nation, separating it from the negative image of the "Korea Discount." In the past, large Korean corporations did not promote their products as "made in Korea" due to the devalued perception of Korean products stemming from the production of cheap and unremarkable products in the 1970s. Although the main export industries in Korea were high-tech—semiconductors, automobiles, mobile communications—many believe that the national image lagged behind that reality.[31]

In order to meet new global demands, "Dynamic Korea," an umbrella slogan, synthesized the goals of export promotion and an increase in foreign investment through IT, tourism, and culture under one slogan.[32] Jin Nam-gung of the MCST said that the administration planned to promote the 2002 World Cup as a "cultural World Cup," "tourism World Cup," and "IT Korea," with emphasis on biotechnology and cultural products.[33] Bottom-up participation seemed to be successful. During the World Cup, people cheering enthusiastically on streets caught international attention. For Koreans, soccer was not just a sport, but how Koreans united and expressed national identity and pride as Koreans. Chanting the nation's name, "Dae-han-min-kuk," and wearing red T-shirts with the logo "Be the Reds," a reported 7 million Koreans had gathered in the streets to cheer during the June 25 semifinal against Germany.[34]

The government did not miss out on opportunities that arose because of this new phenomenon. Post–World Cup projects were soon introduced. On June 19, 2002, at a meeting with CEOs of big corporations, President Kim asked that the government and business sector work together to maximize the phenomenon through exposure and exportation.[35] A similar announcement was made public during the semifinal.[36] Although the Korean Information Service; MCST; Ministry of Foreign Affairs; and Ministry of Commerce, Industry, and Energy had been engaged in public relations, the Committee on Nation Image Improvement was established under the control of the prime minister on July 2, 2002, composed of ten highly ranked government officials and ten civilian members tasked with promoting the slogans "Creative Korea," "Friendly Korea," and "Bright Korea."[37] The sports World Cup would thus be transformed into an economic World Cup,[38] a policy protocol continued by President Roh Moo-hyun in 2003.

With a very close margin of victory in the presidential election, Roh Moo-hyun, a former human rights lawyer and National Assembly member who served in Kim's cabinet, took office in 2003. Strongly supported by the generations in their twenties, thirties, and forties and by civil society groups, his win meant a generational change in Korean politics. The support from President Kim also meant a continuation and extension of the Kim administration's policies; economic and nation branding policies were no exception.[39] Having emphasized social integration, national integration, and balanced development, particularly regional, the Roh administration ironically insisted on nationwide policies for enterprise and neoliberal market reform.[40] Transitioning to an innovation-driven economy and win-win growth were the main concerns in industrial policies.[41] "Innovation" was the key word: technical innovation, system innovation, and cultural innovation. Roh emphasized science and technology, with a special focus on biotechnology as "next-generation growth engines."[42]

The administration endeavored to replace the negative image of cheap and low-quality products "made in Korea" with the high-tech industry. The "Dynamic Korea" slogan was more effectively materialized and intensified to support science and technology and the cultural industry under the Roh administration. The government sponsored "Dynamic Korea" through TV promotional video in 2003 and extended it as a public campaign during international events in 2005.[43] The slogan characterizes a partnership of government agencies, business sectors, research institutes, and academia. Academics discussed the post–World Cup phenomenon, soft power, and cultural industry, and government-sponsored academic institutions were actively engaged in this discourse. The Institute for Industrial Policy Studies, a think-tank institution of the Ministry of Commerce, Industry, and Energy, kicked off the Korean Brand Conference in 2002 as well as the annual survey on the nation's image; foreign scholars, such as the French neoliberal economist Guy Sorman, were often invited to government-organized academic conferences on economic growth and nation branding to support market privatization; the government planned to open a graduate school focused on cultural industry and technology at Korea Advanced Institute of Science & Technology (KAIST);[44] KAIST finally established the Graduate School of Culture Technology sponsored by the MCST in 2005.

The post–World Cup projects were reinforced by stressing the importance of foreign investment and image promotion. In the early 2000s, branding and marketing professionals began engaging in political campaigns and government agencies. Online civic participation, grassroots campaigns, and new media characterized the presidential election in 2002,[45] resulting in Roh Moo-hyun's win with massive support from younger voters, though he was often redbaited as a leftist. The election also meant the demise of old-fashioned politics and was often called the "Internet election." A series of TV commercials emphasized his touching personal history and images, as a human rights lawyer and progressive politician. A government official in the Seoul Metropolitan Government's City Branding Division told me in 2017, "Advertising professionals began getting involved in political campaigns. It was very intensive. . . . They grew to play an important role in the elections. They work with a presidential candidate for campaign commercials. Some worked at the Blue House for public information and media promotion." This official, who also worked at an advertising agency company before working in the public sector, explained that professionals in the advertising industry have shifted the public understanding of politicians. Such business strategies have indeed penetrated political campaigns and the government, as politicians and policy makers across the planet increasingly recognized and engaged in the branding assets in global flows of neoliberal state agendas.[46] He also became a part of the trend, later working in the Seoul Metropolitan Government and developing various city branding policies and strategies.

After the presidential election in 2002, President Roh made his first foreign visit to the United States on May 11, 2003, for a summit meeting with President George W. Bush on May 15. In addition to the perennial issues of nuclear arms, conflict with North Korea, and reinforcement of the Korea-US military alliance, Roh also sought to enhance commercial ties and economic cooperation between the two nations. As the visit was "sales diplomacy," thirty-one business leaders, including CEOs from Samsung, Hyundai, and LG, accompanied the president;[47] likewise, Roh and the business leaders met with their Wall Street counterparts to encourage investment in Korea and emphasize the administration's intent to build the basis for an appropriate market system.[48] Roh thus encouraged foreign investment by branding the nation as more market friendly and technically advanced, confirming his administration's desire to follow an Anglo-American neoliberal path of deregulation and market privatization,[49] facilitating financialization but at the same time investing in itself.[50]

New Industries, New Opportunities

As was the case in the previous Kim administration, the IT industry became the backbone of economic policies. Mobile technologies, including Samsung and LG, were key for Korea's commercial success in the global IT market. As "next-generation growth engines" and a part of research and development investment, the Roh administration aggressively invested in the biotech industry. The government continued with nation branding efforts by connecting them to the IT industry. During the APEC summit in Busan in 2005, the government marketed Korea as an IT nation under the slogan "IT Korea." The Ministry of Information and Communication played a critical role, having worked with Samsung, LG, KT, and others, to demonstrate new technology and showcase high-tech products.[51]

Likewise, there was investment in the cultural industry and products. With a clear agenda for the future culturally leading nation, Lee Chang-Dong, a leading film director, screenwriter, and novelist, who won the Silver Lion at the Venice Film Festival for *Oasis* in 2002 and later the Best Screenplay Award at the 2010 Cannes Film Festival for *Poetry*, was appointed as the minister of culture and tourism (now Ministry of Culture, Sports, and Tourism) in 2003. In 2004, Lee announced a mid-to-long-term cultural policy, "Creative Korea," and the Art Policy in New Korea. Creative Korea put forth its plans for promoting cultural creativity among citizens through education as the basis of a multicultural society.[52]

If Creative Korea is a more philosophical and broad approach, C Korea 2010—announced in the following year—emphasized the cultural industry and products. C Korea 2010 straightforwardly called for the promotion of culture, tourism, and leisure, based on three Cs—content, creativity, and culture—with a goal of $30,000 USD per capita gross national income.[53] Video games have created the most revenue by far for Korea; its synergizing of technology and cultural content is in line with administration strategy. The online and mobile gaming industry has grown dramatically since the early 2000s with the development of IT infrastructure; Korea is a leading exporter of games. Like the game industry, other types of Korean companies—including cosmetics, fashion items, and electronics—have become popular in China and Vietnam through product placement in various Hallyu content.[54] The popularity of Korean TV dramas in Japan, China, and Hong Kong attracts Hallyu consumers to Korea for travel. A particularly successful Hallyu-related marketing outcome is the popularity of Korean food in Asia due to the traditional Korean food drama "The Great Jang Geum," first broadcast in Korea in 2003 and later exported to over ninety-one countries as of 2013 (including Iran, Turkey, Zimbabwe, and Rwanda).[55] In fact, like the gaming industry, technological advances have become one of the driving forces in distributing Hallyu content overseas. Cultural industries, rather than culture itself or arts, were espoused as resources for national revenue, encouraging government investment in marketizing and industrializing the culture under the nation branding strategy "Dynamic Korea."[56]

Although the liberal administrations of Kim and Roh recognized, underlined, and invested in the importance of nation branding, their strategies and slogans were not integrated into the umbrella slogan "Dynamic Korea." Diverse government agencies proposed branding strategies.[57] For instance, in addition to the promotion of popular culture, the MCST kicked off a project to commercialize traditional culture, called "Han Brands" or later "Han Style." Categorizing traditional culture into six categories—Hangeul (language), Hansik (food), Hanbok (clothes), Hanji (paper), Hanok (house), and Hanguk-eumak (Korean traditional music)—was essentially a way of rebranding traditional culture, with the expectation that these traditions, newly connected to modern culture, could also act as a source of cultural product profit. Han Brands became the basis for the key Korean food projects in the following administration.[58]

In 2007, during the last year of Roh's presidency, the Korea Tourism Organization introduced a slogan promoting tourism based on a survey among tourism experts in nine countries and potential foreign tourists in seventeen countries; "Korea, Sparkling" was meant to convey the revitalization and freshness of the country and symbolize its interconnection of tradition and highly advanced modernism. With domestic and international experts such as Simon Anholt participating in the process of brand making, the organization planned to promote the national brand in major cities, such as Tokyo, Beijing, New York, and London. The marketing budget increased to 22.5 billion won (about 22 million USD in 2007), producing television commercials promoting tourism that were seen on major broadcast networks, including CNN and BBC.[59]

Korea Inc.: Nation Branding Policies

The Kim and Roh administrations focused on paying back the IMF bailout and revamping the economy through rapid economic restructuring and new branding strategies after the financial crisis of 1997, shaping the government's role as a facilitator of the neoliberal state. The following conservative Lee and Park administrations (2008–2013 and 2013–2017, respectively) even further expedited the neoliberal order by branding its nation as a business-friendly country and by emphasizing the cultural industry.

CEO of Korea

During the presidential election campaign, Lee Myung-bak, as a former CEO of Hyundai Engineering and Construction and CEO-style mayor of Seoul (2002–2006), gave credence to his 747 plans, calling for 7 percent annual growth in gross domestic product (GDP) and $40,000 USD annual income per capita and establishing Korea as the world's seventh largest economy.[60] In the five years of his presidency, Lee's economic policies centered on what was often called "Korea Inc.": corporate-friendly economic policies such as a high exchange rate, reductions in corporate and real estate taxes, market and financial deregulation, welfare reduction, privatization of public enterprise, and healthcare marketization—all of which greatly aided the chaebol. Although this market orientation of the state was also part of the two liberal administrations—in part to redeem the 1997 IMF bailout—the Lee administration more vigorously supported neoliberal economic practices; this included a reduction in social security benefits after the 2008 recession.[61] Probusiness state intervention was present in a number of Lee's policies, particularly green growth,[62] nation branding, and

Korean food projects. (The overseas food project will be discussed in detail in chapter 2.)

In a speech on August 15, 2008—Korean Independence Day—President Lee Myung-bak, who had taken office earlier that year, announced three new core values in Korea's future: the development of green growth, encouragement of nation branding, and enhancement of law-abiding spirit.[63] The Lee administration kicked off a "Nation Branding" project, under the president's direct control, due to concern over Korea's ranking as thirty-third out of fifty countries in the Nation Branding Index. This index, a tool developed by the custom research company Anholt-GfK to measure the image and reputation of the world's nations and to track their profiles as they rise and fall,[64] has strongly influenced how the Lee administration creates strategy regarding the nation's image and reputation by transnational investment.

Several public and private actors participated in the nation branding project. The business sector, conservative media, and domestic and international academia worked together closely to achieve the promotion of positive images of the nation. The government is a main actor in this project, via the Presidential Council for Nation Branding (PCNB); Yoon-Dae Euh, a former professor and president of Korea University, nicknamed the CEO of the university for the accumulation of college development funds in his term, was appointed as chair. To make the branding project international in scope, a group of "global advisors" to the Korean president consisting of market-friendly academic and public figures was formed, including Heizo Takenaka of Keio University and Japan's Koizumi Cabinet, Michael Porter of Harvard University, John Thornton of the Brookings Institution and former CEO of Goldman Sachs Asia, and Bill Gates of Microsoft. Guy Sorman, a neoliberal French scholar, was also appointed; his presence exemplifies how the Korean government worked with international scholars to academically justify neoliberal economic policies.[65]

What Forbes magazine calls the "Korea discount"—"the amount by which investors undervalue Korean stocks"[66]—was often referenced by policy makers and chaebol leaders as the phenomenon by which Korean products are devalued because of the low national reputation. As a result, chaebols have worked directly with the PCNB. Samsung, Hyundai, LG, SKT, and Kolon agreed to lend middle-ranked staff members to the council for their marketing expertise; this staff as a body was considered volunteer workers, as they are paid by the companies lending them out.[67] Samsung has been particularly active in the administration's nation branding efforts. Samsung Economic Research Institute (SERI, now Samsung Global Research), a private academic institute focusing on economic issues, released a series of economic reports that emphasized the importance of nation branding. SERI and the council also consented to devise a new index—the Korea Brand Index—to measure achievements in nation branding and systematize a management system; the funding of the project by SERI in the name of social contribution was well publicized.[68] SERI and the council devised the SERI-PCNB Nation Brand Dual Octagon and have published an annual report on nation branding between 2009 and 2012;[69] likewise, the Hyundai Research Institute also published several reports on international competitiveness and nation branding.

More indirectly, sports have been a popular venue for business-based nation building efforts. For instance, the chair of Hyundai led a campaign for Yeosu Expo 2012. Similarly, the campaign for the 2018 PyeongChang Winter Olympics was run by the former chair of Samsung, Lee Kun-hee, although this required a special amnesty granted by President Lee.[70] While the economic benefits of the Winter Olympics offered an excuse for the special pardon, it also clearly showed the exceptionalist attitude toward Samsung and chaebols in general in the Lee administration.

Internationally, the nation branding strategy aims at achieving a positive image of Korea overseas, hailing its transition from one of the poorest nations worldwide to an economically and technically advanced nation, from a recipient to an aid country, and from a country lacking an international voice to a country strengthening global communication. The G20 Seoul Summit, the fifth meeting of the G20 heads of government, should be noted as a factor in the Lee administration's nation branding efforts. Held November 11–12, 2010, in Seoul, Korea was the first non-G8 country to host a G20 meeting; the Lee administration publicized this as a turning point for Korea's integration into the economically advanced nations through its important role in new global governance. Media continually aired special news programs dedicated to the meeting and its economic impact on the nation,[71] and pro-

Lee journalists wrote countless articles assuring citizens that the event would boost the nation's status in the world economy. SERI published a report that Korea would reap direct economic effects worth 102.3 billion won (about 92.1 million USD in 2010), with indirect economic effects benefiting Korean companies anywhere from 21.45 trillion to 24.54 trillion won (about 19.3 billion to 22.1 billion USD in 2010).[72] However, these forecasts were criticized as exaggerations by progressive scholars and media.[73]

Domestically, nation branding aimed at enhancing the integration of a multicultural Korea and a sense of citizenship as enhancement of law-abiding spirit in the Lee administration.[74] Social integration had become an issue in the late 1990s due to an increase in foreign brides and guest workers from Southeast Asia and China; social integration of foreign-born brides and their biracial or bi-ethnic children was often emphasized by Yoon-dae Euh at press interviews and conferences. The council also created several projects to develop the sense that "every citizen is a single individual diplomat to represent Korea." For instance, in 2010, the PCNB and LG, a conglomerate, worked together for the "Love Korea" TV campaign, which had a theme of "a memory about you is a memory about Korea," raising awareness of "global etiquettes" and manners among Koreans to greet foreign tourists who visit Korea.[75]

Creative Economy and Hallyu

In 2012, Park Geun-hye, a daughter of the former president and military dictator Park Chung-hee, was elected as the first female president of Korea with strong support from conservative politicians and citizens. During the presidential election campaign, economic revitalization was a key issue. Park ambiguously argued that revitalization would be propelled by a creative economy and economic democratization—an economic reform restructuring the existing chaebol-centered economic system; this was ironic and strategic because it was the opposite of what she and her party had long focused on—economic growth rather than wealth distribution. Many of her supporters missed the rapid economic growth of her father's era, and they expected that she would carry on her father's legacy. In order to touch on nostalgic memories, often romanticized and shared by conservative voters, she purposely used nuanced propaganda of the developmental state, reminiscing about her father's tenure, even though Korea had already reached an advanced stage of economic development with relatively low GDP growth.

In order to inherit her father's legacy, Park introduced the "Second Miracle on the Han River" as a new agenda for the new administration during her inaugural speech on February 25, 2013. "The Miracle on the Han River" is a symbolic term, referring to the rapid economic growth with intensive labor of the 1960s and 1970s during her father's dictatorship. Her usage of this term was very strategic and clear: to declare herself as the president to revamp the economic downturn, while still denouncing the Kim and Roh administrations as "The Lost 10 Years," even after Lee's five-year-tenure. Within a year, of course, Park and her administration switched gears toward more economic growth rather than distribution and economic reform.[76] However, once she was elected, the administration's economic policies and development paradigm brought the creative economy to the fore; there was a shift from manufacturing industries to new industries, ultimately aiming at creating more job opportunities and revitalizing the economy.[77]

In 2013, the Park administration established both the new Ministry of Science, ICT and Future Planning and the Presidential Committee on Cultural Enrichment in order to implement the infrastructure and ecosystem for the creative economy.[78] As part of the public-private partnership, the Public-Private Creative Economy Committee was established by the Ministry of Science, ICT and Future Planning, consisting of representatives from the private sector—such as economic organizations, corporations, and research centers— and government officials.[79] In 2014, as a part of the public-private partnership efforts and the Three-Year Plan for Economic Innovation, the Center for Creative Economy and Innovation (CCEI) was established to support startups and small- and medium-sized companies. Although seventeen CCEI offices were spread out across seventeen metropolitan cities and provinces in Korea, in each region, a CCEI was paired with a chaebol with their own specialization in order to provide legal services, financial investment, marketing strategies, and mentoring services as well as opportunities for overseas market expansion; this offered a new model for local industry to network with big corporations, such as CJ Food and CJ E&M (a media company that produced and distributed the movie *Parasite*) among many others, and learn from their experience.[80] Yet, despite its nonprofit status, the CCEI is controlled by the government and chaebols, including Samsung, LG, and Hyundai; it aims to be an "entrepreneur ecosystem" establishment, and represents a typical Korean top-down economic strategy,[81] or as some call it, the cozy relations between politics and big businesses.[82]

Likewise, in 2015, as part of the cultural enrichment policy, the MCST and CJ E&M jointly established the Culture Creation and Convergence Belt—"a cluster of cultural and content-related industries," where cultural content meets and "converges" with Information and Communication Technology (ICT)—in order to realize the government's vision for the creative economy and build the cycle of planning, production, realization, and reinvestment in the cultural content industry.[83] The belt included the Creative Center for Convergence Culture, the Culture Creation Venture Complex, the Creative Economy Leaders Academy, and the K-Culture Valley. Invested in by CJ E&M, the Creative Center for Convergence Culture was located in the CJ E&M Center of the CJ Group in Seoul, offering startups and cultural creators free space and a mentoring system with music producers, filmmakers, drama directors, and food experts and focusing on planning, development, and incubating.[84] The Culture Creation Venture Complex offers spaces for venture companies to be housed, while the Creative Economy Leaders Academy provides training programs to cultural creators. The government even planned to construct a theme park—K-Culture Valley in Goyang, Gyeonggi Province—in addition to other multiuse facilities such as K-Experience complex cultural space and K-pop Arena.[85] K-Culture Valley, a theme park, featuring six zones from K-pop to TV dramas, has been planned and constructed by CJ Consortium, while K-Experience—a urban cultural hub—has been undertaken by Korean Air.[86]

"Creative Korea," a nod to the "creative economy," was announced as a new nation brand slogan in July 2016 by the MCST; this new slogan replaced "Dynamic Korea" and was the result of design contests and asking keywords about Koreanness. The MCST explained that creativity, passion, and harmony were identified as major keywords, thus, they decided to include "creativity" in the slogan, because creativity was embedded in Korean people's DNA."[87] The word "creative" was everywhere during Park's tenure, from cultural and economic policies to the nation branding slogan. Yet, it soon became controversial because of the design similarity to the logo for "Creative France." In fact, this brand logo was abolished in 2017 during the following Moon Jae-in administration.

President Park Geun-hye was accused of and admitted to leaking official state documents to a friend, Soon-sil Choi. Choi was found guilty of numerous offenses, including intervening in state affairs and benefiting from government-sponsored projects, including nation branding, the *Hallyu* industry, and sporting events, particularly in preparation for PyeongChang's 2018 Winter Olympics. Choi engaged in developing Korea's "Creative Korea" branding slogan and devised other related projects, including working with K-pop video director, Eun-taek Cha, who was accused of abuse of power, coercion, and embezzlement to win the right to work on these projects, including the Culture Creation and Convergence Belt. Furthermore, the administration and the MCST blacklisted thousands of artists and cultural figures who criticized and satirized the Park administration; in addition, these individuals were barred from receiving government funds and benefiting from government programs. The list includes well-known directors and actors, such as Bong Joon Ho from *Parasite* (2019) and Park Chan-wook from *Old Boy* (2003) and *Decision to Leave* (2022). They were also blacklisted from the National Intelligence Service in the Lee administration. In addition to the blacklist, Lee had been accused of receiving bribes from chaebols (including Samsung), embezzlement, and corruption in defense and military industry and resource diplomacy.

Korean citizens voluntarily organized candlelight vigils in various cities to call for President Park's resignation starting from October 29, 2016. The most visible of these protests in Gwanghwamun, Seoul, which occurred for twenty successive weeks on Saturday nights, became known as the "Candlelight Revolution" and represented a symbol of new democracy of Korea. Park's impeachment was filed by the opposite parties at the National Assembly on December 3, 2016, in part the result of weekly protests by Korean citizens, and approved on December 9, 2016, and was waiting for the Constitutional Court's decision. Park's impeachment was approved by the Constitutional Court on March 10, 2017. She was later arrested on March 31, 2017, and sentenced to a twenty-year prison term.

Pandemic, BTS, and Global Audience

Shortly thereafter, Moon Jae-in, a former human rights lawyer and politician who served in Roh Moo-hyun's administration, was elected as the president of Korea in 2017. Korea was in the process of mending its democracy that had broken in the nine years of two corrupt presidencies. In the following year, former President Lee Myung-bak was also arrested for corruption, including bribery, embezzlement, and tax evasion on March 22, 2018; the court upheld a seventeen-year jail term. However, both Park and Lee were pardoned by later administrations.

After a series of political scandals swept over Korea in late 2016 and the early presidential election in 2017, Koreans witnessed two things that they had not anticipated. As introduced earlier in this chapter, Korea's entertainment industry experienced a series of successes of movies, dramas, and K-pop groups while the entire globe was suffering from the COVID-19 pandemic. Korea became one of the earliest and largest epicenters of COVID-19 outside of China by February 2020, due to its geographic proximity and close trading relations with China. However, the pandemic became a turning point for the Moon administration and nation branding strategies in two different ways. First, with aggressive testing and contact tracing utilizing digital technology such as GPS data, Korea was showcased as a global exemplar of dealing with the COVID-19 pandemic[88] and practiced what became known as "mask diplomacy."[89] Second, coinciding with the pandemic and quarantine, Korean pop culture achieved its highest-ever level of global popularity, and the Korean government did not miss the opportunity to connect pop culture to the broader nation branding policies, though they did not necessarily use the term "nation branding." Though the pandemic closed borders and called off cultural events, the quarantine enabled the Korean Wave—Hallyu—to hit the global market like a tsunami,[90] particularly in the West. According to the MCST, Korea achieved the highest export in cultural content. According to 2021 press release by the MCST, Korea's cultural content export reached $11.92 billion in 2020 in the middle of the pandemic by increasing 16.3 percent from the previous year.[91]

The Korean government took advantage of the opportunity provided by the immense global popularity of Korean popular culture. When BTS was invited for the United Nations (UN) General Assembly, President

Moon officially appointed BTS as "Special Presidential Envoys for Future Generations and Culture" in Seoul on July 15, 2021, and he granted the boy band diplomatic passports to the UN General Assembly in New York. President Moon and BTS attended the UN General Assembly and gave speeches at the Sustainable Development Goals Moment on September 20, 2021. In his speech, President Moon claimed that Korea would work closely with the global community in order to combat global crises, including the pandemic and climate change, and to attain sustainable development. As a part of the nation's efforts, he pledged the equivalent of $200 million USD to COVAX AMC for COVID-19 vaccines to be available in low-income countries and promised to "strive for an equitable and expeditious supply of COVID-19 vaccines" as one of the global vaccine production hubs.[92] Introduced by President Moon, the seven members of BTS made their second UN speech, sending messages about climate change, vaccination, and the power of youth for future changes. In line with the president's pledge to provide international aid for vaccines, BTS also encouraged the youth to get vaccinated. "All seven of us. Of course, we received vaccinations. The vaccination was a sort of ticket to meeting our fans waiting for us. And to being able to stand here before you today,"[93] J-Hope of BTS said. More importantly, they tried to send a positive message to the youth, often called the "lost generation," during the COVID-19 pandemic. "Instead of the lost generation, a more appropriate name would be the welcome generation. Because instead of fearing change, this generation says welcome and keeps forging ahead,"[94] Jin of BTS said. This speech and the subsequent performance were viewed or streamed live by more than one million people and discussed on various social media platforms.[95]

During their visit to the Sustainable Development Goals Moment, President Moon and BTS had interviews together with the UN and ABC and talked about the Sustainable Development Goals Moment's messages to overcome poverty, disparity, and the pandemic. During the interview with the UN, the president said that "there is no better candidate than BTS that can represent and speak up for younger generations," and he commended them because they "made much more effects on the younger generations than any other politicians' speeches."[96] BTS also joined the First Lady, Kim Jung-sook, at the Metropolitan Museum of Art to visit the Arts of Korea Gallery and celebrate the artisans of Korea;

in addition, they joined the First Lady in donating Korean contemporary artist Haecho Chung's *Rhythm of the Five Color Luster* art piece to the Metropolitan Museum. At the gifting event, RM, the leader of BTS, said, "I believe that we could be here today thanks to those who have been trying to promote and increase awareness of Korean culture. . . . It is true that K-culture, including K-pop, K-dramas, and K-movies, has taken prominent positions in many areas, but there are still some great unknown Korean artists working very hard. As Korea's special presidential envoy for future generations and culture, we will strive with a sense of mission to help increase awareness of Korean culture's greatness and potential."[97] As shown in RM's speech, BTS has emphasized that their global success did not come out of the blue, but rather as a result of the efforts of other Korean artists and fellow Koreans who came before them in raising awareness of Korean culture.

The trip to New York with President Moon was not their first time working on spreading awareness of Korean culture. When BTS was awarded the Hwagwan Order of Cultural Merit at the Korean Popular Culture and Arts Awards in 2018, Suga of BTS said at the acceptance speech, "I will make efforts to raise awareness of Korean culture worldwide, with a mindset of a representative of the nation."[98] They have incorporated hanbok, traditional Korean clothing, in their stage costumes. They also performed a couple of their hit songs at Gyeongbokgung Palace in Seoul for NBC's *The Tonight Show with Jimmy Fallon* in late September and early October of 2020 as part of the late-night talk show's #BTSWEEK. In fact, BTS has served as the Honorary Tourism Ambassador for Seoul since 2017, and they have filmed and released a new tourism promotion video every year.[99] Their collaborations are rooted in the hope that their cultural popularity would eventually bring tourism roaring back, appeal to foreign investment, and bring more revenue to other associated industries that have shrunk during the pandemic.[100]

Likewise, the Moon administration developed a new branding strategy to directly connect Hallyu with export industries and nation branding. In 2019, the Ministry of SMEs and Startups (MSS), a ministry that supports small and medium-sized enterprises and startups, launched a new branding project with entrepreneurs: Brand-K. Brand-K is a government-authorized label of consumer goods from small and medium-sized companies that look for global outreach. Simply put, Brand-K is also a public-private partnership project among the MSS, Small & Medium Business Distribution Center, and corporations that help smaller corporations from cosmetic brands to small home appliances extend their market overseas. After the application process, goods and brands with good quality but relatively weak brand power are selected, displayed, and sold through the public home shopping channel in Korea.[101] In order to celebrate the launch of this new project, the MSS organized an international launch event in Bangkok, Thailand, a cultural and economic hub of Southeast Asia, on September 2, 2019. President Moon also attended the launch event at the Central World Shopping Complex, along with Korean soccer icon Park Ji-sung and several K-pop stars, including Ailee, Sandeul, Weki Meki, and Verivery. At the opening speech, President Moon stated that Hallyu is a driving force to connect the two nations.[102]

Does Top-Down Nation Branding Really Work?

While working on this project since 2008, I, a Korean national who resides outside Korea, have observed various political and economic challenges in Korea through traditional and new media. I often felt out of the ordinary during those years. Two former presidents, Kim Dae-jung and Roh Moo-hyun, who initiated nation branding projects after the financial crisis, passed away in 2009, while two other former presidents, Lee Myung-bak and Park Geun-hye (who became the first impeached president), were arrested in the middle of political scandals. President Moon Jae-in, who was deeply engaged in the Roh administration, took office after Park's impeachment in 2017.

Amid these political controversies, I returned to Seoul for some follow-up research. While attending the Saturday candlelight vigils leading up to Park Geun-hye's impeachment, I conducted some interviews in December 2016 and January 2017 with those who participated both directly and indirectly in nation branding-related projects. It was also very challenging to bring up such sensitive topics around the political scandals in the middle of controversies. However, some interviewees who were no longer affiliated with the organizations, like Seunghee, a thirty-two-year-old former employee of the Korea Culture and Arts Education Service (KCAES) under the MCST, and Juyeon, a twenty-seven-year-old graduate student in Seoul, talked honestly about their experiences.

I met Seunghee in Seoul in late 2016. At a small coffee shop in Gwanghwamun, central Seoul—near the site of months-long major protests—she shared her memories and frustrations about her work at the KCAES during the Park administration. She reminisces that the Park administration emphasized certain cultural content—both traditional culture and K-pop (but less at the KCAES but more at the Korea Creative Content Agency). She remembers pressure at the KCAES to develop "Arirang"-related projects at work: "For example, this administration often pushed to develop Arirang-related projects. Well, I do not necessarily think these Arirang-related contents are bad, but when you have pressure that the order is made at the BH [Blue House, Cheongwadae] by the VIP [the president], I do not think anyone really understood the contexts. We just had to do it."[103] Arirang is a lyrical folk song, varying from region to region, and symbolizes the cultural roots of the Korean diaspora. It is, thus, not uncommon that Arirang, added to the UNESCO'S Intangible Cultural Heritage, is often celebrated at various domestic and international events. However, the pressure was not ordinary in the Park administration.

Likewise, Park Geun-hye's administration also pushed Saemaul Movement–related projects both domestically and globally. The Saemaul Movement, also known as the New Community Movement or New Village Movement, was a government-launched political initiative that modernized Korea's rural economy in the 1970s. Notably, it was started by former President Park Chung-hee, who was a military dictator and also Park Geun-hye's father. Seunghee said, "The current administration [the Park administration] highlighted and pushed the Saemaul Movement. It was obvious that those who developed Saemaul-related projects got easy budget approval. . . . The budget distribution was not systemically practiced in this administration." As a part of nation branding, Park believed that the Saemaul Movement could become a model for international development cooperation and contribute to overcoming poverty in developing countries. Yet, this movement symbolized the rapid economic development during the military junta or her father's dictatorship by taking advantage of cheap labor and labor oppression. It is often understood as a strategy to reinstate and carry out her father's legacy, awakening old right-wingers.[104]

Likewise, Juyeon, a twenty-seven-year-old graduate student, also shared her memories with nation branding projects in the Lee administration. Juyeon was a college student participant in the Korean Brand Supporters program in 2011, organized by the Presidential Council on Nation Branding. Juyeon shared that she was initially very excited to be part of these opportunities as a college student. Having learned about the values of nation branding from an early age, she believed the project would succeed as it had been widely promoted in various national media outlets. However, she expressed disappointment, noting that their roles were very limited. College students were invited for branding-related events, but she thought they were mainly there so the administration could show them in the press release photo, and they did not do much work. From that point, she did not have high expectations from the government-led nation branding projects, and the scandals that followed in the past months did not much surprise her.

By undergoing national political scandals, impeachment, a series of trials, and an unexpected early presidential election, fundamental issues of top-down nation branding projects and public-private partnership have been raised in the past few years. The Korean government after the financial crisis, whether liberal or conservative, has quickly adopted neoliberal market strategies into political entities, namely nation branding. They argue that they have focused on building the infrastructure and promoting positive images of the nation for future investments and economic benefits rather than directly interfering in the market, as a government official at the Korean Food Foundation (now Korean Food Promotion Institution, or KFPI) told me during the interview in 2012. Yet, simply, did these top-down policies really work?

As political uncertainty in Korea stabilized under the new administration, albeit being still polarized by gender and generation, the pandemic hit Korea hard. Within a short period, Korea became one of the earliest and largest epicenters of the COVID-19 pandemic outside China. While Korea has undergone a series of political and economic uncertainties, I have also witnessed something while writing this book that I never could have imagined in the past—the global popularity of Korean culture. Since I returned to New York City in 2019 after three years of work in Ohio and upstate New York, I have observed that non-Korean consumers fill Korean restaurants and shop for K-pop goods at a bookstore in Koreatown in Manhattan. Unlike K-pop fans who I spoke with at the earlier stage of my research, newbies in K-pop no longer feel that they are weirdos.

However, a series of political scandals and the unexpected global popularity of Korean pop culture during the pandemic made me reflect on my project in various ways. I was often struck by questions about nation branding, our own inferiority complex, and longing for the West both in Korea and in overseas Korean communities. How do I understand and interpret top-down policies amid political scandals? If I define nation branding as neoliberal agendas driven by a neoliberal state, but also reshaped by bottom-up participation by citizens, the diaspora, and even noncitizens, how and why do Koreans in the government, in franchises, in the home country, and abroad, whether Korean nationals or diaspora, sell the nation and its identity to the world? Why do we want positive confirmation of the nation and culture by the white West? Who is included and excluded in this process? Why do many racial minority interviewees – particularly Black Americans– openly express their frustration about the Korean entertainment industry and media and even Koreatown in Manhattan? If Koreatown is a microcosm of Korean society, how do we address such concerns within a small strip in cosmopolitan New York?

In chapter 2, I turn my attention to New York City and Manhattan's Koreatown as a transclave by paying particular attention to Korean food. New York City has been one of the most important global markets in Korea's nation branding project, and Koreatown in Manhattan continues to be of interest to and an investment of the Korean government and corporations. The Korean government and corporations consider New York City the United States' cultural and economic center, making it one of the most critical overseas markets for Korea's nation branding projects. I discuss the role of local entrepreneurs—Korean immigrants and Korean Americans—and analyze how and why they promote Korean culture and food by targeting non-coethnic New Yorkers.

2

Transclave

Selling Korea in a Global City

KFC has gone mainstream in American food world. I am not talking about Colonel Sanders; I am talking about Korean fried chicken.
—James Park, *Eater New York*, January 25, 2018

It is on the 16th floor of a building in the heart of K-town [in Manhattan]. It isn't a neighborhood with many Michelin-starred restaurants so many people have expressed to me their concerns about the location. However, it is the perfect place for us to take on this new challenge.
—Chef Chang-ho Shin of Joo Ok, a two-Michelin-star restaurant
Interview with Michelin Guide, December 7, 2023

On a cold gloomy morning in December 2022, I was speaking with Minjae in his office in Midtown Manhattan. As a businessperson who owns several restaurants in Koreatown, he often appears in the Korean ethnic media in New York City, due to his success in the food and beverage industry and deep involvement in Korean business organizations in New York City, including the Koreatown Association and the Korean Cuisine Globalization Committee USA (KCGC USA). After seeing him on the ethnic news, hearing his stories, and trying to connect with him for an interview, I was finally introduced to Minjae by a Korean student who I happened to get to know by chance earlier that year.

It was an interesting time. After witnessing a series of political scandals in the Lee Myung-bak and Park Geun-hye administrations, I thought the globalization of the Korean food project was over in New York City. The committee was no longer active, though I saw them making a big bowl of bibimbap on 32nd Street during Chuseok (Korean autumn harvest) festival in 2017. However, Koreatown businesspeople seemed to maintain their transnational ties with their home country in different ways. Minjae told me that Koreatown businesses did not lose much traffic during the pandemic and that some even gained new clients since then because of the global popularity of Korean culture (illustrated by the success of BTS, *Parasite*, and *Squid Game*) and the city's Open Streets program. In fact, according to New York City Department of Transportation, the Open Street corridor in Koreatown saw a 15 percent increase in taxable sales compared to before the pandemic.[1] Korean food is as popular as ever in New York City—both in and outside of Koreatown. Koreatown businesspeople were busy incorporating global trends into their businesses by offering dalgona (honeycomb candy) from *Squid Game* and jjapaguri (also known as ram-don, a combination of Chapagetti and Neoguri, two popular Korean instant noodle brands) from *Parasite* to both old and new clients who were recently hooked by this "new" Asian culture and cuisine. However, during this time period, several older Korean restaurants, including two of the oldest ones on 32nd Street, closed down, while Koreatown was gaining young and new business owners. I thought that Koreatown's transnational ties with the Korean government were over and the committee was buried in the past.

However, earlier that year, both Korean media and local ethnic news coverage about Kimchi Day designation efforts in New York's Korean American community and the Korean government caught my immediate attention. The Korean American community, including Ron Kim, the representative of the 40th Assembly District, the KCGC USA, and the Korean government had worked together to push the State of New York to pass the state bill, recognizing Kimchi Day in New York. November 22 was originally designated as Kimchi Day in Korea in 2020. This government effort in Korea was driven by a cultural dispute over kimchi against China. During an interview with the current president and a staff member of aT Center New York in 2024, both officials—dispatched from Korea—pointed out that the global popularity of Korean cuisine led Chinese, particularly online, to claim that it originated in China. "We needed to announce that kimchi is Korean," said the current president of aT Center New York during the interview. After pao cai (a general term for pickled vegetable dishes from the Sichuan

Province in China) received certification from the International Organisation for Standardisation (ISO), the *Global Times*—a China's state-run media outlet known for various political controversies—referred to the event as "an international standard for the kimchi industry led by China." However, the ISO clearly stated that "this document does not apply to kimchi." In fact, kimchi is often served under the name pao cai in China, but pao cai is a distinct Chinese dish with its own variants. This international dispute has become a key moment for the government agency to further engage with the Korean diaspora and showcase the originality of kimchi abroad.[2]

Furthermore, the Korean government and its agencies worked with Korean American policymakers and community actors to recognize Kimchi Day in states with prominent Korean American communities, including New York, New Jersey, California, and Virginia. Bill K00574 was passed, "recognizing November 22, 2022, as Kimchi Day and honoring the history and importance of a beloved food staple first introduced in the United States and the State of New York by the Korean American community."[3] The celebratory reception was hosted by Ron Kim with aT Korea on May 24, 2022, in Albany, New York, recognizing kimchi as a national symbol of Korea and the Korean diaspora. Chun-jin Kim, then-president of aT Korea, and Byung Hwa Chung, Consul General of the Republic of Korea in New York, also attended. Chun-jin Kim said, "Kimchi Day in New York, a capital of world economy, will be a momentum to enhance the reputation of Kimchi."[4] The efforts continued on the federal level. On April 6, 2023, at the 118th Congress, H.Res.280 was introduced to the House by ten policymakers, many of whom are Korean Americans, in order to support the designation of Kimchi Day on November 22, 2023.[5] A few months earlier in December 6, 2022, the Museum of Korean American Heritage, together with aT America and the KCGC USA, organized a Kimchi event at the Library of Congress in order to introduce Kimchi-themed Korean cuisine and push Congress to pass the resolution.[6]

Minjae is one of the key local players in such efforts. He actively supported New York State's legislation for Kimchi Day, attended the celebratory reception in Albany, and organized various Korean food promotion and fundraising events with Korean American community leaders both locally and nationally. Although the presence of Korean government agencies and officials in these recent events are obvious, Minjae weighs the role of Korean businesspeople in New York City. He said, "Korean restaurant owners have organized Korea-related events as poomasi (exchange of labor or communal efforts/help)" even after the First Lady scandal in the Lee administration and the following budget cut, which will be discussed later in this chapter. He reemphasizes that "these events have been always for the local community" in New York City rather than just for the effects of government policy.

This chapter focuses on transnational and local efforts to create positive images of Korea through pop culture and cuisine overseas in order to bring their own financial benefits by utilizing Koreatown as a platform. This chapter explains how and why the Korean government and corporations, particularly franchise stores, have expanded overseas market and financial investments by collaborating with the Korean diaspora—mainly transnational entrepreneurs in New York City since the mid-2000s. New York City is one of the most critical overseas markets for Korean government agencies, like aT Center, and Korea-based franchises and chains; and the landscape of Koreatown in Manhattan reflects these transnational engagements both in cultural and economic policies and in business investments. However, the government agencies' transnational efforts have shifted to heavily focus on support for food exports to the US market and cultural event support since the mid-2010s, while Korean businesspeople contend that such food promotion efforts are a local community endeavor, as Minjae calls it, "poomasi." Yet, interestingly enough, the partnership between Koreatown businesspeople and the government and its agencies still continues, though its intensity has declined over time and their approaches are very different from each other. How and why do they see nation branding and transnational investment differently? Why do they carry on with this uncomfortable but necessary partnership?

Korean Food and Nation Branding in a Transclave

As Korean culture slowly gained popularity in New York in the 2000s, the ethnic media pointed out that lack of promotion would hinder the consumption of Korean products, including food in Koreatown. The question of inadequate preparation for the introduction of Korean culture to the US mainstream has often been brought up.[7] In a *Korea Daily* article on August 12, 2005, "New York is Unprepared for Korean Wave," a reporter claimed that Koreatown was not ready to magnify Hallyu, the popularity of Korean pop culture, for the American market.[8] The absence of promotional materials, such as a guidebook to Koreatown shopping or a map of Koreatown—even the lack of a clear signboard—obstructed access to Korean culture in New York.[9] Although there have been efforts by local businesspeople to establish a sign or symbol for Koreatown at the corner of 32nd Street and Broadway, some entrepreneurs in Koreatown believe that the Korean government should support the promotion of Koreatown.

The Government: Branding Korean Food in New York

Korean Cultural Center New York (KCCNY, then Korean Cultural Service), a government institution under the control of the Consulate General of the Republic of Korea, also agreed that they should work with other agencies to promote Korean culture in New York; at a press interview in 2005, Jinyoung Woo, then-director of the KCCNY,[10] said, "I absolutely agreed that we should provide appropriate information for those Americans who are interested in Korean culture. If we'd like to widely kindle the Hallyu fever, rather than to limit itself in just a brief introduction, thorough preliminary research, systematic data collection and collection of public opinion should be preceded and the Korean Cultural Center is preparing for them." [11] This interview elaborated on an ongoing government project on nation branding during the Roh administration—Hallyu—an institutional engagement in the overseas promotion of the cultural industry, though Hallyu had not yet arrived in New York. "*Han brands*" or later "*Han Style*," as devised by the Roh administration, classified traditional culture into six categories; it arrived in New York City through collaboration with megacorporations, entrepreneurs, and other agencies. Hansik (Korean food), one of the six categories of the *Han Style* project, was promoted by government agencies such as the KCCNY, KTO New York office, and aT Center.

In 2005, following Korean food festivals at the United Nations in 2002 and 2003, a series of Taste of Korea events were designed. The first Taste of Korea event was held on August 31, 2005, at Don's Bogam, a Korean

BBQ restaurant in Koreatown. Attendees for a cooking demonstration and food tasting included marketers, as well as about eighty journalists and critics from media outlets including *The New York Times*, *News Day*, Food Network, and *Wine Spectator*.[12] Three other events at the end of 2005 were designed to introduce Korean food to such tastemakers, with the hope that Korean cuisine would receive attention from mainstream US media. However, the government's earlier efforts to globalize Korean food in New York mostly targeted food-related professionals and the media rather than the wider audience of ordinary New Yorkers. It also sought to enhance bilateral ties with a small number of people through national food and dining experiences in New York.[13]

As explained in chapter 1, the Korean government began aggressively engaging in the globalization of Korean food projects during the Lee administration by establishing several government institutes, such as the Korean Food Foundation (KFF), now known as the Korean Food Promotion Institution (KFPI). As a global project, the KFPI also selected target markets and organized committees at the city level for large investments; global cities were particularly attractive to the KFPI for investment, including New York, Los Angeles, Tokyo, Shanghai, Hong Kong, London, and Paris, among others. Selected based on the global city index by *Forbes* and by *Foreign Policy*,[14] these cities became the main nodes for each region or country. New York is the main market in North America.[15] An official at the KFPI (then the KFF) whom I interviewed in Seoul in 2012 said, "Both LA and New York are critical cities in our project. But New York plays a role as an antenna [for a bigger market]. The market is there; Koreatown is there. You cannot create a global trend by ignoring New York. It you make it there, you are going to make it anywhere." For the KFPI, New York is one of the most racially and ethnically diverse cities in the nation; it is associated with multiculturalism, a history of immigration, a sizable foreign-born population, and business opportunities. Although LA has the largest Korean population in the United States, New York is understood to be a cultural trendsetter and a hub of world economy and media, especially in the context of multiculturalism. Jeongwoo, a staff member at KCCNY, explains that this agenda is still shared in 2024. "New Yorkers tend to embrace a variety of ethnic cultures, showcasing diverse groups of people. You might have Chinese food for lunch and then want to try

Ethiopian cuisine for dinner. This is absolutely possible in New York City," said Jeongwoo. In such a multicultural environment, "exotic" ethnic culture meets with and delves into the desires of an external tourist gaze. The government understands these "tourists" of Korean restaurants to be consumers who seek out aesthetic and authentic experiences.[16] While recognizing New York City as a marketing outpost for the food globalization project, the Ministry for Food, Agriculture, Forestry, and Fisheries (MFAFF), now known as the Ministry of Agriculture, Food and Rural Affairs (MAFRA),[17] also announced that they would provide various hands-on experience events and media promotion and carry out annual surveys in order to measure public opinion of its cultural policies overseas.[18]

The Korean government's emphasis on New York in the globalization of the Korean food project in North America is particularly prominent in "the flagship restaurant project." In 2010, the MAFRA and the KFPI launched a new project to purchase space and establish a "New York Flagship Korean Restaurant" in Midtown Manhattan. The MAFRA and the KFPI planned to invest 5 billion won (about $4.3 million USD in 2010) in "seed money" and recruit private companies to invest 10 billion won (about $8.6 million USD in 2010) in the hope that this government-sponsored high-end restaurant would help popularize Korean food in New York and, in turn, help extend the project to other global cities overseas, such as Paris, Tokyo, and Beijing.[19]

The project was often referred to as the "First Lady project" due to the deep engagement of the First Lady at the time, Kim Yoon-ok, from the project's early stages. Often praised as a Korean food missionary and food diplomat by the conservative media, she had shown personal interest in the globalization of Korean foods overseas. During President Lee Myung-bak's official visit to the United Nations General Assembly in 2011 in New York, the First Lady made visits to three Korean restaurants in Midtown Manhattan and praised the efforts of the KCGC USA,[20] Korean and non-Korean chefs, food truck entrepreneurs, and Korean food bloggers for the promotion of Korean food in New York and emphasized the importance of networks among New York Korean restaurants in the promotion of Hallyu. In fact, the First Lady had been deeply involved in the globalization of Korean food projects early on; she participated in the Korean Food Globalization Task Force as an honorary president in

2009 and published a book, *Hansik: Stories of Korean Food*, with photos of herself cooking Korean food in 2010. She also made appearances on TV news programs on networks such as CNN advertising Korean food to overseas audiences, particularly in New York.[21]

The KFPI's aim was very clear: to promote Korean food to non-Koreans through various media outlets. For example, the KFPI was deeply involved in Marja Vongerichten's PBS documentary series, *Kimchi Chronicles*, which aired between July and September 2011. The series was the story of a biracial Korean adoptee's journey to her motherland with her husband Jean-Georges Vongerichten, a well-known Michelin-star French chef, to discover Korean food. The documentary attracted both Korean and non-Korean viewers.[22] *Kimchi Chronicles* was produced by a Korean American director, Eric Rhee, but was heavily subsidized by the Korean government and Korean corporations. Its underwriters were Visit Korea Committee, the KFPI, Samsung, and H Mart, and it was further financially supported by Korean corporations, including CJ, Hite, Jinro, Amore Pacific, Korean Air, the Western Chosun Hotel, and Yido (a gallery in Seoul), among a handful of other non-Korean corporations.[23] In order to promote this documentary, events were organized by the Korea Society and the KCCNY, funded by Korean corporations and government agencies.

Food was clearly a tool for corporate market expansion beyond the Asian market. The KFPI did not expect to instantly profit from television programming and food-related events, understanding that the plan should be long-term, "spending at least 4 or 5 years only for PR," and designed to brand and market Korea's culinary culture for future national profit, the staff emphasized in my interview in Seoul in 2012.

Government Collaboration with Korean Entrepreneurs

In addition to targeting New York City, the KFPI has also attempted to exert direct influence on businesses in Koreatowns and other communities. Many entrepreneurs in Koreatown have been involved in the KFPI's project launching the "globalization of Korean food." Although the government budget for the globalization of Korean food was secured, it was important to establish a project in New York by local businesspeople and to propose ideas gathered by locals to the central Korean government.

The KFPI has closely worked with entrepreneurs and agencies on the East and West coasts; the Korean Cuisine Globalization Committee USA (KCGC USA) was launched on January 29, 2010, and some Korean restaurant owners in the New York City metropolitan area participated in the committee. By extending bottom-up participation to its diaspora, nation branding included Korean entrepreneurs who both produce and live the brand.[24] More importantly, they also function as intermediaries between the government and consumers. These entrepreneurs, particularly those who are older, have operated their businesses for decades and established ethnic networks while knowing consumer's needs. As transnational migrants, they understand the Korean system and generally do not have language barriers.

These multifaceted efforts to globalize Korean food turned out to be good timing for these Korean entrepreneurs. Korean food, once thought of as "weird" and "strange" in the West, especially compared to other Asian cuisines such as Chinese and Japanese, has slowly been gaining popularity. By 2010, the popularity of Korean pop culture and food was mainly limited to Asian communities in the form of transnational consumption, with goods directly imported from Korea. However, the expansion of Korean food to non-Asian communities in New York intensified in 2014, as food critics, celebrity chefs, food experts, and the mainstream media took notice of Korean food.

The KCGC USA, together with the KFPI, devised and implemented several projects in New York. New York's "Discover Korea's Delicious Secret" campaign was originally created by the KFPI to promote Korean food overseas in China, the United States, and Europe; it is a product of KFPI and the MAFRA, sponsored by the KCGC USA and the KCCNY. As part of the New York campaign, a mobile kitchen offered complimentary Korean fare in eighteen public spaces (with pop-up locations announced via Facebook and Twitter) in Manhattan, including Bryant Park, Union Square, and Koreatown, from April 18 to May 20, 2011. Nine Korean restaurants participated in this project.[25]

Likewise, later that year, on August 16, the committee organized the second annual Korea Day in Central Park, aimed at promoting diverse aspects of Korean culture. The most outstanding component was the food. Organized by the KCGC USA, this event was sponsored by the KFPI, MAFRA, the consulate general of the Republic of Korea in New

York, and the KCCNY and supported by Korean food companies such as Bingree and Nongshim. As a part of the event, the committee organized a Korean Food Exhibition that offered samples of Korean food to the audience.[26] Then-president of the KFPI, Il-sun Yang, flew to New York to participate in this event and announced the importance of New York in the series of food projects, noting that "the KFPI aims to create a boom in the popularity of Korean food in New York and spread to other countries."[27] These major projects, one centering on food and the others on Koreatown itself, show the intensive government involvement in New York as well as the cooperation of entrepreneurs.

In order to target non-Korean populations, the KFPI also actively reached out to Korean entrepreneurs and chefs who had opened upscale restaurants outside of Koreatowns, introducing Korean cuisine to non-Korean gourmet omnivores within the context of what the Korean media calls "the second generation of the Korean restaurant business."[28] Hooni Kim is a good example. When his restaurant, Danji, received one Michelin star in 2012, Kim immediately received attention not only from local media in New York, but also from Korean media, praising his success as the first "Korean" restaurant to win a Michelin star. The KFPI and MAFRA promoted his success through press releases. Though he was not a member of the KCGC USA, he participated in the food projects from the beginning.

Collaborations with the sending state also provide new business opportunities in the homeland. Despite his open criticism of government policies, Hooni Kim of Danji, Little Banchan Shop, and Meju worked closely with some Korean corporations and the media in Seoul.[29] His unique human capital, transitioning from a Berkeley graduate and a medical school student at the University of Connecticut to an owner-chef of Danji and Hanjan (now closed)—one of *The New York Times'* Top 10 Restaurants of 2013[30]—prompted the Korean media and corporations to create a new trend in Korea, where food and lifestyle industries have grown in recent years. He signed a contract with Jookjangyeon by Young-Il International, an artisanal brand based in a small village in Korea that makes fermented sauces, to commercialize "Hooni Kim's Special Ssamjang (a condiment comprised of fermented soybean paste and red pepper paste commonly served alongside Korean meat dishes)."[31] He also served as a celebrity judge for Master Chef Korea's third season in 2014 and fourth season in 2016. He regularly visits Korea and has been on Korean TV shows to promote his business.

Ironically, although the fundamental mission of the globalization of Korea food in the Lee administration was to improve international recognition of Korean food, the responses and press release by the KFPI and MAFRA, as well as media reports in Korea, show that the project targets citizens in Korea using nationalist sentiments to market food.[32] By linking the banal and everyday aspects of nationalism of its citizens to the private sector and state,[33] the food project, in fact, promoted nationhood and belonging, as many Korean national interviewees express that they, as Koreans, are "proud" that their food has become embraced by New Yorkers.

Several restaurant owners participated in this project, attending meetings in hopes of benefiting from the popularity among consumers of Korean food in New York. Restaurants that participated in the project back during the Lee administration put the KFPI's logo, Taste of Korea, in front of their restaurants, despite the fact that most customers do not know its meaning.

However, not all Koreatown restaurant owners are active in this project, and those who are involved participate to different degrees. During the interview in 2012, Insook, an entrepreneur on 32nd Street who played an active role in the KCGC USA in the early 2010s (albeit being at the peak of the project), told me that only twelve entrepreneurs from Koreatowns in the New York–New Jersey area who actively participate in the project "pay the membership fee and suggest their own opinions . . . and have rights for voting." Despite their less-active involvement in the projects, other entrepreneurs also recognize that the popularity of Korean culture and food as a whole could benefit their businesses. Jaesu, a first-generation businessperson who has run a restaurant since the early 1980s on 32nd Street and is involved in the Business Association of 32nd Street shared a similar opinion in 2012. He told me that "now Koreatown cannot hold up without non-Korean customers." About a decade later, Minjae agreed with Jaesu: "We no longer target Koreans. We keep in mind that half-baked fusion would not work particularly in New York City. . . . Of course, we try to bring what Koreans like [or think of as being authentic]. On top of that, we target what foreigners [non-Koreans] like. . . . My BBQ restaurant offers more banchan [side

Figure 2.1. The "Taste of Korea" logo at Kang Suh Restaurant. Kang Suh, one of the two oldest restaurants on 32nd Street in 2013. Photo by the author.

dishes] that Koreans like but particularly pick what foreigners like out of them. We are trying to meet our clients' needs." Some restaurants, bars, and noraebang (karaoke establishments) devise their own business strategies to take advantage of the popularity of Korean pop culture and authenticity of their food. Such transnational business strategies seem to be more prominent during the pandemic than ever. I visited Koreatown a few days after Halloween in 2021. I saw a variety of *Squid Game*–themed Halloween decorations. At Food Gallery 32, the Guards, also known as Pink Soldiers in *Squid Game*, were welcoming clients, while a two-dimensional replica of Young-hee, the scary doll featured in the first episode of *Squid Game*, was constantly showcasing K-pop music videos from a television monitor mounted where her head should have been.

Likewise, bb.q Chicken, a popular Korean fried chicken franchise, held the 2021 bb.q Chicken Halloween *Squid Game* Party on Friday, October 29, offering games from *Squid Game*, including the dalgona (honeycomb candy) challenge; the restaurant advertised this Halloween event on a banner in front of their entrance. Grace Street Coffee & Desserts also seized opportunity by actively adapting the global online sensation from the pandemic, featured in Squid Game—dalgona and honeycomb candy-themed drinks—to their offerings.

Their business strategies are in line with the past globalization of the Korean food project by actively collaborating with Hallyu stars. For example, in the mid-2010s, a Korean restaurant called Five Senses offered free appetizers for those who had concert tickets to see the popular K-pop boy band, Big Bang. Likewise, Roll & Katsu Kitchen, a small Korean-Japanese food restaurant at the Food Gallery 32 food court, incorporated K-pop stars' names into some of their menu items, such as the Big Bang roll, Sistar roll, and T-ara roll. However, interestingly, the origin of their foods has nothing to do with authentic Korean food. In fact, these rolls are not even Korean. Kimbap, a Korean version of a rice roll wrapped with dried seaweed, is not on their menu. Instead, these K-pop-themed rolls are Americanized Japanese food that is popular in Korea. Yet, Koreatown businesspeople do not miss an opportunity to take advantage of the growing popularity of Korean pop culture and food by incorporating K-pop into their business promotions.

The entrepreneurs aim to offer their consumers a form of experience economy, rooted in themed, often aesthetic or authentic, ex-

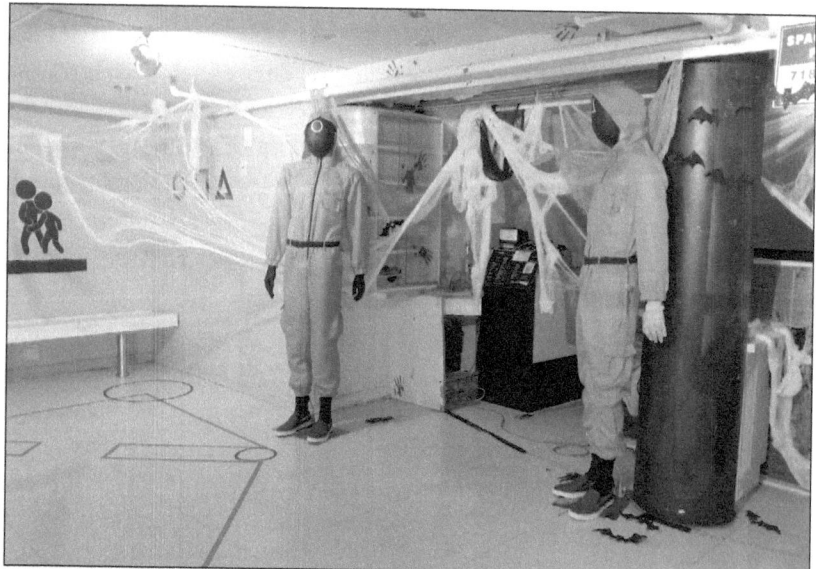

Figure 2.2. *Squid Game* Pink Soldier mannequins on Halloween at Food Gallery 32 in 2021. Photo by the author.

Figure 2.3. Dalgona Coffee & Candy being advertised at Grace Street Coffee & Dessert in 2021. Photo by the author.

periences.³⁴ The cultural experience of a nation's cultural industries, in fact, becomes "the objects of both marketization and aesthetic consumption."³⁵ In this way, these entrepreneurs, regardless of their involvement, play the role of mediator, connecting the transnational presence of Korean culture and overseas investments with bottom-up participation of consumers, whether they are Korean or not. These businesspeople are proactive in building Korean businesses in Koreatown as a bridge between Korean cultural strategies and mainstream America. Establishing cooperation between the public and private sectors in this way enriches both parties.

Conflict Between the Government and Entrepreneurs

Collaboration between the government and entrepreneurs seems to work, at least at first, as it offers new economic opportunities for both parties. However, marketing collaborations are not free of conflict. Moreover, Korean government bureaucracy is often a hurdle when it comes to collaboration.

There was quite a bit of controversy when the MAFRA embarked on establishing a flagship restaurant on behalf of the Korean government. Despite substantial objections by opposing parties and the public, the then-ruling Hannara Party (now the People Power Party) rushed through a budget bill to secure 5 billion Korean won (about $4.3 million USD as of 2010) to open the restaurant. It was rejected during the budget examination at the National Assembly, but ultimately passed.[36] However, the plan did not work as expected. The flagship restaurant project failed to recruit even a single private investor. Furthermore, it faced objection from local businesspeople concerned about new competition; they insisted that the government-owned restaurant would harm smaller businesses despite the fact that the scale of business in Koreatown is different from "traditionally immigrant-owned mom-and-pop stores," as many of them own multiple businesses across New York and New Jersey. In a press interview, a manager of a restaurant furiously predicted that "once customers taste the high-end luxurious food in the flagship restaurant, they might complain that we wouldn't offer the same [quality of] food. Those government officials, diplomats and resident employees at Korean companies will have meetings and gatherings at the flagship restaurant."[37] The concerns of low-end or mid-level food businesses countered the government's initial plan highlighting the "luxury" of Korean dining.

Yet, during my interviews with non-Korean consumers as well as through observations I conducted as a language teacher in the past decade (described in chapters 5 and 6), I learned that many consumers are not necessarily affluent and are often racial and sexual minorities. And despite its growing popularity and expansion, Korean food is still located outside of the US "gourmet" foodscape, unlike elite and upscale French and Japanese cuisine. In fact, for many non-Korean, particularly non-Asian, consumers, Korean food is novel and exotic, despite the long presence of Korean businesses across the city in the post-1965 era. At the macro level, the popularity of Korean food has probably benefited from the US culinary scene's gradual move toward openness and diversity since the 1970s and shift from food snobbery and exclusivity to omnivorousness,[38] as discussed in chapter 6. In this case, the needs of local entrepreneurs—particularly first-generation Korean Americans—clearly conflicted with the government's goals.

Jaesu, who engaged in the Business Association of 32nd Street, actively collaborated with the KFPI yet was similarly unenthusiastic about the flagship restaurant in 2013. He explained: "There was too much attention. I do not think anyone can overcome that much attention. . . . Obviously, we are stuck in the time when we immigrated. . . . If some chefs come and teach us about a new trend, it would be great. . . . But buying a building is nonsense. . . . Rather, they should focus on PR [instead of competing with us]." The possibility of PR as beneficial for both parties required limiting the government's role as a cultural transmitter and supporter of Korean business. In this context, inviting Korean chefs funded by the government to New York would provide entrepreneurs with an opportunity to network with trendy Korean chefs without harming their own businesses.

Though local entrepreneurs insisted that the flagship restaurant would create more competition between the government and local businesspeople, the foundation argued that they did not mean to distort a market mechanism during the interview in Seoul in 2012: "That's what the market does . . . but what we do is to construct infrastructure for 'demand generation' and media advertisement." For the government, state economic intervention through policy reform would be replaced by facilitating the process of global changes and investing in research and development and infrastructure.[39] The official at the KFPI also said during the interview that there is a wide gap between the KFPI and entrepreneurs, and to understand what the globalization of Korean food means. He said, "they [entrepreneurs] should change their paradigm. They've only targeted ethnic Koreans, yet is it really globalizing Korean food?" However, New York entrepreneurs clearly stated that their main consumers were no longer ethnic Koreans, and they developed business strategies to respond to this new trend during my interviews between 2012 and 2015.

Similarly, bureaucracy is also a serious problem for food projects, because of a gap between the government and individual entrepreneurs' expectations. Conflicts around standardization projects show how the policies would be understood differently by various actors. Standardization was indeed frequently brought up by government agencies and local media in Korea during the Lee administration; efforts to standardize the Romanization and translation of Korean words regarding food and recipes have been highlighted. Although the government's efforts to standardize Korean food vocabulary trace back to 1998,[40] the Lee administration most intensively actualized policies and devised overseas projects. For instance, the "Restaurant Menu Romanization Guidebook" was initially published in 1998 by the Korea Tourism Organization.[41] The MAFRA announced an intensified project in 2009, in collaboration with MCST, Ministry of Foreign Affairs, Korea Tourism Organization, and Korea Foundation, particularly targeting Korean restaurants overseas. The project focused on the standardization of the Romanization of Korean dish names for English, Japanese, and Chinese. For example, kalguksu, a noodle soup dish with seafood or meat broth made with knife-cut noodles, has been translated in various ways, from "knife-cut noodles" to "noodle soup" in English. Through this project, kalguksu is now officially described as "noodle soup." Through this project, they target not only Romanization for English, Japanese, and Chinese written languages, but they also introduced ingredients used in food as well as back stories or histories that each food has.[42] This was published and released to overseas Korean restaurants, Korea Tourism Organization branches, and embassies and consulates in 2012.

Although government agencies have emphasized standardizing recipes and Romanizing Korean food vocabulary from the beginning of the Korean food globalization projects, the reception of these efforts by local actors in New York have varied. Standardizing the Romanization of Korean food vocabulary was largely uncontroversial. The project was even promoted by some Korean students in New York, organized by New York University's Korean Graduate Students Association.[43] They conducted a campaign to Romanize proper nouns with English translations, rather than writing translated Korean; Jaeho, the Korean graduate student at New York University, who initiated this campaign, told me during an interview in 2012 that he shared his idea on his blog, spread word to other online groups, and sent petitions to Korean companies and Korean restaurants to consider the change. Claire seems to agree with Jaeho. Claire, a general manager at an upscale Japanese restaurant in her mid-forties, has been involved in the Korean food project for years by offering some workshops for Korean restaurant businesses. During my interview with Claire in 2022, she recalled that "Yukhoe [a dish consisting of raw beef] was translated as 'six times.' Gomtang [beef bone soup] was translated as 'bear soup.' I told them to change it, but it took probably around four years for them to make changes."⁴⁴

Yet standardization of Korean recipes was very controversial. The Korean government as well as some opinion leaders in Korea believed that Korean food, relying on families' "traditional" recipes, required too many steps for cooking, making them difficult to export. They wanted standardized, modernized, and simplified recipes with accurate measurements that would be more market compatible and would allow consumers to anticipate what a dish would taste like. Some entrepreneurs agreed with the government's plan. Kyung Rim Choi, an owner of the Group KFF that operated twelve restaurants as of 2019 and a participant in the KCGC USA, said, "Customers said that they go to the restaurants with a hope that they would taste Korean food after hearing about and looking at photos, yet the food was so different from what they saw and heard about."⁴⁵

However, chefs viewed the plan as an infringement on their creativity. Hooni Kim did not hesitate to criticize the project at the workshop at the Korea Society in New York on October 24th, 2012. He said, "Standardizing recipes is like communism. They are telling every cook you can cook one way, but that's what they are promoting."⁴⁶ However, the government did not push chefs to follow standardized recipes. Rather, despite controversies in Korea, the project was devised with the hope that these standardized recipes would entice potential non-Korean customers by introducing consistent flavor profiles and allowing them to cook Korean food themselves. The KFPI wanted to target American foodies and omnivores through government investment in infrastructure and market involvement, yet they regularly emphasized the role of the market and limitations of government involvement, because the MAFRA is an economy department.

Likewise, cultural differences sometimes caused misunderstandings between the government agencies and individual entrepreneurs. In particular, Korean Americans and non-Koreans who do not fully understand the mechanisms of Korean bureaucracy have more trouble with government agencies. As Hooni Kim noted at the Korea Society in 2012, the government often cancels small projects at the last minute:

I was supposed to be cooking at James Beard Awards. The first time James Beard Awards allowing a Korean chef to cook Korean food, and I thought it was great opportunity, so I asked Korean government for little stipend that I can get hanwoo, Korean beef from Korea and all this great ingredient. We ordered them all, but two weeks before the event, sorry we are the org not to support one chef but the entire cuisine. . . . Really upset. Korean government does not get it. . . . The government will never get.[47]

Hooni Kim's experience with the Korean government was disappointing and he did not mind openly criticizing it during the talk at the Korea Society in New York.

The ensuing First Lady scandal, related to the globalization of Korean food projects and its failure, that followed political scandals during the Lee administration was a blow for the KFPI as well. Budget curtailment due to the scandal and massive objection both in Korea and among entrepreneurs in New York City turned local businesspeople's attention to projects such as the plan to offer Korean lunch menus at New York public schools. In 2012, Insook of the KCGC USA said, "We planned to sell lunch boxes at public schools [in New York City]. If we get sponsored by the government, we can reduce the price." Introducing Korean culture through "cultural familiarization" to younger New York residents appealed to local entrepreneurs as a long-term goal, as potential customers would get accustomed to the taste of Korean food and eventually visit Koreatown. Yet this particular project shows the difficulties of coordinating across nations for smaller projects. The most challenging obstacle for the school food plan was the different budget cycle in Korea. Insook explained, "We cannot assure the budget from Korea by mid-June, but schools in New York are closed during that time. We should contract with them earlier for fall semester, but then we cannot do it because we are not sure about the budget by mid-June." Budget spending and varying budget cycles can indeed obstruct a project's continuity. When I asked the president of aT Center New York and a staff member about general budget-related issues during an interview in 2024 (without specifying persons and events in the past), they explained that budget matters are very tricky. For public officials and staff members at government agencies, the nature of government funding is not as flexible as it is in the business world. "This is tax money. Because the budgets come from taxes in Korea, there must be strict restrictions and regulations for budgeting and spending at government agencies.... We all have to undergo annual budget investigations to successfully secure funding," said the president of aT New York. From a business perspective, however, this bureaucratic process was indeed a hindrance to the public-private partnership.

Local entrepreneurs and government also understand public-private partnership differently, particularly at the earlier stage of the project in the Lee administration. "Education" came up several times in various newspaper articles and government documents. In order to educate immigrant entrepreneurs, the KFPI planned to devise an "overseas Korean restaurant recommendation system": "There is a lack of information about Korean restaurants.... We plan to investigate overseas Korean restaurants in major cities. And we promote the restaurants by publishing guidebooks and apps if they are qualified. If not, we will offer the educational opportunity.... We need the business paradigm shift by enticing more non-Koreans." The staff at the KFPI points out that the government pays more attention to providing overall guidelines for overseas Korean restaurants if they do not meet the government's proper qualifications.

During the interview in 2012, staff at the KFPI strongly emphasized the role of the market while underscoring the role of marketing in the food project. They did not aim to engage in the market mechanism. However, for local entrepreneurs, the government does not seem to fully grasp the mechanism of ethnic business in the United States. For the government agency at the earlier stage, these entrepreneurs do not clearly deliver the values of authentic Korean food, unless they capitalize on a new trend. Though the government wanted to encourage banal or everyday nationalism through foods or gastronationalism among individual actors in the diasporic community, they are, in fact, entrepreneurs.[48] Despite their clear transnational connections and possible patriotic sentiment toward their homeland, their priority in nation branding is profit. In fact, despite their efforts to promote Korean food through public-private collaboration, the projects seem to lack consistency due to conflicts of interest among various parties, leading to inefficiency and project failure.

However, these conflicts did not always lead to negative outcomes for chefs and business owners in New York. Even a decade later, local businesspeople continue to collaborate with government agencies to promote Korean food. For example, the media exposure in Korea enabled Hooni Kim to work with Korean television networks such as tvN, MBC every1, and Arirang TV. He appeared on *Little Big Hero: The Challenger* on tvN in 2020, *Video Star* on MBC every1 in 2020, and on *The Globalists* on Arirang TV in 2023. Additionally, he maintains collaboration with government agencies like KCCNY (Korean Cultural Center New York). In 2022, KCCNY launched an online Korean Cuisine Cooking Series titled *Kimjang: Making and Sharing Kimchi*, featuring Hooni Kim.[49] As part of the Korean Food Culture Education Program, this four-episode series aims to introduce various types of kimchi and showcase the kimchi-making process with his own recipes. The series begins with an episode on baechu kimchi (napa cabbage kimchi) and suyuk (boiled pork belly), traditional dishes enjoyed on Kimjang Day after a day of communal labor. In this episode, which aired on December 20, 2022, Hooni Kim briefly explains Kimchi Day and kimjang, the annual process of preparing and preserving kimchi. "November 22nd is Kimchi Day in Korea and here in New York, as well as California, Washington, DC, and other places. Also, UNESCO has recognized kimjang as a traditional Korean cultural heritage."[50] After briefly introducing Kimchi Day and telling viewers that UNESCO designated kimjang as a cultural heritage—likely influenced by the cultural disputes over kimchi with China—Hooni Kim shares his recipe and demonstrates how to make different kinds of kimchi. In the next three months, the KCCNY released three more episodes, "Kkakdugi & Chonggak Kimchi" (radish kimchi and ponytail radish kimchi) on January 24, 2023, "Baek Kimchi" (white kimchi or non-spicy napa cabbage kimchi) on February 23, 2023, and "Kohlrabi Kimchi" on March 27, 2023.

Despite disagreements and conflicts with the government, the food project became a bridge for Hooni Kim to reach the Korean market and the media, as explained earlier in this chapter. Jeongwoo, a staff member at KCCNY, explained to me in 2024 that "the major role of the KCCNY in this context is to build a ground for these stakeholders to create their own network [between the United States and Korea]." Likewise, Yeongji, an aT New York staff member, who is dispatched from aT Korea, emphasized that one of their key focuses in New York is connecting Korean restaurant owners with Korean corporations, particularly when these restaurant owners seek Korean ingredients, such as jang (fermented paste) including doenjang (fermented soybean paste), ganjang (soy sauce), and gochujang (fermented red chili paste). "As the president mentioned, we are a food export corporation. Even if they [restaurant owners] do not use exported ingredients, we strive to maintain connections and offer support when needed," said Yeongji in 2024.

Not in Koreatown, but K-Town-Adjacent

Despite the controversies and conflict over the globalization of Korean food project in New York City, Korean food is more popular than ever. The year 2023 was big for Korean cuisine, particularly fine dining in New York City. When the Michelin Guide announced seventy-one restaurants that received Michelin-star status in New York City, eleven Korean or Korean-fusion restaurants were included.[51] This happened about a decade after Danji in Hell's Kitchen received the first Michelin star for Korean cuisine in 2011. The following year, Jungsik in Tribeca earned its first Michelin star, followed by two stars in 2013, and ultimately became the first Korean restaurant in the United States to earn three Michelin stars in 2024.

In the past few years, several Korean newspapers and magazines have highlighted the Korean foodscape in New York City by categorizing it into three distinct generations of Korean cuisine. During my interviews with consumers and producers of Koreatown and participant observations between 2008 and 2016, respondents tended to agree that unlike Thai, Japanese, and Vietnamese cuisines, Korean food is mostly available in Koreatowns in New York and New Jersey. Therefore, most consumers have to travel to Koreatown to buy Korean ingredients and enjoy "authentic" Korean food and nightlife, which the Korean media has dubbed first-generation Korean cuisine. However, recent trends indicate that Korean cuisine is being adopted in the US foodie scene.

While Koreatown tends to serve "traditional" ethnic cuisine to co-ethnics, where Koreans would go and eat their food, as Jungsik Yim of Jungsik said in an interview with NBC News, a new generation of Korean chefs who offer high-end Korean dining experiences began exploring opportunities beyond Koreatown—the so-called New Korean Cuisine.[52] Those businesses are operated by what are deemed second- and third-generation Korean chefs in New York City. Second-generation Korean chefs are Korean American, such as David Chang of Momofuku and Hooni Kim of Danji, Meju, and the Little Banchan Shop, while the newer, third-generation Korean chefs include Korea-born-and-raised chefs like Jungsik Yim of Jungsik in Tribeca (though he was a pioneer of the generation who opened his first New York restaurant in 2011), Junghyun Park of Atoboy and Atomix in Flatiron, and Brian Sehong Kim and Tae Kyung Ku of Oiji in the East Village (now Oiji Mi in Flatiron). As Matt Rodbard, one of the authors of *Koreatown: A Cookbook*, mentioned at the Korea Society's talk in February 2020, Jungsik in Tribeca was one of the first fine-dining restaurants expanding its scope outside of Koreatown.[53] Restaurants outside Koreatown, often run by younger Koreans and Korean Americans, tend to offer high-end culinary experiences that do not always conform strictly to or are not limited to "authentic" Korean food.

Interestingly, many of these new-generation Korean chefs differentiate themselves from typical and traditional Korean immigrant restaurant owners in Koreatown. First, many of them attended and were trained at US culinary schools like the Culinary Institute of America (CIA) and the International Culinary Center (ICC) and worked for fine-dining establishments across the globe, such as Eleven Madison Park, Gramercy Tavern, and Per Se.[54] Hooni Kim, for instance, worked for Michelin-starred restaurants Daniel and Masa before opening Danji and Hanjan (now closed) and more recently Meju and Little Banchan Shop in Long Island City, Queens. Jungsik Yim also attended the CIA and worked at Aquavit and Bouley, in New York, and Zuberoa and Akelarre, in Spain. Both Brian Kim and Tae Kyung Ku of Oiji went to the CIA; Kim worked for David Bouley, while Ku worked at Gramercy Tavern.[55]

Second, they target non-Korean clients or omnivores who look for novel tastes. In an interview with *Korea Daily*, Kim and Ku of Oiji said, "we 'Americanized' our recipes to make Korean ingredients more approachable to non-Korean customers."[56] Simon Kim, a proprietor of Cote Steakhouse in Manhattan's Flatiron District, told the audience at the talk at the Korea Society in 2020 that he chose Flatiron for his business because he thought that "there [are] certain demographics that feels not necessarily very comfortable going to K-town," leading him to the neighborhood for his business. Indeed, he did not want to be "the 'authentic' version of the Korean barbecue, because I didn't want the restaurant to be the best second place," in an interview with *JoongAng Ilbo*.[57] In fact, Simon Kim, a 1.5-generation Korean American from Seoul who immigrated to the United States when he was in the seventh grade and grew up in Long Island, noted good aspects of both societies. He said during the interview with *Korea JoongAng Daily* in 2019, "As a Korean American, I have seen what's good in both cultures as well as what lacks, and I wanted to adopt what's better in each culture, and marry them together to make something that resonates well to many. We don't promote it as a Korean restaurant in New York. It is a restaurant in New York that serves Korean food."[58] The transnational experience that Simon Kim grew up with, as a 1.5-generation Korean American who vividly remembers his childhood in Seoul, has made him develop a unique perspective on his business by bridging two societies but clearly targeting non-Korean foodies.

Finally, many chefs were born and raised in Korea and actively incorporate their Koreanness into dishes that accommodate the American palate by maintaining transnational ties to Korea. All four chefs in the third generation—Jungsik Yim, Junghyun Park, Brian Kim, and Tae Kyung Ku—were born in Korea, and some were also raised there. Jungsik Yim gained his fame as a rising young chef in Korea in the 2000s, bringing creativity to his plates, before he opened his New York City restaurant. Junghyun Park of Atoboy and Atomix used to work for Jungsikdang in Seoul, and joined Jungsik in Tribeca, a two-Michelin-starred fine-dining Korean restaurant—now holding three Michelin stars as of 2024—as the chef de cuisine, before he and his partner opened their two restaurants. Likewise, Simon Kim of Cote began his hospitality career at the MGM Grand Hotel and Casino and worked for celebrity chefs Jean-Georges Vongerichten and Thomas Keller.[59] Yet, he reminisces that though his experience working with the "demi-god[s] of the culinary world," including Vongerichten and Keller, taught him how big-name chefs really play the game, it also made him think about what could differentiate him from these chefs. At the talk at the Korea Society in New York in 2020, Simon Kim said: "I was born and raised in Seoul, where one of my favorite restaurants was obviously Korean barbecue. . . . It is casual but expensive. . . . That's my nostalgia childhood growing up and when I came to New York, I fell in love with Peter Luger. . . . This is also authentic representation of who I am and what I like." While working for the culinary empires by Vongerichten and Keller, Simon Kim's vision for his own business was, in fact, rooted in where he came from and who he is, channeling memories of his childhood in Seoul, particularly the barbeque restaurants. His dream was actualized and materialized not only through what he learned in the culinary world in Las Vegas and New York, but also through his own roots in Korea. Likewise, Hooni Kim also shared a similar story at a talk at the Korea Society in 2012: "[At Daniel,] I saw these French cooks cooking French food that was more than technique, flavor, and taste. It was they were cooking who they were . . . the history, heritage. That's the pride that they had. . . . What I realized earlier on was I may have been as good as cooking French food, compared to them, I was sort of like a pretender. . . . That's why I started cooking Korean food. I sort of wanted to have that pride."[60]

During this talk, Hooni Kim emphasized the importance of authenticity and his own frustrations as a Korean American chef who cooked French cuisine.[61] Yet, his decision to marry his Western techniques with Korean flavor has brought his uniqueness and authenticity into the culinary world in New York. In fact, this innovative combination has made him successful, as one of his restaurants earned a Michelin star. During an interview with the local Korean media in the United States, he emphasized his Korean roots and tastes, inherited from his grandmother in Soan-do, an island in Southern Korea, where he has traveled to every year since he left Korea at the age of three. He said that his experience with Korean restaurants in New York was different from his grandmother's sonmat (literally translated to "hand taste," or an individual's unique flavor and sense), which originates from one's own creative cooking skills and talent rather than standardized measurement.[62] This authenticity, as a Korean chef who was born in Korea and has maintained strong transnational ties since a young age, was, of course, a plus.

In fact, their authenticity as new-generation chefs is in line with a new worldwide culinary trend that "pairs global techniques with familiar Korean flavors."[63] The food is Korean and the chefs are born-and-raised Koreans, but the dishes are presented in a Western manner and prepared with European techniques, like tapas-style Korean dishes at Hooni Kim's Danji and multicourse prix fixe menus at Junghyun Park and Ellia Park's Atoboy and Atomix. Atoboy and Atomix are probably the hottest Korean restaurants in New York as of 2020, as Atomix received two Michelin stars in 2018, the year it opened, and three stars from *The New York Times*. Danji received its first Michelin star in 2012. The Michelin Guide noted, "The opening of Atomix in 2018 brought about a paradigm shift in the city's appreciation of Korean food."[64] Likewise, Pete Wells, a *New York Times* food critic, emphasized that their representation of creativity and imagination "recalls the early days of the Four Seasons, which moved beyond European models of formal dining by hiring an American architect and American industrial designers."[65] The chef and owner of Atoboy and Atomix Junghyun Park, and his wife and co-owner Ellia Park, regularly travel to Korea to bring their old-aged soy sauce from Damyang, a southern region of Korea, in order to infuse "traditional" Korean flavor into their dishes in New York.[66]

However, despite the fact that they tend to stay away from Koreatown in terms of business locations by choosing Tribeca, Hell's Kitchen, the Flatiron District, the East Village, or even Brooklyn, some of these "new-generation" restaurateurs recognize the importance of Koreatown as a mecca of Korean food. Ellia Park of Atoboy and Atomix explains that when she and her husband Junghyun Park decided to open Atoboy, they did not want to be far from Koreatown. She said at the Korea Society, "We want to *stay around* Koreatown but *not in* Koreatown so you can represent your Korean food to American people at the same time to Korean people together." She pointed out that they wanted to stay near Koreatown, because of its symbolic place in the Korean foodscape in New York, but not in Koreatown. As will be discussed in chapters 3 and 4, before the pandemic, Korean nationals often saw Koreatown as an old and outdated space—a misrepresentation of their nation. Yet, despite stereotypical images of Koreatown, as businesspersons, the Parks knew the value of Koreatown as a Korean food mecca in New York, bringing foodies and clients who are already familiar with Korean food to their new and unique restaurant. In addition, skyrocketing rent on 32nd Street also was a factor for them to "become K-town-adjacent" rather than opening their first restaurant on 32nd Street, as she said in an interview with *Eater*.[67]

During the talk at the Korea Society, when Ellia Park said that they wanted to stay around Koreatown, another panelist, Simon Kim of Cote, jokingly said, "That's great, because after the great dinner, you have to go to karaoke."[68] Simon Kim understands typical Korean nightlife—eating dinner with some drinks, having more drinks, and ending the night at a noraebang, the Korean term for karaoke, which literally translates to "singing room" or "room for singing/songs." Koreatown, in fact, offers the total cultural package to both Koreans and non-Koreans.

Though Ellia Park and Simon Kim might disagree, their understanding of Koreatown is in line with the government's vision. The Korean government saw Koreatown as replicating, albeit with a bit of a time lag, what Korea is all about. As part of a larger initiative, the government completed the construction of the New York Korea Center at 122 East 32nd Street (between Park and Lexington Avenues), just two blocks from Koreatown. The New York Korea Center relocated from its previous site—KCCNY at 460 Park Avenue (between 57th and 58th Streets)—to Midtown Manhattan, and now houses other culture- and tourism-related government agencies, including the Korea Tourism Organization, King Sejong Institute Foundation, and Korea Creative Content Agency. Although the government purchased the land—formerly parking lots—back in 2008, the project took more than fifteen years to complete due to various budget-related issues. The new building aims to serve as a comprehensive cultural institution, offering a range of experiences including a theater, exhibition space, and cooking studio. "I heard that not everyone was happy with the final decision about this location, but in the end, it worked out well," said Jeongwoo, a staff member at KCCNY in 2024.

Interestingly, Jeongwoo, like Ellia Park of Atoboy and Atomix, highlights that "this new location is Koreatown-adjacent, but Park Avenue psychologically divides the two spaces [Koreatown and the KCCNY]." He believes this physical and psychological divide provides interesting opportunities for both Koreatown and KCCNY. The new building's various facilities, such as a cooking studio and a gallery, enable KCCNY to showcase Korean culture beyond just consumption. Additionally, the KCCNY has launched a group visit program for students and teachers from Korean schools and public schools that offer Korean language classes since moving to the new location. Koreatown, thus, extends its imagined territory, actualizing ideas about Korean consumer culture to more total cultural space, as Jeongwoo puts it in 2024, "beyond consumption."

During the talk at the Korea Society in February 2020, I was surprised by what Simon Kim said about how and why Korean food became popular. He said,

> Japanese cuisine probably is very good thing to look into for the relative comparison. So Korean restaurants, last year, we have six Michelin restaurants.... That's the most amount of stars awarded to any other cuisine other than Japanese that comes from Asia. So if I look at the history of what happened, we kind of resemble very similarly to what Japan did, so I feel like the manufacturing like Sony, Panasonic, Toyota, they kind of made big and then that money went into the financial institutions and they made it even more and then they invest those money into cultural things like restaurants and art and different things and then had a golden age of culture.[69]

While he didn't explicitly say "nation branding" or "public diplomacy" in his talk, Simon Kim is clearly aware of the cultural power of the nation by comparing the emergence of Korean cuisine to the popularity of Japanese cuisine in New York in the 1980s and 1990s.

What Simon Kim said at the talk lingered in my mind for a while. This talk, "Beyond 32nd Street: Korean Restaurants of the Moment," was organized by a senior director of arts and culture in the Korea Society on February 27, 2020, as part of a series of talks on Koreatown and the Korean foodscape in New York. Three weeks prior to this event, on February 6, 2020, I gave the first talk, entitled "32nd Street: Then & Now," about the history of Koreatown in Manhattan. While I explained the history of Koreatown, which evolved from a space for wholesalers to a transclave, I heard the stories of three panelists in the second talk—Simon Kim of Cote, Jenny Kwak of Haenyeo, and Ellia Park of Atoboy and Atomix—that I found to be very refreshing. I had been away from the city for three years, after studying Koreatown in Manhattan for almost a decade, but the Korean foodscape was obviously evolving and expanding its boundaries beyond Koreatown. Their business approaches were very different from what many first-generation Koreatown entrepreneurs would have imagined.

If Simon Kim was right, in some ways, isn't it true that the cultural power of the nation brought Korean cuisine into the US mainstream? If so, despite their disagreement about the role of the government, wouldn't these chefs have also participated in a larger project of globalization of Korean food by bringing their creativity into the marketplace?

Territorial Expansion

Kyung Rim Choi, an immigrant from Korea, is the president of Group KFF Inc. that operates eleven restaurant and dessert brands in New York, including Don's Bogam and Hong Chun Cheon, as of February 2024. Choi also introduced two bakery chains from Korea—Koryodang and Tous Les Jours, a bakery chain owned by CJ Group in Korea—and opened the first food court in Koreatown, Food Gallery 32, which he sold a year later. He was also an active member of the KCGC USA and worked closely with the Korean government in the 2000s and 2010s. Finally, he served as a representative of the Business Association of 32nd Street.

According to press interviews, he emphasizes his business trips to Seoul for his unique position in New York's Korean business world. According to *Eater*, he splits his time between Korea and New York and samples the latest food trends in Korea. He has brought these new trends to Koreatown and even beyond. He signed a contract with the CJ Group to turn his Koryodang bakery outlets into Tous Les Jours in Manhattan in 2012. Seven years later, he signed with a new Korean franchise, Hong Chun Cheon, which specializes in dak-galbi, or spicy stir-fried chicken, and operates over two hundred restaurants across Korea, and established it in New York.[70] After success in Manhattan's Koreatown, he planned to open a second location in Flushing in 2020.[71] In 2019, his group announced that they had invested $6 million in a new food hall called K-Food Gallery, featuring sixteen food stalls. The plan was to open it just northwest of Koreatown in the summer of 2020.[72]

In several interviews with journalists both in New York and Seoul, Choi did not hide his passion about promoting Korean food in New York. He said that he would like to "continue building awareness around Korean cuisine."[73] He highlights the cultural power of Korea, just like Japan did in the past, as Simon Kim also pointed out at the Korea Society in 2020.[74] He also visits Korea once a month in order to ship two containers of items and ingredients for his businesses to New York, even including interior decorating materials, because his clients like the feeling of Korean-style design.⁷⁵ He explains that the group wants to "create Korean enclaves in other parts of the city" and "expand Koreatown westward into the Times Square area."⁷⁶ Even a few years after being deeply involved in the KCGC USA, he still planned to continue making efforts to increase "awareness around Korean cuisine" at the heart of New York.⁷⁷ As of December 2024, his plan seems not to meet his expectations. The food court is not open yet. However, whether his plan has been actualized or fallen apart, his original plan was in line with the recent expansion of Korean restaurants across the city. Is it a sign of a territorial expansion of Koreatown?

Likewise, Hooni Kim also relates his business with his diasporic roots and actively promotes them both in the United States and Korea. He said on *Little Big Hero: The Challenger*, a tvN (Korean cable channel) show in 2020:

> For the past ten years, when I have been cooking at my restaurants, I felt like I am an Olympic athlete, because I am representing my country and my culture through food. Almost feeling like the whole country is supporting me behind my back to make sure that I cook the best food that I can to show off the best of Korea . . . All chefs who cook Korean food need to have a responsibility to make sure that the food is good. And the customers, after they dine at your restaurant, will be curious to dine at other Korean restaurants and ultimately maybe even come to Korea.⁷⁸

On the show, he was introduced as a national chef representing his country who was brave enough to give up his career as a medical student to become a chef. He said he always brings and uses gochugaru (red chili pepper powder), sesame oil, and jang (fermented paste), produced in Korea, in order to deliver authentic flavor. Of course, his ideas are envisioned beyond the Koreatown territory.

Yet, after the globalization of Korean food project failed in the Lee administration, the KCGC USA switched gears toward local projects, as introduced earlier this chapter. Koreatown entrepreneurs in New York and other cities, such as Los Angeles and Chicago, among others, met to discuss if they should still collaborate with the Korean government to promote Korean food in 2019. At the time of the interview in April 2022, Claire, who was involved in the KCGC USA, told me that there were more people who objected to this plan because of past conflicts with the government, particularly around the budget, but they had not come up with an agreement. Minjae from KCGC USA told me that the Korean government does not take any particular actions to improve the situation. However, in New York City, these entrepreneurs still wanted to promote Korean food in their own ways, though there is no longer much financial aid from the Korean government. Claire shared her thoughts in 2022: "The best part of their activities is to donate food to schools. They organize parties in order to publicize Korean food. Popularization at a community level. . . . You send a message that Korean food is not just about grills or meat. We have galbi [beef or pork short ribs], but we also have ddeok [sticky rice cakes], jeongol [hot pot], eel, and hoe [raw fish]." I was very surprised by their current efforts, even after the globalization of Korean food died down in Korea with a series of political scandals in the Lee administration. After interviewing Claire and Minjae in 2022 and reading news articles about Kyung Rim Choi and Hooni Kim, I reflected on an interview with Insook, a businessperson and participant of the KCGC USA, that I conducted more than a decade ago. Claire told me that they were very disappointed with the government, particularly because the budget did not arrive in the United States, which resulted in entrepreneurs donating their own money for local food-related events. Their businesses thrived, while Korean food has received much attention in the past decade. Many might not need any public promotion for their businesses; in addition, organizing such a committee and events requires a great deal of time and energy. Yet, why were they still willing to promote their culture and food on a community level, even after experiencing broken promises from the government agencies in the past? How do we locate these entrepreneurs in a map of Korea's nation branding overseas?

About a decade after two interviews with businesspeople on 32nd Street, Insook and Jaesu, it was refreshing to learn about how the next generations of Korean chefs and entrepreneurs, from Simon Kim to Hooni Kim to Minjae, reinvent and bring the meaning of the nation and the national culture to the diverse food scene in New York City—a home to various ethnic cuisines; and, arguably, a global culinary capital. These

Korean entrepreneurs both in and out of Koreatown bring their national and ethnic roots into their businesses in various ways, from collaborations with the government and transnational corporations to cultural events. Nation branding is not only driven by top-down policies but practiced by various individuals from citizens to diaspora and nondiasporic individuals, reconstructing the traditional meaning of the nation and nationhood by extending it to their national and ethnic territories. However, their efforts might not be rightly called nationalist sentiments or ethnic solidarities. As businesspeople, their priority is to maximize profits. In fact, the meanings of nation and nationalist sentiment are indeed redefined and reinvented as "commercial terms" and "narrative for domestic consumption" by the diaspora in the marketplace.[79]

In the next four chapters, I turn my attention to three groups of consumers—Korean nationals, Korean Americans, and non-Koreans—and how they respond to nation branding strategies by paying attention to their intraethnic, interethnic, and interracial relations. Chapter 3 analyzes how the collective memories of ethnic Koreans—Korean nationals and Korean Americans—help them negotiate the meaning of "Korea" and (re)shape Koreatown as a space for homemaking and nostalgia in a transclave.

PART II

Consuming Ethnicity

3

(Re)Making Koreatown

Nostalgia and Collective Memories

I am a foreigner in this city. But at least I feel like I'm a part of the majority on this street.
—Jieun, a twenty-eight-year-old PhD student at NYU

My friends and I, when we would go out we'd be like, K-town, this is our town, we own this street and saying dumb stuff like that (laughs).
—Emily, a twenty-three-year-old second-generation Korean American

In the 1980s, when she was a middle-school student, Sunmee would often visit a friend who lived on the third floor above an old Korean restaurant on 32nd Street. A forty-two years old second-generation Korean American who was born in Korea and came to the United States when she was five years old in the 1970s, Sunmee would go across the street to get food to cook for her father. Her friend was a twice-migrant who was "born in Korea, moved to Brazil, and her family was all into the garment industry." The friend lived in a studio apartment with her divorced father, who was sometimes away, allowing her to "play hooky" and invite Sunmee for sleepovers. When Sunmee visited her friend, they would go up to the rooftop. She vividly remembers how 32nd Street looked back in the 1980s, recalling that it was "the weirdest block ever" and very dangerous, where "women would be clutching their handbags because there will be lots of bag stealing. It was very common in the '80s to steal a woman's bag," and "a lot of restaurant owners will say be careful when you go out." This resonates with what one of the early store owners recalled, and what many American cities were like during this time of urban disinvestment.

Though 32nd Street was "dangerous," with a high crime rate in the 1980s, Sunmee remembers it having a strangely diverse mix of people, including the mostly Black residents of the welfare hotel, Korean customers who were the target clientele at the restaurants in the area, and Korean wholesalers in the Korean Business District a couple of blocks away. After the welfare hotel closed in 1987,[1] the landscape of the space started to change. In the 1990s, it had become a space mainly for Koreans, and "exploded, little by little, little by little," though its main population, unlike today, was mostly Korean immigrants and their children. Sunmee remembers that a generational divide existed in Koreatown; she felt that the "the business that was catering on 32nd Street was for Korean speakers, there was never for Korean Americans." She often avoided those places, where ajeossi (middle-aged men) were hanging out, and "didn't want to bump into my parents" in her twenties. Instead, she and her friend "went to the Village . . . which was a hotspot."[2]

In the 2010s, 32nd Street became more bustling and vibrant in different ways. Sangjin, a twenty-four-year-old language student, was a newer consumer in Koreatown in 2012. As an active and outgoing person, he wanted to expand his social circle and enjoy his temporary stay in New York City as a language student. Expecting to meet new friends, he joined "NYC Meetups," an online social group. Among several other groups, he belongs to a "Meetup" between Asian men and Black women. When he began hanging out with Black women in the social group, he was surprised that many of them were intrigued by Korean culture and food and by the nation itself. He sometimes brought his friends whom he had met in the social group to Korean restaurants in Koreatown, not just because he wanted to share his culture with them. Of a woman he met through the group, Sangjin said, "This woman from Gabon was really into Korean food, so I took her to Koreatown. . . . When I asked her if she had specific food in her mind, she was like, 'I would not mind anything if it is Korean.' . . . She really wanted to make Korean friends." As a newcomer to New York without much international experience back home, he was pleased that non-Koreans were interested in his culture, and he wanted to introduce it to them.

Unlike old-timers of Koreatown such as the ajeossi that Sunmee wanted to avoid back in the 1980s and 1990s, these younger consumers in the post-2010 era are more diverse, younger, and cosmopolitan. The pandemic and the popularity of Korean culture have unexpectedly made Manhattan Koreatown even more diverse. Jinsun, a fifty-two-year-old former Koreatown restaurant employee from the late 1990s to 2009, now calls "the K-town" a hot destination both for tourists and locals. She talks about the scale of restaurants in "a three-story building" and "a long wait line" with young and diverse groups of people in the post-pandemic. In particular, the holiday seasons are a peak time for Koreatown businesses, according to her husband, who still works on 32nd Street as a cook as of 2024. Koreatown has attracted a new consumer population and new types of businesses and is different from more typical Koreatowns such as the one in Queens encompassing Flushing and Bayside.[3] Immigrant-owned small businesses have left and been replaced by Korean franchise stores, either because they could not afford the high rents or because the proprietors retired. By the 2010s, Manhattan's Koreatown had attracted a new Korean population: Korean nationals (including temporary residents such as students on F1 visas), Korean tourists, and young Korean Americans (including college students, graduate students, and those who work or live in metropolitan New York City). In addition, non-Korean locals and tourists have joined Koreans as people who frequent Koreatown. Sangjin and his African friend were part of this new trend in Koreatown.

In this chapter, I turn my attention to the role of collective memories in the process of making and remaking Koreatown, representing the Korean nation and its culture embedded in a small commercial section of New York City. I pay more attention to how various individual consumers in New York have shaped Koreatown as a space for homemaking and nostalgia in a commercial neighborhood by exploring how the consumer groups, especially ethnic Koreans, have perceived and utilized Koreatown as a cultural platform for cultural and ethnic consumption. Nostalgia is often defined as a yearning for home and a sense of loss and displacement, thought to be associated with individual emotions and longing.[4] However, this nostalgia is not only limited to the segmented and fragmented memories of individuals, but also limited to collective memories and practices because the past was no longer something to be forgotten, but preserved for social cohesion and tradition.[5] I emphasize those bottom-up voices and narratives of individuals about their nostalgic yearning and longing for time and space. Introducing their narratives and acknowledging their own stories in their voices is critical to understanding both their individual and group identities and their sense of belonging within particular communities and collectivities.[6]

Two Tales of Koreatown: Nostalgia and Collective Memories

Nostalgia provokes "meaningful events, relationships or things" that require "the form of general practices (for example, sustainability or solidarity) or more particular ideas (for example craftsmanship or ethnic identity)"[7] and encourages us to take "the politics of loss, attachment to, and uses of the past and present" into consideration.[8] Though many scholars have emphasized that nostalgia is about time,[9] I paid attention to how it is situated, embodied, and anchored in space,[10] mainly because space "house[s] the remembered experience" and reconstructs their collective memories.[11] If this is the case, how do we reimagine and reconstruct our lost home, our loss, and our attachment in collective forms in a commercial space? In this case, Koreatown?

By integrating nostalgia and collective memory, I understand Koreatown as a symbolic space for each group, where individuals negotiate the meaning of "Korea," nation, or the motherland, rooted in their respective relationships with their groups, and each respective group's unique collective memories and histories, real or imagined. I introduce two tales of Koreatown by Tiffany and Emily.[12]

Tiffany

During her freshman year at New York University in the late 2000s, Tiffany sometimes rode the train from her dorm near Greenwich Village to Herald Square, a busy commercial area in Midtown Manhattan near Koreatown. Unlike many other New Yorkers who come to shop in this major commercial district, the purpose of Tiffany's visits was rather different. As soon as she would get off the train, Tiffany would walk two blocks to be reunited with her high school friends—young people who, like herself, attended one of the most prestigious specialized high schools in Seoul but who were attending college in the United States. She did not like the idea of hanging out in Koreatown.

She would often ask herself, "Why the hell am I hanging out there when there were so many other fun and cool neighborhoods in New York City?" Her favorites were the East Village and Alphabet City, where she could experience a vibrant and creative arts scene. Yet, she recalls that it was a common event for her and her friends to gather in Koreatown, particularly during the first two years of college. She recounted, "We're not just seeing people from New York or the East Coast, but people were coming from the West Coast and the Midwest. We met during Thanksgiving and spring breaks or just before a new semester begins. We felt lonely and missed friends, and, of course, they wanted to visit New York. It was very special for us to see each other and hang out, because we are high school friends."

Tiffany was born in Seattle in the 1980s, thus she is a US citizen by birth. However, she does not necessarily identify as second-generation. Her upbringing was somewhat different from many other US-born Korean Americans. She is part of a group that I refer to as "new transnational generation Koreans," whose upbringings are uniquely transnational due to their family's decisions to relocate to two or more countries and enroll their children in British or American schools at an early age. She has lived in a number of countries throughout her life, and when asked where she is from, she "need[s] to answer for like at least fifteen minutes." She moved back and forth between Seattle and Toronto for the first five years of her life due to her father's job. When she was in kindergarten, her family returned to Korea, where she went to elementary school until the sixth grade. She moved back to Seattle for junior high school and then came back to Korea for high school.

Her high school experience was very special for her, and she often questions who she is and how she defines herself. She gradually became more "comfortable" during college, as she got to know many other new transnational generation Koreans who shared similar upbringings. However, she reminisces that her high school was the only school where she felt she "belonged." Unlike Tiffany, who is a US citizen, speaks fluent English, and has experience in US education, her peers who had an elite high school education in Korea still feel "nostalgia" for their time in Seoul while learning a language and struggling to fit into college culture in the United States. Tiffany shared with me that they were visiting New York from all over the United States.

Tiffany recalls that their routine was a "very Korean" night out and that their activities did not change for two years. They would meet at a humble pub in Koreatown, where customers could get both anju (food consumed with drinks) and soju and beer to make somaek (soju and beer bombs) and they would get drunk. They then would go to a noraebang to sing, dance, and let loose in a private room to release their stress. That was what they did back home in Korea, and they brought their "very Korean" routine to a small street in New York City. Many Koreans perceive New York as a city of consumption, fashion, sophistication, and culture—mostly constructed through media—and they do not necessarily like the images of Koreatown. However, Tiffany and her Korean friends' routine in Koreatown is common among many Korean international students, despite the fact that food and drinks were generally too expensive for college students' limited budgets, as Tiffany recalls. However, as time went by, her friends acclimated to life at their own colleges and were less motivated to travel to New York City. However, Koreatown was their main destination in New York whenever they visited.

Emily

Emily, a twenty-three-year-old second-generation Korean American, grew up in a middle-class family in Maryland. She might be categorized as a "typical" Korean American in terms of being perceived by outsiders as a highly assimilated child of immigrants. She studied journalism and English at New York University (NYU) and recently started a job in New York. Despite having grown up in a predominantly white neighborhood in Maryland, she still vividly remembers her adolescence in terms of her differences and isolation from her peers: "I went through a lot of confusion about my identity because I was going to a predominantly white school" and felt "nobody could understand me." Like most of my informants, whether they grew up in white or Korean communities, Emily expresses that she often did not "truly belong anywhere" or "fit into" the American mainstream, particularly among white peers.[13] She shares one vivid memory in high school that sticks with her. "I was in class and my teacher accidentally called me—there was another Chinese American, the other Asian American girl, her name is Kaleen. So the teacher called me Kaleen by accident. And I was like, oh, you know, that's not my name. And then this kid who was next to me was like, 'Why don't you shut up, it doesn't matter anyway, you guys are like the same person anyway.'" Emily's unforgettable memory of her teacher and white peer treating her as "the same person" as the Chinese American classmate is a common experience among other Asian Americans: hearing that they are interchangeable Asians.[14] Feeling marginalized and rejected, or at least not embraced or properly recognized by the dominant group is often rooted in the anti-Asian racism that Korean Americans collectively experience.[15] Anti-Asian racism can take many forms; sometimes it is obvious and overt, as in the murder of the Chinese American Vincent Chin.[16] More recently, it has manifested as violence and hate crimes against Asians during the COVID-19 pandemic, including the murder of six Asian women by a white man in Atlanta. And perhaps most commonly, it occurs as racial microaggressions in daily life.[17] These microaggressions are more subtle and not easily recognizable or even necessarily identifiable.

Rather than confronting the white peer, Emily could not say anything and did not know how to respond. She also talked about her Korean American church friends. She recalled that "basically, my whole life in high school was church." The Korean church was, in fact, a safe home for Emily, where her parents maintained ties with a Korean community. Her mother both encouraged her children to learn about their ethnic roots and wanted them to assimilate into the American mainstream; she regularly drove forty to sixty minutes to take the children to the Korean church, not only for the service but also for Saturday Korean classes, where she herself was a teacher. Emily, who became an atheist in college, feels that her family's emphasis on a relatively conservative and religious lifestyle further isolated her. She recalls that her white friends would focus on "partying and cursing," which she would not participate in because she felt "that's against God's law or whatever." She explained why she became so dedicated to her church. "I actually really began to feel it, maybe towards the end of high school when I completely sort of shut myself off from my school friends. So I slowly began to lose a lot of my high school friends because I had just started to focus all my efforts on my church friends, because I felt like those are the people that truly understood where I came from and could understand my background—my experience." While struggling with her racial and ethnic identity and feeling different from her white peers, she became deeply involved with the praise team, where she was the leader, and she attended church on Friday, Saturday, and Sunday every week. This emotional attachment to her coethnic religious community combined with her confusion about her identity permitted her to develop a keen interest in Korean culture.

Yet, for Emily, her college experience at NYU was very different from her teenage life in Maryland, as she moved to a big city from a small town. As she summarizes it, "It's such a cliché story but it's like the Christian conservative girl moves to the city and becomes free." New York City is racially diverse, and so is NYU. Emily was able to meet Asian peers in her program and beyond, which she had wanted for so long. She also joined the North Korea human rights group, where she was able to meet many other Korean and Asian Americans.

During her freshman and sophomore years, she missed the Korean food her mother cooked for her. As a response to this longing, she frequented Koreatown with Korean American friends whom she met in school, who also grew up eating Korean food at home. "In the beginning, I felt very at home there. Like what I said before, that's where other people who are like me go to eat and interact. If you hang out there you can meet other people who . . . yeah, who look like me and—especially my programs, there were too many Asians so it was definitely very familiar to go back to that area." Emily felt at home in Koreatown when she was new to New York City. As a metaphor, home is a place of belonging, a safe place, a place where people do not get hurt, and a place that one longs for.[18] It is also about emotional attachment.[19] Having been surrounded by white peers who did not understand who she was and diminished her existence by telling her that she and her Chinese American peer were interchangeable, this space, albeit commercial, was comfortable, safe, and familiar. Emily's excitement about being around people "who look like me" is akin to how Laura, a thirty-year-old second-generation Korean American, initially experienced Korean society while living in Korea for about three and half years; she compared being ethnically Korean in Korea to "[like being] white in America" (as will be discussed further in chapter 6). Despite struggles due to cultural differences, language issues, or mistreatment, Korean Americans' status as a racial and ethnic minority is less intense, or even somewhat disappears in Korea. It does in Koreatown as well.

Yearning for Seoul

Immigrants and their children often feel nostalgia—longing for the past and emotional attachments to their homeland. Rather than entirely cutting themselves off from their past, these individuals speak with their past selves in order to serve the present.[20] Yet, interestingly, the past that my research participants yearn for, as seen in Tiffany and Emily's cases, is often different from that of many traditional immigrants discussed in the immigration literature. It is mainly due to changes in the immigration patterns from Korea to the United States since the 1990s. It is particularly true for international students, as seen in the cases of Tiffany's friends.

First, their motivation for migration tends to be more voluntary, particularly for higher education. According to the Institute of International Education, in the 2022–2023 academic year, Korea sent 43,847 students to the United States and ranked third for countries of origin for international students, following China and India.[21] Second, many young Korean nationals are in the United States on student or work visas, granting legal status for temporary stays, while their family is in Korea. Their parents and families tend to be well-off, enabling them to support their children in school.[22] Only three of the Korean nationals I interviewed identified as working-class, with one identifying as between working and middle class.[23] Many Korean nationals I spoke with regularly travel to Korea—typically once a year, or in some cases twice—and their parents, siblings, and friends also tend to visit them in the United States too. This trend has accelerated since the Visa Waiver Program, which allows Korean nationals to travel to the United States without a visa for up to ninety days, was implemented in 2008, facilitating visits. Third, due to technological advancements in recent decades, Korean nationals frequently talk and text with family and friends in Korea via Kakao Talk, a Korean messenger app, and consume Korean media in the United States. Unlike students from earlier time periods who had limited access to Korean media, Korean students today are able to easily watch Korean dramas and TV shows—which are now available on various media outlets such as Netflix and YouTube—and listen to Korean popular music, which will be further discussed in chapter 5.

This high level of transnationality between the United States and Korea, mainly due to their temporary status in the United States, enables them to maintain strong ties to their home country. Their nostalgia is complex, and doesn't necessarily indicate a yearning for a return to the past.[24] It is not the same loss that permanent immigrants often feel about the country they left, but rather, it is a temporary and transient type of nostalgia. For these younger transnational Koreans, their memories of the past are recent, enabling them to easily catch up once they are back home, though it isn't always the same. Many Korean nationals point out that the pace of change in Korea is very fast and even faster and more intensive than in New York City. Regardless, the temporality of this loss reduces the time lag between home and the United States.

Though nostalgia is often triggered by being far from one's homeland, modern understandings of nostalgia center on temporality, and tend to downplay the importance of place that emphasizes mobility, environment,[25] and landscape.[26] Yet, the loss of local and national identities in a globalized world, ironically and paradoxically, motivate new ways of claiming and reclaiming localities and cause "contrary and reflexive mechanisms of reterritorialization."[27] Instead of the deterritorialization of belonging, there are multiple forms and sites of belonging here and there,[28] often connected to place, landscapes, monuments, and urban architecture because these are places where past events are often celebrated and collected.[29]

Therefore, Koreatown is a place of nostalgia where people's identity and collective memories are embodied, rediscovered, and negotiated in their lives while communicating with diverse agents, from coethnic strangers to non-coethnics.[30] As in the case of Tiffany, her friends, and many Korean nationals, their choice to dine, drink, and enjoy nightlife in Koreatown is rooted in nostalgic memories, which are anchored in spaces such as home, neighborhood, and even Koreatown. The memories of certain spaces—mostly popular and trendy commercial areas in Seoul such as Gangnam—are reified and realized in Koreatown, albeit with a time lag. Place-making and a sense of place in a transclave reify and enable ethnic minorities and transnational migrants to deliver their own nostalgia narratives because they struggle with them and challenge and redefine those meanings. Therefore, belonging and nostalgia are situated between the local and global through individual interactions in a transclave,[31] where transnational culture and consumerism intersect with the local contexts.

Safe Home and Belonging

Unlike Korean nationals, whose nostalgia is rooted in collective memories of Seoul's recent past or present, Korean Americans like Emily tell different stories. Their stories are rooted in their complex upbringings in childhood and adolescence as racial minorities in the United States. Furthermore, their collective memories are shaped by their unique processes of rerooting their (transnational) identities through a wide range of transnational activities from family trips to Korea to return migration to their ancestor home, to, of course, Koreatown consumption.[32]

Our Town, Our Street

Jenny is a thirty-seven years old second-generation Korean American and moved to New York City for college in the early 1990s. Like Emily, Jenny also grew up in a predominantly white neighborhood in Washington, DC. She remembers that some of her white peers made fun of her, saying "things like, even in junior high, 'Ching Chong' or yeah, those kinds of ridiculous things." She explains one specific vivid memory of a microaggression in junior high school: "Some guy said, 'Oh I don't want to dance with her, that Ching Chong.'" The "Ching Chong" slur directed at Jenny mocks Asians who are assumed not to be fluent in English and have heavy foreign accents. Jenny, who was born and raised in the United States, does not have a foreign accent, yet this racial insult was nonetheless regularly used to debase and separate her based on her racialized appearance.

Having experienced a series of anti-Asian microaggressions and lacking advice or other guidance from her parents, Jenny honed her identity as a woman of color in general and an Asian American woman in particular during her years at Barnard College in the 1990s. Jenny developed her identity by participating in organizations led by women of color as a young adult. In doing so, she found and nurtured a sense of racial affinity and commonality, not only with Asian Americans of Korean descent, but with "other Asians."[33] Outside of college life in New York City, she also felt connected to Koreatown. Though she visited Koreatown with her parents as a teenager, she returned as a young college student in the early 1990s. Even though Koreatown wasn't her favorite space to hang out with friends, she was glad it was there, saying: "Yeah, I think I was happy that there was at least one street dedicated to, you know, Koreans, for Koreans, yeah." When Jenny revisited Koreatown as a college student, it represented a rare space devoted to Koreans in New York City. Her relief to be able to reconnect herself with the space shows that it represented and accentuated Koreanness for her; in her predominantly white neighborhood of DC, Koreanness wasn't part of public space and was only practiced privately. Furthermore, Koreatown constructs a novel local identity through Koreans' narratives,[34] counteracting the racial inequality of normalized whiteness.

For some Korean Americans, Koreatown reflects their personal history and the struggles their parents experienced in the United States. The sense of ownership is more fraught. As Emily, a twenty-three-year-old second-generation Korean American, says, "My friends and I, when we would go out, we'd be like, 'K-town, this is our town, we own this street' and saying dumb stuff like that (laughs)."

"We own this street." Emily did not grow up in New York, but five years prior, she started going to Koreatown with Korean American friends regularly while she was a student at New York University. This short commercial strip soon became theirs, feeling a part of a larger community that reinforces familial and emotional bonds with others and to place.[35] In fact, some Korean Americans have developed their own symbolic ownership of the street's identity "in order to secure the neighborhood's degree of distinction in the city."[36] For Korean Americans, I use the term "symbolic ownership" to describe their understanding of spatial identity or urban imaginary as a safe space or home where their racial or ethnic distinction or insecurity in the larger society is diminished. In addition, they can claim their Koreanness in distinctive spaces or streets such as those in Koreatown. This space can be understood as rooted in the history of Korean immigration and Koreans' struggle in the US racial hierarchy.

This process is one of "the new ways of home-making" in the "caring community," where Korean Americans find "their place among 'normal' people rather than being isolated in institutions."[37] Clearly, it is a "comfortable space," even if they cannot pinpoint why. Considering this question, Eren, a thirty-year-old second-generation Korean American from North Carolina, has a hard time explaining why she feels this way: "Why do I feel comfortable? I mean I don't feel uncomfortable. I don't know, I am just so comfortable there. Maybe because I am familiar with it."

Others, despite expressing emotional attachment, do not realize that they construct the space based on collective ethnic identification. Although Sunmee, a forty-two-year-old building manager who grew up in Brooklyn, does not think that she owns the space, her interpretation parallels Emily's feeling of the space being *her* street.

> I do feel more comfortable on 32nd Street because I grew up there in a way. I mean, I've seen it over the years as something I know very well . . . I see the changes. Yes, definitely over thirty years, I've seen the change and I feel comfortable with it. And in a sense, I feel like it grew as I grew. . . . I don't know. Koreatown is just Koreatown. I never really felt—I don't feel like I own it, I just feel like I know it and it's always there. . . . Like Chinatown is also comfortable but I don't feel like it's mine—Koreatown is like mine.

Sunmee, whose parents were greengrocers in Brooklyn in the 1970s, recalls being taken with her siblings to Koreatown on special occasions. She remembers taking a photo of 32nd Street in the early 1980s on the roof of the building, where one of her best friends from junior high school used to live, as introduced earlier in this chapter. She used to eat in Koreatown with her friends when she was in her twenties and had coffee or drinks downtown in the Village. Koreatown was specifically for consumption of Korean products and services, and it seemed like a space for immigrants, not for younger Korean Americans doing typically "American" things. Although she does not believe that she has ownership of the space, she uses the word "mine" in comparing Koreatown to Chinatown; while the latter is also a comfortable space for her, she feels that Koreatown is hers, a part of her personal life as it relates to her experiences and identity. Eren also uses the word "ours" when describing Koreatown in comparison to other ethnic enclaves such as Chinatown. "I don't remember thinking about that, I was thinking that ours was 32nd street and there were other places near K-town." Eren is a thirty-year-old second-generation Korean American and grew up in North Carolina and came to New York for work. She was very excited that she finally had easy access to Korean food, given that she was living away from her mother. But after a few years of living in the city, she found that she did not necessarily always enjoy Koreatown. Still, she calls it "ours," since it gives her a feeling of being part of a larger community that reinforces familial and emotional bonds with others and to place.[38]

In line with that, most of the Korean American interviewees say that they prefer hanging out in Koreatown with other Korean Americans—someone "who looks like you" and "who shares your culture." Sara is a twenty-three-year-old second-generation Korean American who was born in LA and grew up in various states along the East Coast. She went to elementary school in a predominantly white neighborhood in Pennsylvania where she felt as though she "didn't face racial discrimination or isolation," mostly because people knew each other and it was such a small town. Yet, when her family moved to Maryland, things changed. She was "thrown in" to a "half African American, half Caucasian" school with less than ten Asian kids, where she began hearing racial slurs like "Ching Chong." For college, she chose to relocate to New York City and attended NYU's Stern School of Business. She recalls her cultural shock because "there are a lot of Asians, especially Koreans" in her program, which she "had never experienced." Sara recounted her first Koreatown dining experience during her freshman year: "I think I went to eat lunch again with one of my classmates [at NYU] that I just met. . . . Yes, Korean American. So we instantly connected. So we went to one of the restaurants there. . . . I think when I first moved to New York, I went every week because I missed Korean food, I just couldn't get used to the dining hall food." While settling down in a new city, she found herself hanging out mostly with other Asians, particularly Korean Americans, because "it was easier" for her. She and her friends' nostalgic memories of home, particularly food, as in Emily's case, led her to Koreatown. (I will explore this more in chapter 6.) The space filled the need she felt to belong in her new city, drawing on emotional cultural attachment, which is often erased or neglected in spaces that lack coethnics.

Matt, a forty-two-year-old second-generation Korean American, would agree with Sara. He said that he would spend time with Korean American and other Asian American friends in Koreatown, because Asian Americans are more "open-minded" to other Asian cultures, unlike a non-Asian acquaintance who called him "the Japanese businessman" when he "went on a bus and had a briefcase and a suit." In fact, people feel a sense of belonging to a particular place and time because they feel comfortable there. Matt feels comfortable in Koreatown, when he is with his Asian friends, who value and respect his culture. In addition, the landscape of the place determines who people are and how they define themselves through several symbols.[39]

Nostalgic Fantasy

Myriad factors can lead Koreans and Korean Americans to seek out a sense of community or reconnect with their ethnic identity in Koreatown. Some examples include receiving microaggressions, being caught between a racialized minority status and the "mainstream" culture surrounding them,[40] or suffering other marginalizing experiences. Many traveled to Korea with their families when they were young or had love-hate relationships with the homeland as young adults. Regardless, their nostalgic ideas or memories of the homeland and their ethnic roots are often abstract and illusory.

On a Thursday evening in the late 1990s, Younghee, then a Columbia University student, should have been preparing for a quiz for her 9:00 a.m. Korean class. Yet she and her classmates were busy with something else. She recounted in 2009, "Like stupidly we would go [out] Thursday night. Every week we would have a language class at nine in the morning on Fridays, there would be a quiz. And we would be like, we're going to take out stuff and go study at a Korean restaurant downtown. We did drink but I just thought it was the stupidest thing in the world. And you know, I would then have to go take a Korean language class the next morning. This was a fairly regular thing." Younghee, a thirty-four-year old biracial Korean American with a second-generation Korean American father and a white mother, was struggling with her heritage language. Her father did not speak Korean, but was deeply engaged in a progressive political organization that focused on Korea-related issues. Her grandfather, who came to the United States during the Japanese colonization of Korea, further influenced Younghee's interest in their ancestral home.[41] Her first Korean class and the Korean culture that she experienced through the classes and the KSA (Korean Student Association) at Columbia University were different from what she thought they would be. Nevertheless, they were crucial as her first exposure to

Korean culture through Korean peers rather than her relatives. Many Korean Americans search for formal paths toward learning about themselves, their collective history, and cultural heritage. This can include taking classes in the Korean language, Korean studies, East Asian studies, ethnic studies, and Asian American studies, as well as participation in ethnic campus organizations such as the KSA and organizations that catered to pan-Asian students, students of color, and religious organizations. This involvement helps people reclaim identities that may have led to their being labeled as outsiders and connects them with a larger community of people who have had similar experiences.

Interestingly, Younghee feels that some Korean Americans idealize a Korean college life that they never had and try to replicate it in the United States. In the first year of college in Korea, students had many formal and informal meetings, the purpose of which was to develop a sense of community and enjoy freedom from the regimented high school tradition of intense academic pressure. These meetings also enabled senior students to introduce social issues and existing student movements to freshmen students, a major part of college culture during the democratization processes of the 1980s and 1990s. After such meetings, students would inevitably have dwipuri (social gatherings or after-parties) to close and recap the meetings, drinking soju or makgeolli (Korean rice wine) on campus or at a bar near campus. They would sing movement songs and discuss social issues, ultimately giving a sense of belonging, community, and collectivity, though it is fast disappearing in Korea. Like Korean college students in Korea, some Korean Americans engaged in dwipuri culture, though not necessarily with a political or social bent. Instead, they went to Koreatown to drink and enjoy themselves. Younghee said, "There was an idea of what colleges are like in Korea, and you can sort of do that here, because New York is so much more Korean than where a lot of people grew up."

Younghee reminisces that her Korean American peers tried to build a Korean community on campus at Columbia University through social events in the 1990s, yet most of the gatherings occurred in Koreatown. She was a self-described "serious kid" at that time who wanted to build a movement culture at the KSA, but she failed and "stopped hanging out with KSA," though she occasionally went to Koreatown for food and drinks. Unlike Korean nationals, particularly graduate students and other temporary residents who moved to New York after college, most US-born and 1.5-generation Korean Americans have only a vague understanding of what Korean college life is like or what dwipuri meant in college in the 1990s.

Yet, as Younghee explains, some Korean Americans romanticize aspects of Korean college life that they never experienced.[42] While many scholars point out that nostalgia is a sentiment of loss and displacement, it is also "a romance with one's own fantasy,"[43] or to "temporarily reunite one with the past in fantasy."[44] This story is an imagined story of the past, driven from personal history,[45] to which they cannot return and "exists mostly as a place in the imagination."[46] For them, Koreatown was a place where these memories could be practiced and reified.

Nostalgia and Koreatown

The loss, longing, and yearning are mobile.[47] So is belonging.[48] Temporary residents, traditional immigrants and their children develop unique and various forms of nostalgia and collective memory through their relationships with shared language, symbols, events, and social and cultural contexts.[49] This is embodied in an urban space and objects brought from their homeland, along with sociocultural means and values. Urban space is, thus, a receptacle of collective memory where "we are never alone,"[50] allowing us to discover and reconnect with the past in the present.[51] Yet, today's memory tends to be more fragmented, rather than being a monolithic kind of national or ethnic memory, due to cultural diversity and its rapid speed of global flows.[52]

The collectivities and group memories of Korean nationals and Korean Americans are, thus, not uniform, despite being categorized as the same ethnic group with shared sociocultural backgrounds in the US racial context. Their nostalgia of the past (time) and the spaces—their home country, their cities, or their favorite commercial neighborhoods or districts, even particular retail stores—is often understood differently, negotiated, and practiced in Koreatown. In this context, Koreatown, thus, showcases a multilayered urban imaginary, both locally and transnationally. Koreatown's local context allows for some of the experiences of being a racialized minority—receiving microaggressions, feeling rejected by the mainstream, being labeled a "model minority"—to be somewhat eased or ameliorated. In the global context, Korean nationals' memories of home are less disjointed, given their more recent experiences in the home country and high levels of transnationality.

Yet, Koreatown's landscape reflects not only diverse voices, but also community relations and judgment about their own and others' sense of belonging.[53] In fact, "the affective experience of locatedness—of being here" are (re)shaped, (re)produced, and embedded through sociopolitical process,[54] while claiming their ownership of the space and beyond. If so, how do Korean nationals and Korean Americans determine who belongs here? In other words, who has the right to claim ownership of not only Koreatown, but of the culture and the diasporic nation? I will bring these questions to chapter 4.

4

"It Is My Street"

Symbolic Struggle over Koreatown

It gives me a lot of pride at being Korean and about non-Koreans wanting to know about or enjoying Korean stuff, like culture-wise or food-wise. It gives me a lot of pride.
—Grace, a twenty-three-year-old college graduate, second-generation Korean American

Physical atmosphere, I mean the street itself is not so much attractive. . . . I do not think it [the street] explains what Korean culture is. . . . I, as a Korean national, feel this is not appealing at all [to non-Koreans].
—Yeun, a thirty-three-year-old Fashion Institute of Technology student, Korean national

In the summer of 2008, I was waiting in my Queens apartment for a friend, Jia, who had just arrived at JFK airport from Seoul. She had planned to visit New York City before traveling to Boston, and I was excited to be reunited with a friend whom I had gotten to know in graduate school in Korea. We made plans to do several fun things together while she was in New York. Following my advice, as soon as she arrived at the airport, she called a Korean cab company that mostly serves a Korean-speaking client base—including immigrants, international students, and tourists—with reasonable prices. While they are now less popular than rideshare services such as Uber and Lyft, these cabs were a rare instance in which Korean nationals—whether temporary residents or tourists—were able to have direct contact with the Korean immigrant community in the United States. When my friend arrived at my apartment, she appeared dumbfounded by her brief conversation with the cab driver, saying that he "asked me if there are apartment complexes in Korea. I was like what? Do they think we still live in the '60s and '70s?"

I was not surprised to hear her story. While still a newcomer to New York City at that time, I had often heard similar stories. In the past eighteen years, while studying, teaching, and working in New York City and elsewhere, I often heard from many Korean nationals that the Korean community in the United States is very different from that in Korea. While clearly recognizing the economic growth in Korea, old-timers who immigrated to the United States in the 1970s and '80s still remember the less developed country that those in Korea today have long since left behind and forgotten. For newcomers, these groups perceive their homeland very differently, as if it is frozen in a different time period.[1] We speak the same language, but the way we speak Korean is slightly different. We also dress and do our makeup differently.

Because of the cultural differences between the two, Korean nationals are often called "FOB" (Fresh off the Boat) by Korean Americans, while Korean Americans are called "kyopo" (overseas Korean), "banana," or "Twinkie" (yellow on the outside and white on the inside) by Korean nationals. Some Koreans, like my friend, feel that Korean immigrants want to denounce Korea by calling their country of origin an underdeveloped nation or by praising the merits of the US system over those of Korea. Some wonder why these immigrants, mostly old-timers, did not know about or seem to have ignored economic and cultural developments in their homeland. Some may have not been able to return to Korea since they left, and their memories may have gotten stuck in the time when they left home, though they might consume Korean media regularly. Others simply see the negative aspects of their homeland and its people in the United States, particularly yuhaksaeng (international students) and jujaewon (employees of branches of Korean Multinational Corporations), whose migration purposes are very different from theirs.

These perceptions sometimes go viral in online communities, where one can share their stories anonymously and also see how immigrants perceive Korean nationals. In the eyes of many Korean immigrants, Korean international students are rich, spoiled, materialistic, and sneaky compared to their "innocent and ingenuous" US-born kids, and jujaewon families take advantage of and milk the immigrant communities in the United States only to turn around and go back to Korea. Their children long for Korea, while realizing the cultural differences and criticizing Koreans' tendency to be judgmental and focus on physical appearances.

In New York City, Korean nationals such as international students tend to not interact much or share residential spaces, networks, or friendship circles with Korean immigrants and their children. Notable exceptions include Korean businesses and services, or religious institutions conducted in the Korean language. These interactions might be more common in small college towns with few Koreans, but not in New York City. Many young Korean nationals, particularly international students, live in Manhattan, particularly in dorms at New York University (NYU) and Columbia, or in nearby gentrifying areas, such as northern Queens (Long Island City, Astoria, and Sunnyside), Jersey City, and Brooklyn, while jujaewon families tend to settle in northern New Jersey. On the other hand, Korean immigrants tend to live in eastern Queens neighborhoods such as Flushing (less now), Murray Hill, Bayside, Little Neck, or Fresh Meadows; Long Island; or northern New Jersey. Younger Koreans might live in the same neighborhoods as younger Korean Americans, but do not necessarily associate with them often because of language barriers and cultural differences.

Both individuals and groups choose to remember and (re)create and (re)construct narratives, drawing meaning linked to a particular time and space.[2] As discussed in chapter 3, memories are not just a rebirth or retrieval from or of the past but new recreations in the present.[3] Memories are expressed from above, particularly through built environments, such as monuments and symbols, street names, and historical conservation, often generated by nation-states and their agencies.[4] However, individuals also collect and accumulate memories from particular times in their everyday lives and the present in particular places.[5] Memory, thus, is place-oriented. Individuals and collectives take advantage of landscapes—"shared spaces, recognizable boundaries, identifiable landmarks, common sites of remembrance" to define and generate relationships.[6]

This chapter follows chapter 3's discussion on collective nostalgia but further investigates how and why collective memories generate symbolic struggles and intraethnic conflicts over space.[7] In Koreatown, there are struggles and conflicts between producers and consumers, or among consumer groups (i.e., Korean nationals, Korean Americans, and non-Koreans), but they are not always visible. Cultural differences, stereotypes, and indifference make these struggles and conflicts often invisible, nuanced, or symbolic and, therefore, often overlooked. I explore how and why each group has shaped a unique spatial identity in Koreatown and developed differences and conflicts, albeit nuanced and hidden.

I pay special attention to how each of these different Korean groups (Korean nationals, Korean immigrants, and US-born Korean Americans) tells their unique stories of collective memories in Korea and the United States and explore why their individual stories should be discussed in larger sociohistorical contexts, both in their homeland and in the United States. How does each group bring their own group identity into the space and draw the line between "us" and "them," creating an urban identity based on unique collective histories in this process of development of symbolic ownership? How and why do such socially constructed identities determine who belongs in the space and, more generally, who belongs in the nation and nationhood across national borders?

Koreatown in a Time Lag

On a sunny afternoon in May of the early 2010s, I was sitting at a coffeeshop with Eunji, close to her art studio in a then-gentrifying Greenpoint, Brooklyn, where she spent a lot of time working on her visual art pieces. Eunji is a thirty-four-year-old artist who came to New York City to pursue her MFA in visual arts after graduating from the most prestigious art school in Korea. She is a US permanent resident with Korean citizenship and an award-winning visual artist in New York City whose work has been featured in mainstream art galleries and media. She lives in Manhattan, works at her studio in Brooklyn, and occasionally visits Koreatown to eat Korean food. Like many Korean nationals I interviewed, Eunji clearly remembers her first time visiting 32nd Street; she had a negative first impression of the space. "I guess I was expecting too much. At first sight, I was like, 'Oh my god, this street is so dirty and gloomy.' And then I was like, 'That's it?'"

Before visiting Koreatown, like many other Korean nationals and Korean Americans, Eunji was excited to see the street with the expectation that she would see something she recognized as Korean—something she missed—but was immediately disappointed upon her arrival. From her perspective as a newcomer to New York and as an art student, she felt that 32nd Street was dirty and gloomy while other parts of Manhattan looked much more glamorous, flashy, and artsy. Those areas made her feel like she could spread her wings and become a part of the city's art scene, while Koreatown, flatly, did not. Further, she was disappointed with the scale of Koreatown. It was too small.

Yeojin, a twenty-three-year-old graduate student, echoes Eunji. She recalls the first time she visited Koreatown while she was an undergraduate at NYU. Her Jewish American roommate, a huge fan of the frozen yogurt chain Pinkberry, invited her to visit Koreatown with her so she could get her frozen yogurt. Upon seeing Manhattan's Koreatown for the first time, Yeojin was very disappointed and underwhelmed. "It wasn't as like nice as it is now, you know, like Paris Baguette and like all these like nice cafeterias that they have now and fancy restaurants. And none of that was there. It was very ghetto. I felt like it was kind of ghetto." Yeojin thought Koreatown was very "ghetto," and, she said, "[I] still think K-town is one of the dirtiest places in Manhattan." Yeojin was born in Korea and came to the United Sates for college, but she is not a typical international student. Rather, she is part of a "new transnational generation Koreans" whose upbringings are transnational by residing in various countries and attending British or American schools, like Tiffany in chapter 3 and many other interviewees. Yeojin grew up in Hong Kong and metropolitan Seoul, where she had an all-English and American education from the first grade through high school before moving to New York City for college a few years prior. Her unique upbringing allowed her to develop a unique "in-between" identity—neither yuhaksaeng nor i-sei (second generation)—though many assume that she grew up in the United States because of her flawless, accent-free English and extensive knowledge of American culture. Yet, her memories of Seoul as a teenager enabled her to observe Koreatown through a transnational lens. Her perception of Koreatown is, of course, juxtaposed by her experiences in Seoul's neighborhoods. Koreatown never met her expectations of delivering an "authentic" Korean experience, though the increased presence of Korean franchises and fancier restaurants made it feel a bit more familiar to her.

Back to the 1980s

Mihee is a thirty-eight-year-old college instructor who attended graduate school in New York between 2002 and 2011. After graduating, she returned to Korea and now works as a college lecture in Seoul. She still, vividly remembers her first visit to Koreatown in the early 2000s, when she was new in New York City: "I was like, wow, it looks like so '70s. Do you know Cosmos Department Store on 32nd Street? There was the Cosmos Department Store in Myeong-dong back in the 1970s and '80s. . . . I still remember how it looked when I was an elementary school kid. Yet you see the store that has the same name. I had a certain image of Cosmos Department Store from my childhood memory." Mihee's first memory of 32nd Street was explicitly linked to her memories of Seoul in earlier decades. Before the emergence of the upper-middle class and the development of the trendy Gangnam district,[8] Myeong-dong was the busiest shopping district in Seoul in the 1970s. It was associated with modern Korea, youth culture, and cosmopolitan consumer culture, especially in the 1960s and '70s.[9] Cosmos Department Store, for example, was an important symbol of economic development and growing consumerism in Seoul until it closed in 1992 due to loss of business. Today it represents the glory of the past as remembered by those who lived through that time period. The Cosmos Department Store in Koreatown connected not only with Mihee's memories, but also the "collective memory" of the nation and its past for Korean nationals.[10]

Figure 4.1. Signboards in Koreatown in 2013. Photo courtesy by Sejung Yim.

Figure 4.2. Signboards in Koreatown in 2024. Photo by the author.

Because Korean nationals recognize that Manhattan's Koreatown is the only space in the city representing Korea, many think that it should showcase contemporary Korea as trendy and technologically advanced. Yet, the landscape of Koreatown mirrors Seoul of the 1970s or '80s, characterized by dwitgolmok (backstreet alleys) with a mass of shabby buildings and hectic streets in underdeveloped neighborhoods in Seoul. When asked, Korean nationals consistently used negative adjectives to describe the space: "gurida" in Korean, translated roughly into "wack," played-out, outdated, old-fashioned, dirty, gloomy, nasty, or even "ghetto."

This outdated image of Seoul in Koreatown is evident in a series of unplanned signboards on 32nd Street featuring old landscapes of big cities in Korea. During the Lee Myung-bak administration,[11] the Seoul Metropolitan Government initiated new urban design projects, demolishing and standardizing disorganized store signboards. As a visual artist, Eunji approaches this presentation of 32nd Street from the perspective of urban design: "It was in New York, but it [Koreatown] was not New York. . . . Look at all the Korean signboards [in Korean]. . . . They were all outdated [before the urban design projects in Seoul]. Look at the fonts and designs of signboards [written in Korean]." Eunji talks about how Koreatown's physical landscape of messy and disorganized signboards showcases the past of the nation or less-developed contemporary areas, portraying an underdeveloped and unmodern Korea. Likewise, Jihye, a thirty-three-year-old graduate student, echoes Eunji and details how the signboards in Koreatown mirror Korea's past: "[I get] the same feeling that I have whenever I visit ji-bang [non-Metropolitan Seoul]." The unplanned and chaotic landscape of Koreatown was criticized by Korean nationals for conflicting with and distorting the present image of Korea as a well-planned, clean, rapidly changing, and cosmopolitan nation, bringing ideas from Korea into a small section of New York City, that has nothing to do with urban policies back home.

Koreatown Is Not Bad, or Nicer

Some Korean Americans might agree with Korean nationals. Jacob, a twenty-five-year-old graduate student who was born and raised in the Los Angeles area, called the Manhattan Koreatown "a very poor imitation of Korea." Still, many strongly disagree. Some Korean Americans remember their first impression of Koreatown as small. This is particularly true among those who grew up or spent time in bigger Koreatowns like LA and Atlanta, or even Flushing, or those who had been to Korea a few times or resided in Korea for some time. Jacob came to New York City to attend graduate school for his master's degree. He remembers the first time he visited Koreatown in Manhattan in the 2000s, soon after he arrived in New York. He thought, "It was more like a street. I thought, 'Why would they call this a town?' It is a narrow street with lots of Korean restaurants."

Jacob was one of the Korean American interviewees who was the least interested in Korean culture and history even though he grew up in a suburb of LA—a city that also happens to have the largest concentration of Koreans in the United States. His parents watched Korean dramas at home, yet he was never interested in learning about his own ethnic culture. When he was young, his parents would take him to Koreatown for food or to meet with coethnic friends, but he did not hang out in Koreatown until he was in college. Nevertheless, he vividly recalls what LA's Koreatown was like in the 1990s versus today. When he visited Manhattan's Koreatown to try some Korean restaurants recommended by his "Asian American friends who have been to New York," it was a bit disappointing compared to the biggest Koreatown in the nation. However, like many other Korean Americans, Jacob did not feel that it was antiquated or old-fashioned, even though he, like all the other Korean American interviewees in the study, had been to Korea before. Some thought that Manhattan's Koreatown being smaller than LA's Koreatown was not necessarily a bad thing. As Tim, a twenty-three-year-old second-generation Korean American law student, said, "K-town is one block—you go there and while we are there we choose somewhere to eat or hang out. The place is just one street so it's easier." Everything from restaurants to bars is crammed into a small area, allowing consumers to enjoy their night without having to go far.

Likewise, Eric shared a story that had parallels to Jacob. A forty-one-year-old second-generation Korean American graduate student and part-time barista, Eric was born and grew up in Atlanta and moved to New York City in the late 1990s, as a young adult. He eventually moved back to Atlanta for several years and returned to New York City in 2010, later moving to Flushing to live with his Korean wife. He remembers that Koreatowns in suburbs of Atlanta, such as Duluth, Suwanee, and Doraville, used to be smaller and less developed when he was growing up in the 1980s and '90s, and he noticed their growth in recent years. When he visited Koreatown in Manhattan in the late 1990s, when there were only a few Korean restaurants, his immediate response was that "they were like that old-fashioned, kind of, small," and "looked like old-fashioned '70s or '80s si-gol [countryside] style restaurants [in Korea]." Initially, he thought Flushing's Koreatown is "just like Korea" because "Manhattan is, obviously, it feels very urban. The buildings are taller, things are just busier." However, his interpretation about Koreatown being "old-fashioned and small" with si-gol style restaurants is somewhat different from what Korean nationals say.

> So you know how like, even in Korea, if you go into kind of like, alleys and golmok [backstreet alleys] or whatever, yeah, you'll still see these really informal restaurants. They look like they could almost be somebody's house, right? Just really informal. And even the way the kitchen looks, it looks like somebody's home kitchen. And you can tell that it's like a husband and wife running the restaurant. And everything tastes really homemade and even like their plates and bowls, like the kind of plates and bowls you have at home. . . . It's very homey and comfortable.

Korean nationals associate old-fashioned, 1970s or '80s-style si-gol with negative connotations, despite the recent rise of newtro (new retro) culture,[12] because it reminds them of Korea's undeveloped past. However, Eric has a different perspective. When I asked him what "si-gol [countryside] style restaurants" means during the interview in 2018, he connected it with informal, homemade, homey, and comfortable. He might be romanticizing the old Koreatown when it was not so commercialized and still offered a cozy and comfortable space for immigrants and their children. Yet, as introduced earlier, Mihee's interpretation of Koreatown, mediated by her childhood memories of Cosmos Department Store, is not all that different from what other Korean nationals say.

Further, unlike Korean nationals, who see Koreatown as dirty and smelly, many Korean Americans do not typically point out that the street was particularly dirty. Instead, they thought of New York as being generally not so clean. John, a thirty-year-old 1.5-generation Korean American who immigrated to the United States with his family in the 1990s, lived in Seoul before his family moved to California and ultimately Connecticut. He is now in Queens with his wife. His family visited Manhattan soon after they arrived in the United States in the 1990s and he remembers going to the top of the Empire State Building to see the spectacular view. Despite its vastness, New York City still felt a bit laid-back compared to Seoul, which he perceived as competitive and busy even as a junior high schooler. Yet, his feelings changed as he got older and started driving with his friends to the city when he was a college student in Connecticut. By that time, he had spent a number of years in suburban America where the Korean food options were very limited: "I have been in the rural America for years since I moved to the US. It [this trip] is like a chonnom [Korean term for a hillbilly or country bumpkin] coming to Seoul, right? I really dislike the fact that the city itself was dirty and complex. . . . Now I get used to 32nd Street, but it was dark and dirty [back then]. It was really dark." He recalled that the trip was not easy; the city seemed to be very challenging in general. Back then, he had no GPS, and parking in Manhattan was hard for those who were not used to parallel parking. Interestingly, the city that felt more laid-back and relaxing than Seoul suddenly became dark and complex. Before coming to the United States, he lived in Gangnam, an upscale neighborhood in Seoul, but now he called himself chonnom from rural Connecticut, who was no longer able to keep up with the hectic pace of big cities. They did not bother sightseeing, but "straightly went to the Koreatown to eat and do grocery shopping at H Mart and left."

Furthermore, those who grew up in places where Korean businesses were scarce especially welcome Koreatown's existence. Erin is a thirty-year-old second-generation Korean American who lived in Philadelphia until she was fifteen years old, then moved to North Carolina and stayed there through college. She is currently a public school teacher in New York City. She reminisced about how excited she was to find Koreatown in Manhattan when she moved to New York City. "The first adult memory . . . I had of it is when I first moved to New York, I went there because in North Carolina it's not so accessible. . . . I remember going to

Woorijip. I was like, oh my god, this is twenty-four hours and I can come whenever I want. And I got the card and the stamps and got so excited. I remember when I first came there, I ate there a lot."[13] In the 1990s, North Carolina did not have many Korean businesses, though this has recently been slowly changing, especially in the Research Triangle region. This twenty-four-hour access to Korean food was new and exciting for her.

Likewise, when asked about her first impression, Danielle, a twenty-four-year-old NYU graduate, instantly compared and contrasted Koreatown with Vancouver's Koreatown and Seoul. "It is kind of similar, but Manhattan's K-town looks much more refined and has more people.... Yes, compared to Vancouver.... Of course, it is not as sophisticated as Seoul is. But I was like, 'It could have been worse!'" Danielle was born in Indiana but moved with family to Seoul when she was four until the third grade. Later she briefly lived in Canada, returning to Korea after a year, and then went to Vancouver for high school. After a few years in Vancouver, she relocated to New York for college. After college, she returned to Korea and is now working in the film industry. She remembers her positive impression of Koreatown. Her perspective of Koreatown was mediated by her experience seeing smaller Korean businesses in Vancouver in the 2000s, though she also contrasts it with Seoul's fancy neighborhoods, which she sees as more sophisticated and well-organized.

Rather than a dirty and old-fashioned neighborhood, Tim explains that many Asian Americans consider Koreatown a popular destination. Tim, a twenty-three-year-old law school student, was born in Manhattan and grew up in Flushing. He went to school with Asian peers and has close relationships with them. Tim and his peers believe that Koreatown is nice.

> K-town is a nicer place to hang out. Chinatown is huge. K-town is one block, you go there and while we are there, we choose somewhere to eat or hang out. The place is just one street, so it's easier. It's just nicer.... I don't know, but for Korean Americans, I don't see them much, but I think Chinese Americans, definitely K-town is like a popular spot. It's just a cooler spot to hang out, I think. For one, a lot of the places, the bars or restaurants, they are pretty nice places.

Some ethnic Chinese, including Chinese Americans, Taiwanese, and Hong Kongers, seem to agree with Tim. Aiden is a twenty-one-year-old college student who was born in New York to Taiwanese parents. Like Tim, Aiden, a twenty-two-year-old Chinese American college student, believes that Koreatown is nice and a great spot to hang out.

> Chinatown always smells like fish. I think Chinatown is a little bit—no offense to my own people, but I think it's a little dirty. The smell of fish and the streets aren't very—I haven't been there for a while, but from what I remember, it's just very crowded, the streets are sometimes very dirty.... K-town is just like one street, it's also very close to a very populated area and the way it's kind of built more efficiently. I think they keep it cleaner in terms of restaurants and stuff.

Aiden sees his "own" ethnic enclave, Chinatown, in a negative way; his comment about the smell resonates with how Korean nationals perceive Koreatown. Ram, a thirty-two-year-old ethnic Chinese Burmese, and Kaylee, a twenty-one-year-old Chinese American college student, echo Aiden. Ram says that "in Chinatown, you're like—[in the] fish [market].... But Chinatown is outdoor, it's on the sidewalk, also wet and all this. Kind of dirty." Kaylee complains that "in Chinatown you go in and people are rude and the streets are nasty and something like that." They do not consider Chinatown a space for spending casual time. However, they find Koreatown to be a fun place to hang out with their friends. Or as Mei, a thirty-two-year-old Columbia graduate student from Taipei explains, Chinatown does not reflect her urban life in Taiwan. She often hangs out in Koreatown, because it reminds her of Taipei, where she could "enjoy the kind of quality of the place." Ethnic Chinese who were born and raised in relatively wealthier countries, like Mei, feel that Koreatown better replicates their country's quality of life than Chinatown. Like Korean nationals who insist that Koreatown does not accurately reflect today's modern and developed Korea, these young ethnic Chinese would agree that Chinatown does not reflect their respective nations. In fact, the global status of their country of origin also plays a role in understanding and perceiving their own ethnic enclaves overseas.[14]

Ossification Effects

As shown in some of the passages from my interviews, Korean nationals tend to see Koreatown as a dirty and gloomy place, while Korean Americans often see it in a positive light as a hot spot. These mismatches in perceptions of Koreatown are rooted in how Korean Americans see the immigrant community by comparing it to homeland. Korean immigrants also recognize their time lagged perception. Those who have closer ties to the Korean immigrant community further explain their frustrations. Jihye, a thirty-three-year-old graduate student, notes how Korean immigrant old-timers have maintained past ideas and images of Korea, which serve to hold back the space:

> This community is extremely conservative. Many older people really ignore women. . . . From my perspective, there is no room for liberal ideas for these immigrants. Ugh . . . They lag behind, particularly in Flushing. They [immigrants] just got stuck in the 1980s and are like stagnant water. . . . Even 1.5-generation folks tend to be much more conservative compared to my friends in my generation back home in Korea. . . . Yes, Manhattan's Korean community is [conservative], but Flushing is even worse.

Jihye came to New York City to pursue her master's degree in New York and planned to go back home after completing it. But she met a second-generation Korean American man at school and married him. She decided to pursue a PhD. Through her work-study program, she has had extensive experience working with Korean immigrants. She often feels that Korean immigrants are extremely conservative and stuffy, an example of what Peggy Levitt calls "ossification effects,"[15] or time-freeze factor.[16] While Korean culture is "fossilized in the diaspora,"[17] the culture in Korea has changed over time. John, a thirty-year-old 1.5-generation Korean American, whose family immigrated to Connecticut when he was in junior high school, shares a similar story. After marrying a Korean woman he met when he visited Seoul, he now lives with his wife in Queens. He often visited Korea after moving to the United States, but noted that he felt that his perception of Korea had been paused at the time of his departure.

In retrospect, I think I considered myself like a middle-school kid until twenty-five years old.... I felt that the time had paused. Whenever I went back to Korea, I just felt like I got stuck in the time I left.... I'd never thought that I did not grow up, but often felt that I was not mature enough.... I do not know but probably because of my memories [of Korea],... I see how Korea has changed whenever I visit Korea and I have changed at each stage of my life.

He has vivid memories of Seoul in the 1990s, when he was a young teenager. Though he was mature enough to recognize his parents' sacrifice for him and his younger brother, he did not fully feel like a grown adult until he was in his mid-twenties. Prior to that period in his life, he felt like he was stuck in the time that he left Seoul. This feeling intensified when he visited Korea, which affirmed that his idea of what Korea is like was "paused" or frozen in the 1990s, despite its inevitable evolution since then.

Many Korean nationals believe that these immigrants think of Korea as it was when they left, and are unable to reflect on the rapid recent cultural changes in the aesthetics. Thus, Korean nationals think that immigrants cannot integrate what contemporary Korean culture is really like into their mental framework. Like many other Korean nationals, Yoojin, a twenty-eight-year-old graduate student, does not explicitly express any emotional attachment or ownership to the space itself. In fact, she rejects it. In particular, this trend was commonly observed before K-pop and K-drama became to permeate the US mainstream during the pandemic. Yet her reaction toward Koreatown is rooted in her feelings for her nation as an imagined community, hence the common refrain, "Korea, as a well-known nation." When Kyujin, a thirty-two-year-old graduate student in Massachusetts, says he "felt proud that Koreatown was doing okay," he is projecting Koreatown as *the imagined property* where the nation and its culture should be given due recognition by non-Korean *Others*. In this process of "authentication,"[18] laying claim to authenticity of Korean food and culture becomes a tool of power for Korean nationals,[19] as they confirm that "we" (i.e., Koreans) define authentic Korean culture—most notably in contrast with Korean immigrants and their children, who cannot claim personal understandings of the nation's culture and taste.[20]

Like Korean Americans who express ownership of the physical space of Koreatown, a few Korean nationals also have a similar feeling. Yet their sense of ownership is strongly linked to Korea as a nation. Sangjin, a twenty-four-year-old language student, feels that his contact with non-Koreans in New York made him think that they associate Koreatown with the country, enabling him to show off his knowledge about Korea and Korean culture to non-Koreans, which he enjoys. Yet, as discussed earlier, most people do not agree with Sangjin. They are often pleased with the popularity of K-pop and Korean food as a part of their own culture from home, which doesn't have much to do with the immigrant community. Korean nationals interpret Koreatown based entirely on their experiences as consumers and social identification as Korean citizens and believe that "others"—immigrants and their children—have modified Korean culture to adapt to a new environment. Some explicitly express embarrassment and shame over Koreatown as the only space representing Korean culture in Manhattan. Minji, a twenty-five-year-old Korean national who attended NYU, expressed her frustrations: "[32nd Street] looks like one of the streets of Seoul in the late '80s and the early '90s from old videos or photos I watched. I feel so ashamed whenever I see 32nd Street, because [non-Koreans] assume that streets of Korea would look like this." Minji felt ashamed in and by Koreatown. Minji's frustration is rooted in her perspective that Koreatown does not represent Seoul's cosmopolitan, fashionable, and rapidly changing urban landscape in a positive or accurate way. In her opinion, Koreatown's urban landscape mirrors "old Seoul," with a certain time lag of global flows from Korea to New York City. For many Korean nationals, Koreatown is familiar but still foreign. For instance, Jinah, a twenty-eight-year-old MA student in New York who was born in Seoul but spent her childhood in North Carolina for seven to eight years, recalls that her first visit to Koreatown was very weirdly foreign, despite the seeming familiarity on the surface. Like Minji, she thinks Koreatown is "trying very hard to mimic Korea, but not really Korean at all, [because it is too old-fashioned]. If non-Koreans come and link Koreatown to Korea, it distorts what Korea really is." It is problematic for Minji and Jinah, because non-Korean New Yorkers and tourists—potential consumers of Korean culture—may see Korea as lagging and dingy based on their pseudo-cultural experiences in Koreatown.

Yet Minji and Jinah's perspective on Koreatown, like that of other Korean nationals, is based on a projection of the nation itself and the nation's reputation. For some Korean nationals, Koreatown is a space where Korean nationals can be confident and proud to be Korean citizens because of the increasing popularity of Korean culture and growing non-Korean presence in Koreatown. As Yoojin, a twenty-eight-year-old graduate student, observes, "I am pleased with these foreigners [presenting themselves in Koreatown]. . . . . because I could see Korean culture finally is getting popular [in New York]." Although Yoojin often expresses her negative impressions of Koreatown, the presence of non-Koreans is one way she confirms the popularity of Korean culture and the nation's international status. Discovery of Korean culture by non-Koreans in New York City marks the city as a center of global culture. The Korean nation as projected in Koreatown is thus a form of cultural success and a statement of global presence.

Symbolic Ownership in Koreatown

Though "we" do not necessarily recognize ourselves as being homogeneous, the boundaries between us and them are bigger than our in-group boundaries.[21] The boundaries are indeed "articulated . . . in the construction, reconstruction and contestation of spaces."[22] This kind of "we-feeling,"[23] or symbolic divide between *us* and *them*, creates and reinforces a city's cultural and political borders,[24] in this case, in Koreatown. Space, thus, becomes a public sphere of symbolic struggles and conflicts in (re)shaping and determining urban identity or symbolic ownership,[25] from a particular sense of community to a certain kind of culture or symbolic economy.[26] Individuals as a group present these discourses around memories, urban identities, symbolic struggles, and conflicts into action and practice. They "work to control the aesthetic presentation, public perception, and social and economic utility of this social space in order to secure the neighborhood's degree of distinction," or what Andrew Deener calls "symbolic ownership."[27]

Signboards and the Past of Korea

Koreatown, thus, is a space where individuals and groups understand and promote a sense of place and symbolic power around representation of national culture. They develop a sense of place, feeling comfortable and reinforcing ownership over place, through symbols showing "certain qualities of that place."[28] For Korean nationals, qualities of Koreatown should be based on the contemporary Korean interpretations of Korean culture directly from Korea. When Korean franchises began investing in Koreatown in the late 2000s and early 2010s, Korean nationals believed that the presence of Korean franchises and newly opened "modernized" Korean restaurants affirmed the global awareness of Korean (consumer) culture and the nation's global cultural status. The Korean franchises and newly opened restaurants on 32nd Street are more connected to "refined, trendy, modern, contemporary, and clean" stores among Koreans, in contrast with the "old, dingy, wack, played-out, and outdated" immigrant-owned restaurants, as most of my Korean national interviewees told me. Korean nationals also believe that these franchise stores and newly opened restaurants help Koreatown promote itself as a more modern, clean, and "better" space, in part because the increasing number of Korean franchises and Korean corporations' direct investment reflect new trends in Korea. In this process, the meaning of authenticity is contested among Korean nationals. In the United States, franchise stores are standardized and therefore less authentic. But for Korean nationals, Korean franchise stores serve the purpose of upgrading an area like Koreatown in a way that makes it more modern and cosmopolitan. As Jinah, a twenty-eight-year-old graduate student, points out, "It is just a picture of New York that is very lightly colored with Korea, yet I would not say that it represents Korea." These visual images of Korea are not looked upon favorably by Korean nationals and are considered something that needs to be improved or even fixed. They want Koreatown to be a space where one can enjoy contemporary "authentic" Korean culture, unadulterated by old immigrants and transferred directly from Korea, specifically Seoul. This will be explored more in chapter 6.

Even the Korean National Assembly echoes this sentiment. On October 14, 2010, in New York, Young-Mok Kim, then–Consul General of the Republic of Korea in New York, directed the assembly's attention toward signboards in Manhattan's Koreatown. As he said at the Inspection of the Administration by the National Assembly in 2010 in New York City, "We have discussed for a long time. However, due to the budget issues, we make a slow progress [on signboard improvement in Koreatown]. I'd like to call for the attention from Korea."[29] Hyo-Jae Kim, a then-elected National Assembly member from then-ruling Saenuri Party, also agreed that Koreatown should improve its physical appearance to give a better impression of Korea: "Particularly, signboards in Koreatown resemble those [oversized and obtrusive] signboards in Korea destroying landscape. . . . It does not match with the images of New York either. . . . It feels so chaotic. It probably will leave a [bad] impression about Korea like that. . . . The signboard should be more modern and standardized. . . . This is a great space for showcasing Korea, but these [oversized and obtrusive] signboards leave much to be desired. But isn't it their own work?"[30] Some Korean policymakers believed that the negative physical appearance and landscape of Koreatown and Korean restaurants would discourage non-Korean consumers from visiting Koreatown, as it could give them a negative impression of the neighborhood and even the nation. This approach is echoed by many Korean nationals. When I asked my Korean national interviewees to specify what made them feel that Koreatown looks outdated, many of them pointed out that design and fonts of signboards in Koreatown reminded them of those signboards back in the 1980s and '90s or those in rural areas. Hyun, a thirty-year-old language student from Busan, a large port city in the Southern Korea, agreed: "You have a certain image of commercial buildings in Korea [particularly in newly redeveloped or refurbished neighborhoods]. Clean and well-organized. Orderly signboards!" The signboards connect Koreans to their past, but some think that they need to be corrected and improved in order to show off what "modern" Seoul looks like.

However, rather than providing financial support, Hyo-Jae Kim insisted that Korean entrepreneurs should take financial responsibility and improve the landscape of Koreatown to make it more closely resemble the more modern, clean, and contemporary Korea that exists today. However, although the government would not take financial responsibility, the nation would still benefit from the improvement as a part of "nation branding." Despite disagreements on finances, Young-Mok Kim agreed that the government should closely work with Korean entrepreneurs to reconstruct the Koreatown landscape to attract non-Koreans and promote the nation. He said, "We plan to persuade the businesspeople to replace their signboards to standardized ones, which are designed in Korea but localized in New York context." Young-Mok Kim and Hyo-Jae Kim ultimately agreed to practice and implement government policies in overseas Koreatowns, just like they did in Seoul—the Signboard Improvement Project.[31] Though the plan was not actualized, it clearly showed the government's claiming of Koreatown as "imagined property" crossing national borders. The idea of exporting the project to the United States was simple: Implement urban policies successfully in Seoul, then send them to Manhattan's Koreatown. For the Korean government, despite the absence of legal rights in Koreatown, Koreatown is not only a platform to promote the nation through public and private partnership but also an imagined property that the government could symbolically claim outside its geographic territory, even though the Korean government does not have the political ability to do so.

Language and Belonging

In addition to buzz around signboards, language is also a notable signifier showcasing belonging, othering, and divide within the Korean community. Jay is a thirty-year-old second-generation Korean American born and raised in Texas, where he was one of only a few Korean kids at his school. Having graduated from a prestigious university in Missouri and a medical school in Atlanta, he is now a physician at a hospital in New York City. Having grown up in a predominantly white area of Houston, his parents pushed their children to assimilate, intentionally erasing language learning and cultural practice at home. During the interview in 2012, he talked about his identity crisis as a Korean American, which lingered until college; part of him wanted to avoid everything Korean. Now as an adult, he regrets not learning the Korean language and recognizes that speaking his mother tongue would reinforce a sense of shared ancestry and provide a level of language skills that would better position him and other individuals in social relationships.[32] But he didn't have this opportunity, and thinks about lost opportunities for his children, as he married a woman from Hong Kong. While language is often learned and practiced in the private sphere for Korean Americans, it also produces tension in ethnic communities. These tensions are often displayed publicly, reinforcing "othering."[33] In Koreatown, his lack of Korean language skills makes Jay feel foreign and uncomfortable in his own ethnic community.

> I think sometimes I feel uncomfortable in my own sense that I'm not Korean enough to be in that area. . . . Yeah, I know about food but I think there's a part of me that just doesn't feel like I culturally related to them enough, because even if I go to a Korean restaurant, I don't order in Korean, I just know what I want because I know what it is. I don't know, this is probably my own prejudice, but I feel like if I'm with my mom or anybody that speaks Korean, I think that it's easier, they treat you differently too. I think the waiters and waitresses treat you differently too. I feel like you get more attention.

Migration separates migrants from one's first language and familiar environment.[34] Language is critical for Korean-speaking Koreans in a new land to make them feel at home, but interestingly, many Korean Americans feel that language constructs cultural barriers in their own ethnic enclave when they lack competency in the Korean language. As Jay notes, his inability to communicate in Korean with employees at Korean restaurants makes him uncomfortable, though he knows the cultural codes and meanings well enough. However, English-speaking Korean Americans are treated differently than their Korean-speaking counterparts—Korean nationals. Jay is not the only one who feels this way.

Alex shares similar frustrations. Like Jay, language is often a barometer for whether Korean-speaking Koreans embrace her as a part of the community. She explains:

> Koreatown has this like symbolism behind it for me, right? But at the same time, it's also very, it's still somewhat inaccessible for me. When you walk into a restaurant, or you walk into a café . . . and you want to order something. And of course, they automatically, I mean, I am Korean. So it's not bad of them to, you know, start to speak to me in Korean, but when I open my mouth, I want to try to feebly say something, you know, order something in Korean or say it in English? Yeah.

You know, there's an immediate judgment. Yeah. And I think the level of serve—a customer service and interest goes down.

Alex is a twenty-six-year-old Korean American adoptee who grew up in upstate New York. Her adoptive parents tried to connect her with her roots by sending her to Korean camps and taking her to ethnic festivals. She recalls her first time visiting Koreatown, in third or fourth grade, when she and her parents "came down in the fall to march in [the] Korean American Parade with the other adoptees." She remembers stopping at Koryo Bookstore on 32nd Street and picking up a couple of souvenirs because she wanted to know "what other Koreans listen to so I randomly picked up a cassette—that's what we had back then." She recalls that "it was the deciding factor for me to move to the city when I was in middle school and high school." And she did. She relocated to New York City when she started college. Since then, she has felt that Koreatown is small and expensive, but it has "a special place in my heart" and was "large to me."

Despite her parents' efforts to connect Alex with her Korean heritage, she grew up in a predominantly white neighborhood with white adoptive parents, limiting her ability to learn and practice Korean culture and language. Nevertheless, she also tried to connect with her homeland, which she has very complex feelings about. In college, she participated in Korea-related organizations, and worked in some nonprofit organizations, including one for Korean Americans. Her own interests and emotional longing for her homeland within her limited access to her roots also seems to be reified in Koreatown, but only partially. Language reinforces the politics of belonging, fortifying the divide between *us* and *them* and constraining others,[35] while awakening a sense of community to those who belong there.[36]

Sunmee, a forty-two-year-old second-generation Korean American, is much more explicit about her experience with language as a vehicle to divide Korean Americans and Koreans. As introduced in chapter 3, she is one of the older Koreatown consumers among my interviewees and has been going to the area since the early 1980s. She also shows strong emotional attachment to Koreatown. She speaks Korean—it is her first language—though she and I communicate mostly in English with a little Korean mixed in, making our conversation a form of "Konglish." She can easily order food in Korean and understand what others say, though when she orders in Korean, food service workers often "repeat it back to [her] in English." She feels irritated by this response because she believes that "they're belittling you." She says that she is not the only person who feels this way. "I have an older brother who actually married one of my high school friends who's a Korean from Korea. She came here when she was sixteen. And when they go out to Korean restaurants, she does all the ordering and when they go to an American restaurant, he does all the ordering. . . . I have another friend who is Korean American, never orders in Korean, always in English because she doesn't want to deal with it. There is a big divide between Korean Americans and Koreans." This "code-switch" as Nicole, a thirty-six-year-old second generation Korean American teacher who grew up in New Jersey, calls it, legitimizes a certain form of identity only among Korean-speaking Koreans in Koreatown, who feel out of place in the wider society, while reinforcing particular solidarities within their ethnic community.[37] It is, as Sunmee highlights, an indicator of the invisible divide between Korean Americans and Koreans, although English has become much more commonly used in Koreatown.

Who Belongs Here?

In my years of research, I also observed that many Koreatown employees, particularly younger people, generally begin a conversation in English, as Korean businesses in Koreatown target more non-Korean clients. As a native Korean speaker who was born in Seoul and lived there until my mid-twenties, I still experience being addressed in English by servers and other workers; even when I speak in Korean, they often respond in English. I've joked with friends that I no longer look like a FOB ("fresh off the boat"). I speak English fluently, but my Korean accent remains prominent. Though it is obvious that I am a native Korean speaker, I've wondered why this happens. And while it makes me feel a bit weird, I don't necessarily feel offended. In fact, as time progresses, the majority of clients in Koreatown are non-Koreans.

However, while teaching Korean language classes and conducting interviews not only for this Koreatown project but also other projects that I am currently working on, I have learned that the Korean language is a very sensitive topic among Korean Americans. It is, in fact, a critical signifier of belonging in their ethnic community and homeland, despite the complexity of their relationships with Korea. Yet, as I noted earlier, though many Korean Americans are frustrated with Korean-speaking Koreans, ethnic Koreans are, in fact, very diverse. Korean international students do not necessarily communicate with Korean immigrants and the Korean immigrant community even though they share the same first language. Some of this may stem from stigma or divisions related to class differences, as workers in Korean restaurants or other retail businesses are more likely to be working-class and even undocumented. However, this social class stigma also seems to be reciprocal. These workers may also think that international students are "rich snobby kids who're just rich and they are just weird and . . . they have shady personality," as Tim, a twenty-three-year-old Korean American student, posited. Korean nationals, particularly international students, feel that immigrants are conservative and frozen in the 1980s and '90s—much like their perception of the Koreatown landscape—while they also think of US-born children of immigrants as being less Korean than they are. Korean nationals also might think the immigrant community is hostile to them, as some hear that old-timers denounce Korea and yuhaksaeng (international students). Furthermore, Korean nationals might think that employees in Koreatown are curt to them, and they attribute this to the assumption that such behavior is a vestige of the "old" Korea they left behind.

This sense of belonging is very complex. During the interviews with Korean Americans, I often mentioned how Korean nationals described Koreatown as a dirty and dingy space. Although their reactions were not always verbal, I observed in their facial expressions that they were offended and frustrated. This is linked to the emotional and symbolic connections they have to the space and their complicated feelings toward the motherland. I often hear my Korean American interviewees say Korean society is too judgmental, overemphasizing one's physical looks. So do Korean nationals and FOBs.

These invisible conflicts are also reflected in Koreatown. The time lag between the contemporary culture of the originating nations and its avatars in other nations in the form of enclaves, transclaves, or other types of urban landscapes reflects the history of transnational migration, as described in chapters 3 and 4. Koreatown was created by Korean immigrants who came to 32nd Street in the 1970s and '80s when the street was unattractive and they were unable to find jobs in the US mainstream.

These symbolic struggles over the landscape, collective memories, and its cultural authenticity are, in fact, a milieu or replica of the symbolic struggle over the nation and nationhood across the globe, provoking emotional affect, acceptance, or rejection to the collective memories of the nation.[38] These "ambivalent and contradictory emotion[s]" are linked to a particular place and time,[39] not limited to the bounds of national borders, in this case in a transclave. These attachments are displayed and reinforced in various ways, based on their own collective memories, migrating back and forth between two nations. These individuals, once assumed to be passive consumers, in fact, have produced and reproduced Koreatown's landscape over the past three decades while negotiating its meanings as it intersects with local contexts.

Jihye, a thirty-four-year-old graduate student, shares her own sentiment and feelings about Korean immigrants, particularly old-timers. Though she is often frustrated with their conservativeness, frozen in the past, she believes that the success of the next generation and social recognition of Koreans in the United States might be a result of the sacrifices of the first generation. Yet, she is witnessing that "the past of Koreatown" and "their stories are disappearing into thin air." If Jihye is right, are we "eclipsing other historical layers of social life that formerly prevailed"[40] in Koreatown? If so, how do we create room for inclusion?

In the next two chapters, I will discuss inclusion by incorporating novel yet significant clients for Korean businesses—non-Korean New Yorkers. I will pay attention to two major aspects of cultural content—pop culture and food—that are advertised, sold, and consumed in Koreatown. More importantly, I will discuss how this imagined space sells fantasies about and constructs narratives of Korea and Korean culture and create various power dynamics in a small section of the global city. Before that, let me take you on a fantasy trip to the K-pop capital of New York City and introduce you to "the ultimate K-pop guide to NYC" here in "K-town."[41]

5

Hallyu in Koreatown

Disneyland or Imagined Community?

Once somebody says they're into K-pop, you feel like you know their soul.
—Kiana, a twenty-two-year-old Black American journalist

K-town was a magical place where K-dramas became real for us.
—Sophie and Isabelle, twins, twenty-five-year-old white Americans

One sunny day in the fall of 2009, Aria felt depressed. A Dominican American and native New Yorker, Aria, who was eighteen at the time, was standing in front of JYP Entertainment—one of the biggest music labels in Korea—on 31st Street near Koreatown. She was waiting to meet up with people she met in an online group. They were gathered to protest against the company's decision to expel Jay Park (Jae-beom Park), a third-generation Korean American rapper and b-boy from a then-popular Korean boy band 2PM, a founder and former CEO of the most well-known hip-hop and R&B music labels in Korea—AOMG and Hıghr Music, respectively—and now a founder and CEO of a record label, More Vision. The Seattle-born rapper came to Korea as a teenager as a trainee of JYP Entertainment in 2005 and soon became successful as a member of the boy band. In the midst of his success, a scandal arose in 2009 when some Korean netizens found that he had written on his Myspace page, in 2005, "Korea is gay," "I don't like Koreans," and "I want to go back to the U.S." The company quickly decided to expel him from the band due to the resulting controversy, despite the fact that it led to fan protests around the world. Aria was one of those fans.

Among the people Aria was waiting for was Taylor, a twenty-two-year-old Black American woman and college student from Queens. A few weeks prior, Aria and Taylor met at the Korean Harvest and Folklore Festival at Citi Field in Queens. Aria was singing all the songs at the festival with a friend, and they began talking with other girls interested in K-pop, including Taylor, who describes the moment as "love at first sight, and [we] never separated after that." Taylor was also upset about the company's decision to expel Jay Park. Protests were held worldwide, from Seoul to Thailand, and Hallyu fans in New York City partook in online discussions and decided to hold their own in front of JYP's New York branch. Several years later, Taylor reflected:

> I was a fan. And I loved them [2PM] together. And when we found out that happened, we were so upset. It was remarkable to see this because people were doing protests all over, not even just in Korea; in Thailand, in Australia. In countries you've never even heard of. It was insane and we were all keeping this together. Somebody made a 2PM forum and everybody was added and we'd keep in contact with everyone and that's when everybody started making flash mobs in all these different countries at 2PM. It was crazy.

Taylor, Aria, and others from the online group protested by putting posters all over the windows of the label's building. Taylor notes that although the protesters were upset about the company's actions, she was young and enthusiastic, and thought that their plan was fun and might actually work. This was where Hannah, a twenty-year-old Mexican American, met Taylor and Aria. After seeing a posting on Facebook, Hannah decided to go to the protest, randomly meeting Aria. The two helped each other put posters and notes all over the windows. All the girls at the protest, regardless of whether they had met before, instantly felt connected to one another. Hannah told me, "[I was] going to see my friends; we're going to have something to speak about and relate to." Taylor continued, explaining, "Yeah. I think we connected right away with that, a lot of us connected right away. Again, we were hanging out with people that were just like us. Most of the people there too were of other backgrounds. So we bonded a lot." Indeed, after the protests dissipated, "it really became about us [Taylor, Aria, Hannah, and others] bonding and finding other people who like the same things we do." They developed a sense of community by attending protests, extending it to build their own community. The community was one in which, as Taylor put it, no one would be the "weirdo" who likes things that most young Americans are unaware of. Furthermore, these ongoing protests brought them to Koreatown. Aria recalls that her fellow protesters told her about Koreatown. "It was with a whole bunch of friends and they were just like, "Do you know about Koreatown? And I was like, 'Is there Koreatown, I didn't even know that?' So we went down and I just saw this block, it was so tiny." Despite being a native New Yorker who grew up mostly in the Bronx, Aria had never heard of Koreatown before engaging in the protests. After the day's protest was over, Aria, Taylor, and their friends had Korean food at an inexpensive Korean buffet. Soon it became a regular thing for them to meet up for the protests in front of the JYP building and then go to Koreatown for Korean food. As Taylor recalls, "We would go there like every day except for the weekends." Although Aria thought that Koreatown was too small to be called a "town," it was exciting.

Coming from mostly working-class families, their financial challenges as young high school and college students might have limited their experiences in Koreatown, an area that is known to be pricey. Yet they saw themselves as dedicated consumers, talking with and getting to know Koreatown workers. They found affordable options in Koreatown and would order fewer dishes at restaurants to share among themselves. Sometimes they wouldn't buy anything at all, and just "walked through K-town, maybe see some stuff." Aria remembers that it was just fun, allowing them to imagine being in Korea, though they were physically in New York. "It was fun, it was like living in Korea. I guess that was the feeling, like you would go there and you would feel like you're Korean or you're at least in Korea because everyone is talking Korean. . . . . Like when you go there, it just makes you feel like you're not in New York anymore, you're somewhere else. That's what I like about it. You're surrounded by a different culture and it's just interesting." Aria, Taylor, their friends, and many other fans of K-pop and K-dramas have never been to Korea. Their experiences with Korean culture have primarily been imagined through the media. Nevertheless, Aria and others still had fun exploring things that they saw in Korean dramas and TV shows. They later realized this in Koreatown, a physical gateway to immersing themselves into Korean pop culture—something simultaneously familiar and foreign.[1]

This narrative explains how Korean culture and food are diffused in online communities, luring locals and tourists alike who have only explored Korean culture virtually to a physical place. Even a decade later, Taylor, Aria, and their friends' stories are replayed by countless other K-pop fans. Koreatown is now much more robust and diverse than ever, with an increasing number of new non-Korean K-pop fans and regular New Yorkers and tourists. This space went from being a block largely unknown to most non-Asian New Yorkers only a couple of decades ago to a mecca for enthusiastic K-pop fans, who browse at Koryo Bookstore seeking K-pop merchandise and waiting to get the latest popular Korean street food, like Korean-style corn dogs covered with potato cubes and filled with mozzarella.

In this chapter, I explore how consumers practice Hallyu in Koreatown, changing the neighborhood's consumer landscape into more of a transclave, a hypercommercial space, in contrast with traditional ethnic enclaves that offer jobs and accommodations for newer immigrants. This chapter focuses on how non-Korean fans—many of whom are people of color—take advantage of the emergence of new media not only to develop an interest in and consume Korean culture, but also to actively create their own community in a physical space, reconstructing the space for transnational leisure, consumption, and entertainment. In this process, the physical space—the transclave—also plays a role in reinforcing a sense of community among non-Korean consumers, though their imaginations of the space are often rooted in fantastical and illusionary experiences presented in the global media. In this vein, are fans passive receivers of new media, only imagining Korean popular culture and Disneyfying a space that was once neglected by the mainstream? Or are they active creators in Koreatown, actualizing cultural fantasies in a real world, as a response to Korea's nation branding strategies?

Hallyu in Asian America

Tyler, a thirty-seven-year-old ethnic Chinese Malaysian social worker who works near Chinatown in Downtown Manhattan, moved to the United States at age twenty-five to attend college. Although his initial contact with Korean culture and people goes back to the early 2000s in Malaysia, he was more heavily exposed to Korean culture while attending college in Albany, New York. Hallyu in New York City became a phenomenon around 2020, when BTS broke through to the US mainstream music industry. Yet, as Tyler explained, certain populations in the United States, particularly Asians and Asian Americans, have a longer history of consuming Korean culture and are pioneers in this trend. He began watching Korean dramas, influenced by his Korean peers in Albany, but he remembers the time when Korean pop culture became very popular back home, and his friends back in Malaysia were "talking about it." His transnational ties to Malaysia also shaped how he perceives Korean popular culture, in addition to his Korean roommates and friends.

By the mid-2000s, this trend had only grown. Tyler noted that Chinese stores in Chinatown stock up on Korean DVDs with Chinese subtitles in order to appeal to Chinese immigrants who enjoy Korean dramas and shows. Tyler said, "In Chinatown, you started buying—in the store, they're selling foreign DVDs, like Malaysia, Singapore, Japan, Korea and maybe 70 percent to 80 percent are Korean DVDs [around 2005 and 2006]." Interestingly, Chinese entrepreneurs in Chinatown promoted not only Korean DVDs but also Korean fashion, including clothing and accessories. According to Tyler, they marketed their businesses with ads like "Our store has a lot of imported Korean dresses." Though Hallyu began with music and dramas in China, Korean fashion and makeup styles and trends seen in music videos, dramas, and movies quickly became popular among younger Chinese consumers since the early 2000s. This new cultural trend also permeated Asian immigrant communities, like Manhattan's Chinatown. Some Chinese entrepreneurs utilized their own ethnic media to promote their businesses, selling Korean clothing and beauty products imported from Korea, targeting Chinese clients.

Likewise, Kaylee, a twenty-one-year-old Chinese Korean American college student born and raised in New York City, also remembers her first exposure to Korean pop culture through her mother who bought DVDs from Chinatown.[2]

> One day my TV in my room broke down, so I was watching Korean dramas with them [her mom and sister].... I was crying. Then there was a

scene in the movie where they were in the hospital and they were finally reunited, I just started nose bleeding. It was like two rows of tears and two rows of nosebleeds and it was kind of ironic to me because that never happened to me. I never cried for a movie before, I was like sob, everything dawned on me.

Kaylee was raised in a Chinese-speaking environment with both parents and believes that speaking Chinese well shows respect for her parents, as it allows her to communicate with them better. Her mother, who was born in China, watched Korean dramas and movies with Chinese subtitles and introduced them to Kaylee and her sister.

The popularity of Korean pop culture slowly extended to younger English-speaking Asian Americans, sometimes through their parents, but more often through peers—either Koreans or other Asians. Nora, a twenty-four-year-old Filipino American from California, recalls learning about Korean pop culture from her close Korean friend in 2006, as a freshman at New York University. "I think I had just gotten very familiar with that [Korean culture] and so maybe that influenced me when I met other Koreans too and maybe I identified with them in a much stronger way—and I just think in the city and in NYU, there was just a very high population of Chinese and Koreans too so it's just pretty much—it felt very natural." Nora immigrated to LA at two years old, growing up in a northeast neighborhood of the city, which she recalls being a half-Mexican and half-Filipino area. Her friends and acquaintances back home are mostly Filipinos, and she did not know many Koreans despite their concentration in LA. She began hanging out with Koreans in college. In Nora's case, her Korean peers at New York University, whether Korean nationals or Korean Americans, played the role of cultural translators. Nora was introduced to Korean pop culture by Korean acquaintances. However, it became even more widespread across communities through the media and other coethnics in their communities.

New Media: Unexpected Encounters

Shared values or cultural proximity might be one of the major factors facilitating the Korean Wave (Hallyu) in Asia and even for Asian immigrants and some of their children living in the United States.[3] Yet this assumption of Asian community as a "relatively homogeneous cultural milieu" does not capture a recent wave of cultural flows beyond Asia.[4] Outside of Asia and the Asian community in the United States, exposure to Korean pop culture is usually unexpected. Lucia, a twenty-year-old college Latinx student, is one of many fans who stumbled upon K-pop on social media.[5] Lucia was born in the Dominican Republic and immigrated to the United States at the age of five. She grew up in Harlem, where she did not have Asian or Korean friends. She was first exposed to K-pop via a YouTube recommendation and "from there, I went on to dramas. I fell in love with everything." This unexpected experience opened the door for her to immerse herself in something new. Most of my non-Asian interviewees who were raised in New York City likewise told me that they did not grow up with Korean or other Asian friends, or at least never established close ties with them. In the past two decades, technological development and social media have been key to accessing Korean pop culture. Yet outside of Asia, the power of new media seems to be even more prominent.[6]

Yet until the 2010s, K-dramas did not get much attention from mainstream US streaming services, such as Netflix. It has been only a few years since Korean cultural content has gotten international recognition on such platforms with the unexpected success of *Squid Game*, *My Name*, and *Hellbound* in 2021. Before mainstream US platforms invested in Korean content and provided subtitles in various languages, the K-drama community in the United States was far more niche. Mila, a twenty-five-year-old Dominican American graduate student, talked about how voluntary translators on illegal and underground websites kept the community afloat in 2012:[7] "It's quick now, when I first started out, I used to have to wait. I remember I was actually waiting every week for them to finish translating an episode. The people were doing it on their free time and they would [have] a website telling us 'we're 75 percent done,' you know." These underground websites were operated by volunteers who dedicated their time and effort to making Korean products accessible to English (and other language) speakers. These types of active engagement and cooperation within the fandom, such as "subbing" (translating and subtitling K-drama episodes), allow them not only to gain access to the content but also to redefine the role of fans as active knowledge creators by breaking from the role of passive receivers in the traditional mediascape.[8] Although remaining somewhat limited to a small number of viewers, online websites for dramas, shows, and music became a platform for these non-Korean consumers in the United States and created new types of hybrid identities in more complex and multilayered ways.[9] Mila found that the popularity of Korean culture in the United States slowly expanded to non-Asian people like herself in the early- to mid-2010s.

However, when I had a follow-up interview with Mila in 2018, she pointed out that "a lot of the underground communities have gone down because they've been, you know, caught," but there are communities "built around" more mainstream platforms. Hulu began streaming Korean dramas in 2011; Drama Fever, Netflix, and Amazon Prime followed its path in 2012.[10] Now various sources, from free websites to legal websites, provide more opportunities for non-Koreans to explore an unfamiliar culture.

Likewise, the role of new media is prominent in the global infusion of cultural products, liberating consumers from traditional adaptation. K-pop stans talk about Korean idols and their labels that heavily utilize social media, such as Twitter, Facebook, YouTube, TikTok, and Instagram as a means of communication with international fans.[11] When I met Emma for a second interview in 2018, she talked about how BTS brought old K-pop fans who were slowly losing interest back to K-pop. Emma is a white Eastern European woman in her thirties whose family immigrated to New York during her late teens. She is one of the earlier K-pop stans who stumbled across K-pop while she was watching a Beijing Olympics promotion song in 2008. In that video, together with other Chinese artists (Nara Jang, a Korean singer included), Han Geng, a Chinese and first non-Korean K-pop idol from a popular boyband Super Junior, appeared. Emma thought Han Geng was cute and wanted to check out his music. From there, Emma was introduced to other K-pop bands through the YouTube algorithm, and that was just the beginning. In the past decade, she has traveled to other cities to attend K-pop concerts, including three trips to LA, and she has made friends from diverse backgrounds in New York City and beyond.

As she grew older, she felt that K-pop was not something new and interesting anymore, and she started losing interest. But the emergence of BTS brought her back. By 2018, BTS was entering the US mainstream music industry. They appeared on popular US television shows such as *The Late Late Show with James Corden*, *Jimmy Kimmel Live*, *The Ellen DeGeneres Show*, and the *American Music Awards*. During my follow-up research, particularly between 2016 and 2018, my interviewees, including Emma, talked about BTS a lot. While speaking about her reunion with K-pop through BTS, Emma showed her phone to me. "See how often they post. Today, today, yesterday . . . ," said Emma, as she scrolled down through the posts. As the group continues to be very active on social media, fans feel that they are connected to their idols and "never get bored," as Emma told me. In return, ARMY,[12] the official BTS stan (fan) club, recreates content made by BTS to keep their exchange with the group afloat. As such, BTS's form of communication is more "reciprocal" than that of most American celebrities, constructing offline friendships and a new sense of community beyond the virtual world.

K-Pop Fandom in New York: From Online to In-Person Community

Hailey is a twenty-three-year-old Black American from Maryland. She went to college in New York City and now lives in Connecticut, where she works as a youth counselor. When she was younger, she listened to Japanese rock music and watched Japanese anime. One day, she went on a website to watch Japanese anime, and it directed her to another site. She ended up on DramaFever, one of the biggest Korean drama platforms. She watched some shows and got "stuck with that for a good couple years in my high school." Likewise, she remembers that she was not "the biggest K-pop fan" until one of her Black friends put on some music from Big Bang, BoA, SHINee, and 2NE1 on her iPod. At first, she thought it was Japanese pop music, but it turned out to be Korean. She remembers that she "just kind of went from there."

Hailey has followed several Korean boy bands and girl groups since high school, including Big Bang and BTS. Her interest in the music has since expanded into physical spaces and real-life experiences with other fans, which entails going to concerts and meeting her idols. She paid over $500 for Big Bang's last concert in New York City years ago, which was only a "regular VIP ticket," and flew to Miami to see G-Dragon from Big Bang. She also traveled to LA from Connecticut for a BTS concert. Hailey has been a fan of BTS for years and didn't mind spending the money to travel to attend concerts. Beyond traditional concert venues, the K-pop industry offers unique opportunities (often monetized) for global K-pop fans to actualize their fantasies of idols in the real world. Two examples of this are "fansigns" and "hi-touches," which offer fans opportunities to meet other members of fanbases as well as their favorite idols face-to-face. "Fansigns" are events where fans can get CDs or vinyl albums autographed by K-pop stars, and "hi-touches" are events that allow fans to receive high fives from K-pop idols after concerts or fanmeets.[13] Both are unique to K-pop culture. Though these events require extra money or luck, for fans in the United States, they are "like a once in a lifetime chance to be able to see them until I go to Korea," as Lucia, a twenty-year-old Dominican college student said more than a decade ago.

In addition to rare opportunities to see their idols in person, concerts are where fans begin to develop a real sense of community and belonging with one another beyond online communities. Madison, a twenty-three-year-old part-time teacher and master's student, shares how friendship-building works through K-pop concerts. She and her K-pop friends planned to go to a GOT7 concert in Washington, DC, in 2017. She is a member of a Facebook fan group for GOT7, and people make different fan pages for each location when there is an event. Madison joined the fan page for DC and asked if other people were planning to go to the DC event from New York. She immediately heard back from about thirty people; she made a group chat with eight people and now talks with them "all the time. We never stopped talking." Unlike American music fan groups, whose members tend to be "kind of mean and snobby," she finds her K-pop friends to be "really nice and sweet" and feels like "we're really close friends" even though they have only met a couple of times in person. They came together because of their mutual interest in a Korean band, whom most of their American friends would not recognize.

Most K-pop fans that I spoke with before the COVID-19 pandemic agreed that the K-pop community in the United States is more open-minded and inclusive of people of color and the LGBTQ community than others, despite the fact that Korea and the K-pop industry are conservative by comparison. Briana, a twenty-two-year-old Black American, describes the K-pop community in New York City.

> In New York City, I kinda want to call us a melting pot. You know, yeah, cuz like, there's so many different cultures within the K-pop community. Yeah, you're gonna meet people who are Muslim, you're going to meet people who are Thai, you're going to meet people who are like, Nigerian, or somebody from Puerto Rico, you know what I mean? Like the K-pop community is very, very diverse. . . . . . I think it's more like, you find a lot of like, friendships into that because as soon as you meet somebody else who likes K-pop, it's like, damn, you're my best friend. Because even though there might, it might look like there's a lot of us, there still aren't a lot of us out there.

Briana calls the K-pop community in New York City a melting pot, explaining that she sees many non-Asian K-pop fans when she goes to K-pop concerts in the New York metropolitan area. This was confirmed by most non-Asian fans that I spoke with. Seeing this diversity and other people like themselves helped non-Korean fans of color feel as though they belonged there. Briana, Emma, and Hailey, like many other non-Korean interviewees, emphasize the openness to diversity of the K-pop community,[14] reinforcing a sense of belonging and allowing for a sense of trust and real-life friendships at meetups and concerts. The music itself was not mainstream in the United States, though the popularity of some artists had taken off, but, as Emma explains, "you get those people who kind of don't really fit the profile, or whatever you're supposed to be." Yet, as Emma, a twenty-seven-year-old white Eastern European woman, said, "you are one of us," regardless of your race, sexual orientation, religion, nationality, and class. You are no longer an outcast among your peers in this community. Interestingly, this in-person friendship allows non-Korean K-pop fans in the New York metropolitan area to navigate into an actual physical space—the transclave in Manhattan Koreatown. This is significant because it is a physical space where their fantastic imaginaries of Korea, which were previously observed and consumed virtually, become reality.

Koreatown: Is It Disneyland?

Sophie and Isabelle are twenty-five-year-old white twins from Pennsylvania. Isabelle currently works and resides in Seoul, while Sophie is a homemaker in Pennsylvania. As young children growing up in a small predominantly white town, they did not have much contact with Asians aside from two Korean adoptee siblings who were raised by a white family. But as I will discuss further in chapter 6, their family was "adventurous" in trying various ethnic cuisines, allowing them to try things like kimchi when they were young. Furthermore, they remember visiting Koreatown with their parents to purchase dresses and jewelry for their business, a formal dress shop, when they were kids. Rather than "a cultural mecca" for Korean culture, their first memory of Koreatown was the wholesale jewelry area, one of the major businesses that Korean immigrants have engaged in for decades.

Sophie and Isabelle were reintroduced to Koreatown during their junior year in the mid-2000s of college at Fordham University by Isabelle's Korean roommate. One day, Isabelle's roommate was alternating between touching her tongue and her nose with her finger several times after sitting on the floor because her leg had fallen asleep. It is a well-known mythical practice in Korea that doing this would get rid of leg pain and discomfort. Isabelle was surprised by this behavior and wanted to know what she was doing. The twins soon became addicted to Korean dramas, music, and food. They said that the first time they watched a drama, they were hooked because "something about the Victorian virtues of K-dramas paired with handsome flower boys was completely refreshing and exciting for us." The standard sixteen episodes, rather than six to eight seasons like American dramas, were "just long enough for you to become engaged and just short enough to make you fall in love and want more." They, like other K-drama fans, appreciated that "it ends."[15]

Sophie and Isabelle began visiting Koreatown to buy cosmetics and eat. Sophie explained why they frequented a particular bakery: "We had seen them on dramas and felt special eating there." The twins knew that Paris Baguette was a Korean franchise because of product placement (called PPL in Korea) in Korean dramas, or embedded marketing, an advertising technique in which a company pays a content creator to show their brand and product in video content. Paris Baguette became a way for the twins to actualize what they consumed in media in the real world.

Likewise, Mila, a twenty-five-year-old Dominican American graduate student, echoes Sophie and Isabelle about how food in K-dramas brought her to Koreatown. Born and raised in the Bronx and Manhattan, she also did not have Asian friends before high school. But her high school in Midtown Manhattan had a good number of Asian students. A fellow student from Japan introduced her to both Japanese and Korean popular culture in 2005, and this friend also took her to Koreatown for the first time. Initially, Mila and her Japanese friend would go to 32nd Street to shop or look around Morning Glory, a character-based stationery store from Korea. Later, they branched out to other stores. Mila developed a real interest in Korean dramas, waiting for new episodes with English subtitles.

Yet, for Mila, the food was what caught her attention: "They eat so much in Korean shows so I'm always hungry when I'm watching Korean TV shows and so I started eating Korean food." When I interviewed Mila for the first time in 2012, she was living in Ohio and would regularly cook her own Korean food, something she never did in New York because of the abundance of Korean options in Manhattan and Queens. The limited supply in Ohio pushed her to learn how to cook Korean food by following YouTube tutorials. After getting into Korean culture, Mila's comfort food was neither Dominican nor American, but Korean: "Korean food is my favorite kind of food, even over Japanese. I don't know, I just love it so much. When I feel sick at home, I eat Korean food."

Non-Korean K-drama fans often point out that there are a lot of food and eating scenes in Korean dramas.[16] Non-Korean audiences find scenes centered on food to be a unique aspect of Korean dramas. Families often have meals together in family dramas or use food as objects to express their emotions or to show social elements. For example, jjapaguri or ram-don in *Parasite*, which is a combination of two different popular instant noodle brands (Chapagetti and Neoguri) supplemented with expensive hanwoo Korean beef, was used to show the class differences between two families. Rather than being "culturally odorless" like manga and anime and removing features unique to one's national origin,[17] Korean drama often maintains cultural differences and unfamiliarity,[18] often becoming a driving force for K-drama consumers to collectively learn social meanings by decoding cultural metaphors and unfamiliar hidden symbolism.

Hailey, a twenty-three-year-old Black American youth counselor, talked about how she was attracted to Korean food while watching Korean dramas. "And like this food. Yeah, it will look so good. Or like, when

Figure 5.1. The Food Gallery 32 in Koreatown, Manhattan. The first floor of Food Gallery 32 offers a variety of Korean cuisines, from street foods and fried chicken to desserts. Photo by author.

the poor girl was like in her house, and she just like took everything like in her fridge and like put it in a bowl. Yeah, like shove it in her mouth, because she was like so upset. It looks so good to me." Hailey's observations about food in Korean dramas seem to be accurate. It is not uncommon to see food scenes in which Koreans take leftover banchan (side dishes) from the fridge and mix it with rice, fried eggs, gochujang, and sesame oil, and put them all ingredient into a big stainless steel bowl, when they have a stressful day. It is a comfort food that many Koreans and even non-Koreans, judging by Hailey's reaction, wanted to try. These fans venture out the boundary of traditional media spectatorship and accentuate fascination with the collectively imagined world, or K-Dramaland.[19] For Hailey, her way of engaging in participatory culture is through buying Korean food at H Mart and eating out at local Korean restaurants.[20]

In this sense, Koreatown is a fantastical place where non-Koreans can marry real life to the Korean dramas they love. It has a unique foreignness, with signs in another language, as a themed ethnoscape,[21] offering "exotic" experiences in the symbolic economy.[22] To them, it is a magical place. Sophie and Isabelle, the twenty-five-year-old white twins from Pennsylvania, said: "After we went home with our bags of K-pop, beauty products, and a golden ramyun pot, we were hooked. K-town was a magical place where K-dramas became real for us. We could eat bingsoo [shaved ice dessert] and see real hanboks [traditional clothing]."[23] The twins' descriptions of Koreatown as magical or fantastical, just like theme parks, is in line with how Hailey views Korean dramas. Hailey likes Korean dramas because they tend to be more fantastical than American dramas, which deal more heavily with realistic issues.

> Um, I think because it all is kind of like a fantasy always like that. The stuff that happens does not happen in real life anywhere, whereas a lot of like American shows, like they try to make it seem like it can happen in real life, which kind of bothered me because then it would make you like a little anxious and paranoid like, you know, people can, you know, really die like that? . . . But Korean dramas were all these so fantastical, so I just really liked it. . . . . . I guess they kind of did like with Disney movies. K-dramas kinda remind me [of] . . . like Disney movies.

Hailey talks about K-dramas as Disney movie-like fantasies. Many fans point out that K-drama plots typically involve love triangles, often including a poor girl who has conflict with a rich guy at the beginning, but ends up falling in love with him. As Jessica, now a twenty-seven-year-old Black American, said during her follow-up interview in 2018, Korean dramas are appealing because they are "completely fantastical"; "I don't want to watch anything in the real world. I live in the real world. It sucks. Let me escape into fantasy," she explains. Korean dramas offer a temporary escape or refuge into the fantastical world, where sensitive, caring, and good-looking men render romantic fantasies to them.[24]

In New York, this imaginary Korea is brought in the unique physical space—Koreatown. Taylor, who routinely went to Koreatown after the demonstration in front of the JYP Entertainment office, thought that Koreatown was beautiful because it had signs like she saw on TV. "I thought it was, in a sense, sort of beautiful because they had the signs where it was like TV going on, signs that were lit up. In a way, I had made at least somewhat of a connection there of being a part of something that was Korean. And I really liked it. It was like a whole other world beyond that corner of a totally different area. So the feel was entirely different." In this image-saturated contemporary world, where depictions are detached from the lived experience and everydayness of individuals,[25] like Disneyland, one observes a "channel-turning mingle of history and fantasy, reality and simulation."[26] As Taylor says, seeing a TV-like landscape allows you to delve into a fantastical lived experience, which is, in fact, two opposite worlds: reality and fantasy. Yet, in this process, time and space are commodified in the exchange of goods and services, while reinforcing the illusion of community.[27]

For fans who are far from Korea, Koreatown is where their mental image of Korea and its narratives in the mediascape turns into an existing space.[28] For them, a trip to Koreatown stands in for Korea itself, just like "a trip to Disneyland substitutes for a trip to Norway or Japan,"[29] sustaining and providing safe versions of the original[30]—in this case, multicultural New York. This "Korea" only exists in the media, but it is also embedded in multicultural New York. As Michael Sorkin contends, "It's the utopia of transience, a place where everyone is just passing through."[31] If this is true, does Koreatown only sell an illusive fantasy?

(Re)creating Koreatown

This understanding of quasi-authenticity, often germinated by the media and actualized in cultural and culinary consumption in the United States, might change or even wane when a person travels to Korea and sees how Korea actually is. Experiencing the culture firsthand can make people renegotiate the meaning of Korean culture and Koreatown.

Camila, a twenty-two-year-old Brazilian American college student, became interested in Korean culture during her sophomore year at college in Florida when she started teaching English to international students. Through this job, she met many Asian students, including Koreans, and they introduced her to Korean pop culture. While she did not realize there was a Koreatown in Manhattan even though she grew up in New York City, she began to spend time there whenever she came back to New York from her college in Florida. She even brought Korean friends from college to Koreatown when they visited her in New York.

In July 2012, she went to Korea. Her original plan was to stay in Seoul from August to December as an exchange student. As it turned out, she only managed to spend a few days in Korea due to a family emergency. Still, she remembers that she "fell in love with Korea" while staying in Busan and Seoul. Even that brief visit led her to question her imagined image of Korean culture before visiting Korea. "After I came back from Korea, I realized that K-town is not as beautiful as I thought it was because at first, K-town was the only source for Korean things and I thought it had everything there. After going to Korea and coming back, it was small and expensive. The smell is not even that good." Camila's images of Korea and Koreatown were reshaped by her brief experience in Korea. Interestingly, after coming back from Korea, she felt that Koreatown was no longer as beautiful as she thought it was. Likewise, Nora, a Filipino American NYU graduate from LA, echoes Camila's thoughts on Koreatown. "I go to K-town now and I think even after I was in Korea too, I went and really it's just like a small street. Maybe one or two blocks. But then if you asked me, like on my freshman year, I would have thought that it was much bigger because I wasn't really aware of my surroundings but now that I have been living in New York for so long now, then I realized it is actually really small." Nora traveled to Korea for about ten days when her Korean friend was visiting Korea. She even thought about moving there and teaching English with the plan that she would learn the culture and history, have fun, and get paid. However, this ultimately did not work out because of the logistics of moving to another country. Nora thought their motherland was less safe and less attractive than Korea. "I also have friends who have experience working in the Philippines and they didn't have . . . it's sort of more uncivilized than Korea, to be honest. Like Manila can be very dangerous," Nora said in 2012. In Korea, Nora was able to stay with her friend who was also teaching English and to visit her Korean friend, who introduced Korean culture to her. Her experience in Korea also shaped how she saw Koreatown. Koreatown became too small, even though it used to feel like a big and nice space for having fun with friends. Her expectations of Korea through media had been actualized. After going to Korea, Nora thinks that Koreatown could never capture the essence of the real Korea.

> I think for me, it's like I absorbed so much when I was in Seoul, there is so much going on there, so many neighborhoods there that K-town can't

really capture all that in two blocks. K-town is more just like a shorter abbreviated Korea of my experience of the Korean culture, whereas when I was in Seoul, there is like really nice parks, tourist attractions, restaurants, different types of neighborhoods and like the palaces. That was my experience there, I tried to make it very broad and when I went to K-town, I was like what can I really do?

Nora says that Koreatown is only an abbreviated version or microcosm of Korea and Korean culture, missing many aspects of Korea, from people to traditional culture to history. Or it only offers a commodified pseudo-Koreanness in a hypercommercialized space.[32] Though non-Korean interviewees who have been to Korea are more likely to have limited experiences there, mostly visiting tourist attractions for example, both Nora and Camila's memories of Korea also include the everydayness of Korean life, thanks to their Korean friends who invited them into their homes and shared meals with their families. Like my Korean American interviewees, whose notion of their motherland is transformed by visiting Korea as young adults, Camila also began to see faults in Koreatown.

> Going to K-town is very like New Yorker style. People are screaming at each other, but in Korea everyone is eating calmly. Maybe not in Seoul? . . . There are so many people in Koreatown. So many people. I do not want to say in a mean way, but Korean people in K-town are very stuck up. . . . Whenever I watch Korean drama, everyone sitting down on the table and homemade meal eating. I've never seen that in Koreatown, but going to my friend's house in Seoul, we actually sat down at the table, to me it was very interesting, having rice for the breakfast, you do not do that in K-town, but in Korea, it's normal, rice and soup.

Camila's and Nora's respective transnational journeys to "places of imagination" in Korea realized and actualized their earlier imagined journeys.[33] Yet, Camila's trip to Korea gave her new insight into what authentic Korean culture means in terms of regular Koreans' everyday lives. She ultimately revisited Korea, and now she tries to distance herself from New Yorkers who love Korean culture but have not had the authentic Korean experiences that she had.

I met Camila in a Korean class that I taught at a non-Korean organization in New York. At the time of the interview in 2012, she was learning the Korean language in New York and in the process of reapplying for an exchange program to Seoul. A couple of years later, I learned that she went back to Korea to pursue her master's degree at a university in Seoul, staying there for several years. Though she had only traveled to Korea for a few days at the time of the interview, she was able to understand how different Korea actually was from how she imagined it to be. In this process, the quasi-authenticity of Koreanness as imagined through the media and Koreatown consumption was reevaluated, recreated, and renegotiated through actual experiences in Korea.

For a relatively longtime resident of Korea like Isabelle, Sophie's twin, some Korean franchises in Koreatown trigger nostalgic memories. Isabelle currently lives in Seoul and teaches English there. The twins explain that their imagined assumptions about Korea and its culture, mostly available via online content, were realized in Koreatown. However, interestingly enough, her transnational experience and her memories in Koreatown are brought back in Seoul. She sees a Paris Baguette on every corner, and for her, "oddly Paris Baguette feels like home" because she "ate it so much in New York." This creates a transnational circulation of culture reverse to what Korean nationals experience.

Conditional Belonging

This chapter explores non-Koreans' constructed narratives of Koreatown, rooted in the growing popularity of Korean pop culture beginning in the mid-2000s, and shaped by new media influences. By looking both at transnational and US perspectives, I analyzed several factors that lead non-Koreans to Korean pop culture and food, and, ultimately, Koreatown. From a transnational perspective, technical advancements, particularly the internet, have made Korean popular culture accessible when it used to be deemed foreign. More importantly, I looked at how and why non-Korean Hallyu fans utilize Korean popular culture as a means to forge a new identity and develop a sense of community. As Tyler said, their community is not just about music, dramas, or other cultural elements, but a sense of belonging. This is crucial for Hallyu fans, particularly those who grew up feeling they were different from their peers, though the trend has been changing slowly in the past five years with a new influx of new fandom, particularly during the pandemic.

Though many believe that the Hallyu community is only active online, many, particularly those in New York City, actively seek out spaces to actualize their virtual consumption in the real world through concerts and Koreatown by eating, drinking, and hanging out. Koreatown, thus, is a fantastical space for some K-pop stans and K-drama fans. However, while some are just happy to be surrounded by Korean culture and people, their belonging is often conditional or rejected, particularly if they are Black or Latinx. Hailey, a twenty-three-year-old Black youth counselor, said, "Whenever I walked in Koreatown, I feel so out of place, because . . . it feels like a place for Koreans only," and "you look like you're not supposed to be there." As Emma said, her whiteness does not make her feel uncomfortable in Koreatown, but she also noted that her Black friends confront uncomfortable situations.

Likewise, Aria and Taylor shared their stories about conflicts with Koreans in Koreatown. When they were spending time in Koreatown almost every day protesting against Jay Park's removal from the boy band 2PM, they remember that some Korean Americans in their group just started talking in Korean with each other, making them feel left out. They noted that "most Americans make you feel weird about liking that. Like constantly reminding you that you're not Korean. . . . They were trying to make it seem like we're pretending to be Korean or we want to be Korean so badly." Various issues around a sense of belonging that came up regularly in interviews with Korean Americans are also shared by non-Korean K-pop stans, particularly those earlier fans who became interested in the culture back in the late 2000s and early 2010s.

Jada, a twenty-four-year-old Black American college student at Rutgers, stated that she recently noticed more Black and Latinx consumers than in the past. But in many cases, their love for Korean culture is not always accepted. So, does Koreatown offer diverse cultural opportunities to people regarding race, ethnicity, gender, religions, and nationalities? Is it really "cosmopolitan," as Alan, a thirty-nine-year-old Chinese American graduate student who grew up in Brooklyn, describes it? Or do they only take "a trip, a fantasy voyage" to an imagined place?[34]

6

Korean Food

Authenticity, Exoticism, and Cultural Omnivorousness

Anyone with a passion and palate for the exotic fare of the Far East would travel far to find a restaurant that fits the bill better than the recently opened Mi Cin at 130 West Forty-fifth Street. The cuisine is Korean.
—Craig Claiborne, "Food News: Exotic Fare of Koreans,"
The New York Times, July 11, 1960

Pretty much any Korean you meet anywhere, you can take it for granted they like food, that they're passionate about food, particularly their food. Which of all the immigrant cuisines, has possibly been messed with the least. Unlike many other new arrivals, Koreans seem to have been the most unwilling to accommodate Western tastes. Maybe that's why it took us so much time to love the stuff.
—Anthony Bourdain, *Parts Unknown*, 2013

On September 8, 2023, the City of New York posted a video on their Instagram account. The video was captioned "Making *kimbap* in a NYC lunchroom. #backtoschool," and it was part of a week-long series that ran from September 4 to September 12, commemorating the start of the 2023 school year, titled "What's in Your Lunch Box?"

In this particular video, Avery, a Korean American third grader, opens and describes the contents of her lunch box to the audience. "Here is what's in my lunch box. Rice, then my mom packed me a foil and seaweed. So I can make this Korean food, called kimbap." Avery gives step-by-step instructions on how to make a simple kimbap with rice and roast seaweed, which are two of the most foundational ingredients ingrained in the everyday lives of Koreans all over the world. She lays out a piece of aluminum foil, puts the seaweed from a package of roasted seaweed seasoned with sesame oil and salt on the foil, pulls cooked rice out of her thermos, flattens the rice on the seaweed, and rolls the seaweed with the rice. When asked "Why do you like kimbap so much?," she pauses for a moment and replies, "I just think the combination of seaweed and rice is very good."[1]

This fifty-second-long video soon went viral. Combined with the online hype of Trader Joe's frozen kimbap that year, this short video was particularly eye-catching not only to Korean Americans, but also to many other immigrants and children of immigrants who often shared traumatic experiences about being teased and ridiculed by westerners because of their ethnic foods. Instagram user "hannabeans" shares a vivid memory about kimbap from her childhood: "I remember these girls wanted some of my kimbap. . . . They took a bite and spat it out, saying it was gross." She felt embarrassed and wanted to eat sandwiches from that moment, but she says, "This video healed a little girl in me!"[2] This emotion is also shared by other minority people. "This also heals the little Jamaican girl in me when they laughed at my fish or curry chicken,"[3] wrote Instagram user "empressngala." In fact, this seems to be a more general sentiment shared by many other immigrants; as "azulgris27" wrote, "She has no idea, but those 30 seconds probably warmed 1000's of immigrant hearts."[4]

Korean food was introduced to the American public as early as the 1950s, even before the massive immigration from Korea began. The *New York Times* article "Food: Korean Dishes; There Are Many Specialties American Cook Can Adapt—Two Recipes Offered" ran on September 2, 1958, and the celebrated *New York Times* food critic Craig Claiborne, a Korean War veteran, introduced the Korean restaurant Mi Cin, considered the oldest Korean restaurant in the United States in "Food News: Exotic Fare of Koreans" on July 11, 1960. However, Korean food did not break into the American mainstream for a long time.

This has changed in the past few years, particularly in New York City. In 2006, Anthony Bourdain, a celebrity chef and author, traveled to Korea to shoot an episode of his popular show *No Reservations*, in which he introduced exotic Korean fare to American viewers, ranging from street food to live octopus; the episode aired on June 12, 2006. He also traveled to Los Angeles's Koreatown for the second episode of a subsequent show on CNN called *Anthony Bourdain: Parts Unknown*, guided by two Korean Americans, Roy Choi and David Choe. The National Restaurant Association ranked Korean food as the second hottest ethnic food in its annual forecast (after Peruvian cuisine), based on an online survey of 1,283 members of the American Culinary Federation, in October–November 2013.[5]

Koreatown's authenticity is now mainly defined by its food. Consumers from various backgrounds, whether locals or tourists, expect to have not only authentic food cooked by ethnic minorities, but also authentic "experiences." Authenticity is centered on not just purchasing things but practicing "experience" in an ethnically themed commercial space.[6] Koreatown has been reframed, marketed, and introduced as a space for authentic Korean flavors and experiences in response to a new cultural trend in US cities that emphasizes authenticity and ethnicity. However, as many scholars have argued, authenticity, originally defined as "origin," loses its meaning and soul in the marketplace.[7] Outsiders, whether foodies, food writers, or ordinary consumers who just like the flavors in Korean cuisine, do not necessarily connect Koreatown's authenticity to its origin. The discourses around Koreatown's authenticity or urban identity do not deliver the history of the space and symbolic struggles that many old-timers and newcomers are part of, nor do they capture the history of urban struggle that swept cities across the United States in the 1960s and '70s. The people who made Koreatown what it is in the past and present are, in fact, mostly racial and ethnic minority groups. During the first decades of the twentieth century, these racial and ethnic minority groups included Jewish merchants and Italian, Irish, and Jewish women workers in the garment industry. By the mid-twentieth century, Koreatown was home to poor homeless families who lived at the Radisson Martinique Hotel at Broadway and 32nd Street, one of the city's largest welfare hotels in the 1970s and '80s. They were followed by Korean immigrants and their families in the post-1965 era and Korean students since the late 1980s.

I unpack the notion of authenticity in Koreatown by delivering the voices of ordinary people. Koreatown's authenticity has been defined by commercialized food in the marketplace in the past decade, which has often been promoted and marketed by entrepreneurs, the New York City government, and, of course, the Korean government and franchises. However, I argue that Koreatown's authenticity represents the collective imaginations of various transnational individual actors, particularly consumers, ranging from Korean nationals to Korean Americans to non-Koreans. Its authenticity also shows symbolic struggles over how we define authenticity—including who has rights to claim it among ethnic Koreans, and who belongs in this space. In this sense, Koreatown is not fixed in a particular time and space but is an ongoing process of ideas and experiences that travel across national borders. I start to unpack its authenticity by introducing three narratives of Inha, Laura, and Tasha, and I connect their narratives to broader themes—immigration, racism, transnationalism, and ethnic culture as a commodity—in order to understand Koreatown's authenticity as a social construction in urban America.

Three Stories

Inha

In the early 2010s, Inha, a twenty-eight-year-old graduate student in Illinois, was excited to prepare for her second trip to New York City. Traveling to the Big Apple was always joyful and thrilling, full of cultural opportunities that she and her fellow Korean students did not always get to experience in the Midwest. She, just like many other Korean students on campus, was making a list of what they called their own "traditions" to fulfill in New York City. One of the main activities that these students usually planned was to eat Korean food. Although her school had a lot of Korean students, their options for Korean food were very limited around campus, and what was available was generally not very authentically Korean for them; as she explains, the offerings were "food full of MSG." The closest Koreatown was located in outer Chicago, but it took more than two hours for them to drive, and they felt it was "waste of their time on the road." They thus actively sought out Korean food and hoped that Korean restaurants in New York City would offer better quality and taste. "We went to Koreatown in Manhattan for lunch, because I heard that the seolleongtang [ox bone soup] at Gammeeok was so tasty. There is a kind of 'to-eat-list' for yuhaksaeng [Korean international students] once one visits New York City.... There are certain Korean restaurants that are pretty famous among yuhaksaeng. We [she and her friends] all had a plan to visit each of them [while in New York City], because we should get our money's worth."⁸ During her first visit to New York, which lasted a week, she visited Koreatown at least four times and tried to complete her to-do-list by eating as many different Korean dishes as she could. She said, "I am finally here . . . I was like, 'let's eat' with so much expectation," fulfilling herself with nostalgic memory of her everyday life in Seoul, where she was born and grew up. Like many other Korean students, she, thus, hoped to develop an imaginary experience of dining at an "authentic," but not "exotic," Korean restaurant before visiting New York City.

Laura

Laura is a thirty-year-old editor who works at a research center housed in a prestigious university in New York City. She is a second-generation Korean American, born and raised in a small town on the East Coast. As with many other immigrants, her parents put enormous effort into and emphasis on their children's education. After graduating from a private high school in a small town on the East Coast, Laura went to Boston College for her undergraduate degree and Columbia University for her master's degree after having lived and worked in Seoul for three years. Growing up in a predominantly white suburb as one of only a few Asian Americans, Laura often questioned the differences between her culture and that of most of her friends.⁹ Ethnic food, although celebrated and consumed on a daily basis in the private sphere, often became a signifier of cultural and racial difference that many Korean Americans confront from an early age. Laura said: "I remember when I was younger, like, some neighborhood kids came over and like, they looked in our fridge and they saw this huge jar of kimchi and they are like, 'God, how is that like, a brain?' Or, I don't know, they are like, 'Why is this so disgusting?' . . . They acted like it was disgusting. I remember up to that point, I hadn't thought about Korean food as being weird and different. . . . . I think I was very conscious of it then."

Foods of many origins have been adopted into American cuisine, with their ethnicity becoming superficial.¹⁰ For Korean Americans, however, Korean foods were not something that they could always celebrate. In fact, Korean food is "a recognized marker of ethnicity."¹¹ This was particularly true for those growing up in the 1970s, '80s, and even '90s, when Korean food was not widely known among non-Koreans. The way Laura's peers reacted to kimchi triggered her recognition of the cultural differences between her and other Americans and, of course, a marker for microaggression and racial discrimination.

At the same time, Korean food is a means for Laura to maintain symbolic and emotional ties and roots. In fact, in some ways, food defines who she is. However, as a young adult, her (re)connection to her Korean roots through food is somewhat different from her childhood. While connections to ethnic food often are practiced in the private sphere—at home—Laura does not often cook Korean food at home because, she says, "I find it really hard to cook Korean food quickly" and "Korean food cooking here [in New York] takes a lot of planning." She travels to Koreatown from the Upper West Side for food. Her continuous connection to Korean food, in fact, is practiced in a commercialized ethnic space, where ethnicity often meets the market, that offers an opportunity for consumers to reidentify with their ethnic roots.

Tasha

Tasha, a thirty-eight-year-old Black American librarian, is one of many non-Korean consumers who frequents Koreatown. She was born and raised in Washington, DC, and came to New York City in 2007. She is a single mother who currently lives in Harlem with her daughter, works on the Upper East Side, and goes to graduate school in Brooklyn. Tasha had tasted Korean food years back as a college student in Maryland. She did not grow up with any Asian friends, yet one of her close friends during college was Korean, and she was sometimes invited over to have Korean food that her friend's mother cooked for them. "Yeah, my roommate was Korean American and we were very close. She's probably one of my oldest friends and I knew all her friends so I spent a lot of time around Korean Americans and Korean immigrants. . . . Her mom would make it. I had this one friend who was first generation and he would cook sometimes and I just really liked it." Unlike many Americans who have not had homemade Korean food, Tasha's experience with Korean food does not solely rely on dishes at restaurants, but rather, is attached to her memory of her close friend and her family during her college years. However, after relocating to New York City, Koreatown became a regular destination for dining and groceries. "I was still eating seaweed—and so I had checked out all the fried chicken places in Koreatown. It's really tasty and delicious. It's just really good. . . . So I love these sort of *Korean interpretations of Americans standards*" (emphasis mine). She has been fond of Korean food for several years. Tasha also enjoys Korean-style fried chicken, which appeals to the American palate, since it infuses Korean spiciness into a familiar American dish. For many Americans, Korean fried chicken may be a little different from what they are used to, but it is not totally foreign to them like other Korean dishes such as kimchi or doenjang jjigae (fermented soybean paste stew) may be.

Korean food is Tasha's family's favorite dining option among the countless types of ethnic cuisine available in New York. She and her ex-husband, who grew up with a Korean American friend when he was younger, used to go to Koreatown to dine together. Even her young daughter likes eating Korean food, as she "loved these little anchovies [dried anchovies], she could eat them like chips" when she was two years old. She often thinks that Korean food and ingredients are expensive in general, but "there's some things" that she "simply can't find anywhere else" but in Koreatown.

Inha's, Laura's, and Tasha's narratives illustrate how diverse groups such as Korean nationals, Korean Americans, and non-Koreans have diverse experiences in their contact with Korean food and Koreatown's commercial space. Those experiences are negotiated within the context of creating a sense of authenticity and, for some, exoticism in the marketplace, created using each group's collective and shared memories. The general public in the United States commonly assumes that Korean food in Koreatown is authentic—and exotic—mainly because it is cooked and eaten by members of the ethnic community.[12]

Ethnic Koreans: Mapping Authenticity in Koreatown

Ethnic Koreans often are perceived as a homogeneous entity by outsiders in the United States. However, Korean nationals and 1.5- and second-generation Korean Americans perceive and interpret the same food and Koreatown differently—including its authenticity.

Korean Nationals

For most Korean nationals, particularly those who reside in New York, Koreatown is unsatisfactory not only in terms of the physical space itself (e.g., outmoded interiors and dirty streets) but also in terms of actual taste and items offered on menus. "Authentic" (or "real" and "traditional") is one of the most frequently mentioned terms when Korean nationals describe Korean food.[13] Korean food produced by immigrants and their children that has been modified to fit different tastes and availability of products in the United States often does not live up to their standards. As discussed in chapter 2, many Koreatown entrepreneurs, particularly younger businesspeople who regularly visit Seoul, try to keep up with Korean trends and bring them back to New York's Koreatowns. Yet Korean nationals did not see their attempts always effectively displayed in Koreatown, particularly before the pandemic. Eunhye, a twenty-two-year-old language student, recounts her disappointment with the Korean food available: "One day we planned to visit New York [from Long Island in 2012]. I just saw a Korean restaurant at the corner of 32nd Street and Broadway as soon as we got off the train at Penn Station. . . . We had kimchi jjigae [kimchi stew]. . . . . Oh, my god, it was too salty." Seasoning frequently came up regarding the taste of Korean food in Koreatown. For many Koreans, the food served at Koreatown restaurants is either too sweet or too salty, as it is modified to cater to non-Koreans unaccustomed to authentic Korean flavors and predisposed to the taste of US-modified Chinese and Japanese cuisines.

For Korean nationals, the overall food experience in New York City is satisfactory in terms of Western-style dining opportunities, as the city itself is known as one of the global culinary centers. Yet unlike Korean restaurants in Korea, Korean restaurants in Manhattan's Koreatown fail to satisfy Korean customers' needs. Restaurants tend to offer as many food items as possible, from Korean barbecue to bibimbap (a popular dish that consists of rice with a plethora of toppings). For example, as of July 2024, Miss Korea BBQ has forty-eight items on their menu on their first floor (while offering more specialized menus on the second and third floors), while New Wonjo has seventy-two items, both excluding lunch specials, combo meal sets, and drinks. In Korea, these restaurants would not attract customers because they do not specialize in a par-

Figure 6.1. bb.q Chicken is one of the most popular and well-known fried chicken franchises in Korea. The banner advertises "Chicken & Beer" as "the perfect duo." Photo by author.

ticular dish or specific type of Korean cuisine. These restaurants also attempt to replicate cheap bunsikjip, inexpensive snack restaurants that provide various inexpensive foods in large portions without any specialties. Nahee, a twenty-seven-year-old graduate student, complains that "these old school K-town restaurants just use the same broth for all the foods," which she believes contributes to these restaurants' distortion of what the food map looks like in Korea. In this context, Korean food in New York City, particularly as practiced by immigrants, is not authentic enough for Korean nationals and distorts the authentic Korean culinary culture that they feel should be displayed in Koreatown.

Until the 2010s, many Korean nationals often preferred to consume from franchise stores over immigrant-run restaurants. During my interview with Jieun, a twenty-eight-year-old graduate student, in the early 2010s, she highlighted this in speaking of her preference for Paris Baguette, a popular Korean bakery with countless locations in Korea and many locations in the United States, because it "tastes the same as I had in Korea." Franchise goods are considered the most standardized but also the least authentic and local.[14] Yet in New York, "Korean" franchise goods deliver different a cultural code. As Jieun says, for many Korean nationals, the standardized baked goods of Korea can be considered more authentic than the Korean food modified by immigrants. The presence of Korean franchises, from fried chicken restaurants and bars to bakeries and restaurants, also confirms the global awareness of Korean (consumer) culture and the nation's status. The Korean franchises on 32nd Street often are associated with "refined," "modern," "contemporary," and "clean" stores among Koreans. In contrast, independently owned immigrant restaurants are seen as "old" and "outdated." Newer and trendier restaurants that directly reflect trends in Korea, including these franchise stores and new trendy restaurants, help Koreatown promote itself as a more modern, clean, and "better" space in which the landscape of Korea's contemporary consumerism is showcased for non-Korean customers.

For Korean nationals, Korean food and Koreatown are, thus, inauthentic, distorted, and reproduced by immigrants who get stuck in the time they left Korea, what Levitt calls the "ossification effect" or time-freeze factor,[15] as discussed in chapter 4. Many Korean nationals even explicitly express embarrassment and shame over Koreatown as the only space representing Korean culture in Manhattan. Yet their perspectives on Koreatown are based on a projection of the nation itself and the nation's reputation. In this process of "authentication,"[16] laying claim to the authenticity of Korean food and culture becomes a tool of power for Korean nationals,[17] as they confirm that "we," that is, Koreans, define authentic Korean culture. In contrast, for Korean nationals, Korean immigrants and their children, who often modify and reinterpret what Korean nationals consider authentic, cannot claim personal understanding of the nation's culture and taste. The perceived inauthenticity of restaurants in Koreatown confirms Korean nationals' claim and status as experts on and representatives of national culture.

Korean Americans

Ethnic food remained "a sign of nostalgia for an imagined time of simple reciprocal exchange" to be celebrated and practiced through family meals.[18] However, as Laura's narrative with her white peers reveals,

Korean Americans' experiences are somewhat different. The way Laura's peers reacted to kimchi triggered her recognition of the cultural differences between herself and other Americans. For her, consciousness of such cultural differences arose from the way other Americans, mostly her white peers, objectified and othered her and her family. Although she is considered to be assimilated into the American mainstream in terms of education, she and her family—and the food they consumed at home—were perceived as outside of that norm. However, this Western perception of "the Otherness of Asian food" becomes a pivotal moment for Laura to realize that their culture differs from the mainstream, and they are racialized and othered.[19]

Food, then, can become something to be hidden. Emily, a twenty-three-year-old second-generation Korean American, vividly remembers the day in elementary school when she was teased by her peers because of her packed lunch, which contained kimbap (a seaweed roll made from steamed rice seasoned with salt and sesame oil, filled with various vegetables and meat) instead of a more typical American lunch item like a sandwich. Her peers said, "Eww ... what is that? That looks so gross." Rather than giving her daughter advice to handle this situation, her mother "never packed me Korean food ever again," keeping their practices away from Western eyes. "My mom, she is a—she always loved cooking things from scratch. I think she studied that or majored in home economics or something. . . . [Yet] it was kind of strange because my mom kept it [kimchi] hidden, sort of, so that when we did have guests over . . . yeah, kimchi was, like, put to the side. She was very sensitive to how other people might perceive us or perceive our family." Her decision was a reactionary strategy designed to mitigate the damage caused by a series of incidents her children had to confront. In fact, for Emily's family, like many immigrants (and their children), safety requires assimilation to the mainstream—and the more visible an immigrant's ethnic "Otherness" is, the more important such assimilation becomes. Thus, for Korean American children and adolescents, ethnic food is most often prepared or consumed at home or in their ethnic community—where their "exotic" culture is the norm.

However, as young adults, many 1.5- and second-generation Korean Americans must seek alternatives, especially once they go to college. Ben, a twenty-year-old business student at New York University, writes about fine dining on his blog. Yet the food he craved on his first day in New York City was kalguksu, knife-cut noodles in soup broth.

> My parents came with me to drop off my stuff, and then they were like, "Where do we go?" I was like, "Don't worry I will take care of it, just leave," but then I called my friends, but they were like, "We are having dinner with parents," so I had a really bad burger and a burrito. So it was a first-day eating experience, it was not very good. So then I had seonbae [senior student] at NYU, and she was like, "Do you want to have something?" Literally what I said was kalguksu [knife-cut noodles] at Arirang. . . . I had my first Manhattan Korean 32nd Street experience.

Ben, who migrated to the United States at the age of seven, was nostalgic for the "comfort food" that his grandmother had cooked for him, which he had eaten on a daily basis back in Seoul. For Ben, the memory of ethnic food primarily found in the home transferred to the commercial space of Koreatown. Memories of ethnic culture, particularly food, confirm and mark cultural difference, both individually and collectively.[20] In Koreatown, Korean Americans can negotiate their relationship with the past through food, navigate the present in search of "home," and confirm the presence of their ethnic culture citywide or even beyond.[21]

For Korean Americans, Korean food is what they have eaten for their entire lives, whether modified or not, in the United States. Despite past experiences with food-related stigma while growing up, Korean food remains a lasting connection across generations, preserving memories of home, where their grandmothers and mothers continually reminded them of who they were. Their ethnic distinctiveness might diminish as they become more culturally akin to the US mainstream compared to their parents' generation, while no longer practicing other ethnic cultures, such as religion and language. Yet, Korean food shows their way of being Korean while navigating and tolerating their traumatic experiences of being racial minorities in the United States.[22] In this sense, Koreatown showcases an authentic space, where personal memories are anchored, racial insecurities disappear, and collective history is rediscovered while being outside or far from home. Korean Americans, thus, interpret this space based on an ethnic identity developed within the US racial hierarchy and through negotiation with the motherland.

Koreatown's authenticity should be claimed by Korean Americans; Sunmee and Emily call it "my street" (see chapter 3). As such, Koreatown offers authentic Korean food to various groups. "That was a really fun time and Jake [a friend] and Ray, the guy's roommate, he was also really into Korean music . . . or he was aware of it. . . . They're very smart and they were very into learning about different cultures, trying to experience the authenticity." Emily believes that Koreatown offers authentic Korean food. When Emily found that her non-Korean friends, Jake and Ray, were intrigued by Korean pop culture and wanted to try Korean food, she was glad that "authentic" Korean food was easily accessible in Koreatown, and that the culture had finally caught the attention of non-Korean New Yorkers.

However, this is not always the case for all Korean Americans. Some even broadly question if ethnic consumption itself is a part of authentic Korean culture, while some later realize that Koreatown does not resonate with what Korea really looks like after they visit the country. Korean Americans who have lived in Korea for several years often compare Koreatown to other consumption spaces, especially Seoul. Laura, who used to live in Hongdae, a trendy neighborhood in Seoul, compares her own experience in Seoul to New York's Koreatown. Her first experience in Koreatown goes back to 2005 when she was visiting New York during a break from her job in Seoul. Having lived in Korea, she wanted to find a space in New York where she could have similar experiences, but she was disappointed with Koreatown.

> I was more disappointed when I got food, because it's obviously more expensive. . . . I was like, this is stupid. . . . Even after I moved [to New York], I still did not like Koreatown. It didn't taste good, it's twice as expensive [as food in Seoul]. . . . Finally, my friends told me to shut up. This was the first big city I lived in since Seoul, and I was comparing everything. I was like, "Korea is better," so my friends were like, "Shut up."

Having lived in Seoul at two separate points in adulthood, she now thinks about what authentic Korean food means rather than reverting to childhood memories of food. When I asked if she was only trying to remember the good aspects of Korean food and culture, she said, "There were stressful things in Korea, I do [tend to] remember the good stuff. I'm not trying to, but it keeps coming to me." Although Laura talks about her identity crisis in Korea, she tries to remember positive things about Korea, like the public transit system and food. Despite the fact that visiting Koreatown is one of the ways that she recollects her time in Korea, she was not entirely happy with the atmosphere, food, and drinks that Koreatown offers.

As a food blogger who is interning in the restaurant industry, Ben believes that, by default, Korean food cannot be authentic in the United States, but authenticity is being used as a marketing tool. "It's not authentic, we're not in Korea. How can you say it's authentic if you're not in Korea? . . . I feel like authenticity is overrated. People say that "oh it tastes better, but it's authentic." I don't care about authenticity. I think about, 'Is it good? Does it taste better?'" Korean Americans who have lived in Korea and consumed authentic Korean culture approach Koreatown in more concrete ways, such as by comparing prices and food quality in Koreatown and Seoul, just like Korean nationals. In this way, their perception of authentic Korean culture has been challenged, rooted in their transnational connections to and consumption experience in the motherland.

However, unlike many Korean nationals, many Korean Americans have developed emotional attachment to the space, as discussed in chapter 3. "The space grew up as I grew up," said Sunmee, a forty-two-year-old building manager. Sunmee was born in a city near Seoul, and her family immigrated to New York City when she was five years old. She remembers that her family was not well-off in Korea. Her family was able to immigrate to the United States through family reunification, sponsored by her aunt who married an American GI. Her parents share a very similar story with many other Korean immigrants in New York. Due to limited economic resources, her father worked for several Korean-owned businesses, including a grocery store, while her mother sewed. They were able to save and even loan some money, and eventually, they were able to open a greengrocery in Brooklyn, where her parents successfully accumulated enough financial means to invest in real estate during the urban crisis. She vividly reminisces about visiting Koreatown as a little kid with her father and remembers the welfare hotel on the street—she truly has witnessed all the stages of change that Koreatown has undergone over the past three decades. She grew up with the space, while seeing that the space itself has developed alongside the history of Korean immigration. In other words, the history of Koreatown parallels Koreans' struggles as a racial and ethnic minority in New York and elsewhere, and their own stories. This is a story often overlooked by their coethnic counterparts—Korean nationals—while they themselves romanticize it.

New Clients in Koreatown

However, outside of the Korean community, the major driving forces for the popularity of Korean cuisine in the United States are different, not surprisingly. The recent K-pop hype (a transnational factor), as discussed in chapter 5, along with the social media buzz around Korean dishes among young Americans—from TikTok to Instagram—appear to be major contributors to the global popularity of Korean food in recent years. However, this is not the whole story.

New Asian Cuisines

This new trend has to do with domestic changes in the US culinary scene, moving from snobbish exclusion to omnivorousness.[23] Because gourmet food culture is a cultural realm, like arts consumption in general, food consumption signals status; rather than maintaining narrow cultural references, these omnivores have a broader range of cultural knowledge due to their embrace of certain forms of lowbrow culture.[24] This change and the ensuing discourse have been shaped and intensified by food media, particularly food writers and critics in food magazines, TV shows with celebrity chefs, and their cookbooks.[25] Food writing started in earnest around the Second World War. *Gourmet* magazine began in 1941, and, by the late 1950s, Craig Claiborne of *The New York Times* had considerable influence on the American culinary scene. *Food & Wine* magazine and other cuisine-focused publications rose during the late 1970s through the 1990s. These mainstream media outlets transformed the US culinary scene. French haute cuisine, only enjoyed by few elites, has expanded to and slowly drawn in the American middle class, while higher classes began to seek exotic foods to differentiate themselves from mass appetites.[26]

Television furthered the widening reach of foodie culture. The Food Network, a cable channel devoted entirely to all things food, first aired in 1993 and has steadily grown in viewership since then.[27] Through this platform, chefs have appeared on TV shows, bringing viewers into their kitchens and making gourmet food available to the general public with their recipes and instructions. And they have earned considerable fame. While earlier celebrity chefs were most often associated with foreign and upscale fine dining, particularly French cuisine,[28] the food and dining industry started to focus on American chefs in the 1980s. Although the Food Network offered Asian food recipes palatable to non-Asians, these recipes were mostly created by non-Asian chefs. The only exception was Ming Tsai on *East Meets West*, who offered various Asian fusion recipes. Asian chefs did not break into the mainstream for some time. However, with celebrity chefs on TV networks and various media, food culture has become a leisure pastime for the general American audience.[29] While the resulting mass audiences for foodie culture carry the implication of lowbrow tastes, foodie culture also works in tandem with the elitist pursuit of novelty and authenticity to bring "exotic" foods to the common palate.

The emergence of Korean food seems to have started with its infusion into other ethnic foods, as seen in the success of fusion cuisine by Korean American chefs both in New York and in LA, such as David Chang (of Momofuku) and Hooni Kim (of Danji) in New York and Roy Choi (of the Kogi Korean BBQ Taco Truck) in LA. More recently in New York City, Korea-born-and-raised chefs like Jungsik Yim of Jungsik in Tribeca, Junghyun Park of Atoboy and Atomix in the Flatiron District, and Brian Sehong Kim and Tae Kyung Ku of Oiji in the East Village have received much media attention, as discussed in chapter 2. While Korean restaurant entrepreneurs highlight their authenticity, particularly in New York City's and LA's Koreatowns, the fusion of Korean food with various other American ethnic cuisines to ease the American palate into the new taste was key. Asian cuisines have become no longer entirely new.

Familiar but Not Too Familiar or Exotic

As discussed in chapter 5, non-Korean consumers' affinity for Korean culture and food is not entirely new. Food is also understood and interpreted as being "familiar" to their own ethnic cuisine; this is most prominent among Asians and Asian Americans. Brandon, a thirty-four-year-old Hong Konger, explains the familiarity of Korean food and its similarity to his family's own ethnic cuisine. But while that led him to explore it in the first place, its "exoticness" led him to delve into it further. "It's nice to have bit familiar, but not too familiar. You know Chinese food, it's great, but I've had it all my life, you know. It becomes more comfort food, you grew up with it. . . . [Korean food is] different enough you have little exotic feeling towards it. . . . Korean BBQ is also interesting. . . . You marry East Asian soy sauce-based marinated meat, with Western-style cooking, which is grilling, and you have something, again, familiar, but different enough to be exotic." Brandon is not necessarily a fan of Korean popular culture, but a foodie who likes to explore new cuisine beyond his ethnic boundary. Korean food is a "bit familiar, but not too familiar" for Brandon, who was born and raised in Hong Kong and lived there until the age of ten. He does not remember his first time eating Korean food, yet clearly recalls how Korean food quickly began to penetrate Hong Kong Chinese palates in the 1990s, followed by Japanese food crazes. He distinctly remembers that he liked Japanese food in Hong Kong because "it wasn't another Chinese restaurant."

The "familiar" taste of Korean food is also noted by some Caribbean informants. Taylor explains her experience with Korean food by comparing it to her ethnic food. "Well, you'd be surprised. . . . You'd be surprised that Caribbean food and Asian food in general is very similar. . . . So I took her [mother] to H Mart [Korean chain grocery store in Koreatown] and she saw that half the stuff we eat at home are here. And she really likes kimchi, I like kimchi too, but she really loves it. . . . She made kimchi spaghetti. She uses kimchi in everything, she just loved it." Taylor was born to Caribbean parents and grew up in a Black neighborhood in Queens. She finds some similarities between Korean cuisine and the food that her mother cooks for her. Likewise, Mila, a Dominican American woman, comments on the similarities between her ethnic cuisine and Korean food: "In Dominican Republic, you don't eat beans, you eat rice. So that's pretty interesting, two cultures surrounded by rice." She dines in Korean restaurants, cooks Korean food, and believes that her comfort food is Korean food. Yet her interest in the new cuisine does not come from out of the blue. Dominican food is somewhat similar to

Korean food, and they share rice as a staple. In this sense, Korean food, for Mila and Taylor, is "familiar but not too familiar."

Some foodies believe that they try to move beyond their scopes to other cultures. Sophie and her twin sister Isabelle are a mix of Irish, Hungarian, Syrian, and Mongolian, born and raised in a German area of Pennsylvania. Although they realized that there were a handful of Korean students at her school, she and her sister did not know "anything about Korea or who was Korean." However, Sophie recalls that she and her twin sister grew up enjoying culinary adventures and appreciating cultural diversity with her family members. "We have always loved spicy food and our family is very adventurous with food. We grew up in a homogeneously German region, but our family always veered toward Asian cooking. Our mother is a wonderful Thai and Vietnamese cook and has begun to learn Korean recipes due to our love of Korean food." Although intensively immersed in Korean culture and food, notably Korean barbecue, as college students at Fordham University in New York City in the 2000s, they were already used to enjoying various Asian cuisines. Without any contact with Koreans, their family often incorporated Asian cooking into their American palate. The family seems to be typical new culinary adventurers who actively hunt for new experiences.

Is It Boundary Crossing?

Many ethnic Koreans—both Korean nationals and Korean Americans—seem to be happy with this new trend that Korean food, once a marker of stigma for many Korean Americans, is finally recognized and celebrated by outsiders. Yoojin, a twenty-eight-year-old graduate student, said, "I am pleased with these foreigners [presenting themselves in Koreatown] . . . because I could see Korean culture finally is getting popular [in New York]. . . . You see many foreigners coming to Chinatown and Japantown, but it was not the case in Koreatown." Although Yoojin often expresses her negative impression of Koreatown, the presence of non-Koreans is a way that she confirms the popularity of Korean culture and the nation's international status. Discovery of Korean culture by non-Koreans in New York City marks the city as a center of global culture. The Korean nation as projected in Koreatown is thus a form of cultural success, a statement of global presence. Yoojin does not explicitly express any emotional attachment or ownership to the space itself; in fact, she rejects it. Yet she understands Koreatown through the lens of national identity and affirms that her nation is internationally recognized and respected.

Likewise, Amy, a thirty-two-year-old second-generation Korean American pursuing a master's degree in art, recalls, "Now you see a group of white guys or African American families having Korean food, it's getting more common." This state of affairs was unimaginable while growing up in the 1980s and '90s, as Amy clearly remembers. Among these Korean Americans, witnesses to a huge change in New York, some think that this trend bridges ethnic boundaries, while others feel a sense of ethnic (or national) pride as Koreans. Nick, a senior at NYU's Stern School of Business, mentioned "Korean pride" several times during his interview, and he seems to be more confident about his culture: "Why? I don't think it's a matter of 'why,' but we are a matter of 'finally,' it's getting like, more popular because it was meant to be. . . . Food tastes good to everybody, the movies are awesome, I feel that the food mostly that people link to our Korean culture. It tastes good, it's healthy, and it's tasty." Nick, who developed his identity and a sense of Korean pride in high school, strongly believes that Korean food's entrance into the US mainstream is due. As he witnesses the growing popularity of Korean culture, particularly culinary culture, his sense of ethnic and national pride is intensified. "Healthy and tasty Korean food," intensively underscored in the globalization of Korean food projects by the Korean Food Promotion Institution and other government agencies, is finally delivered by Korean Americans.

Furthermore, for some Korean Americans, the growing popularity of ethnic cuisines eases racial and ethnic tensions. Emily, who cried while talking about her identity crisis, hopes that diverse groups can come together over shared enjoyment of culture: "I just wanted them to—I guess I wanted them to—yeah, I guess to introduce Korean culture and to— even though I feel like food is a really good way to bridge boundaries and it brought us a little closer, as cheesy as that sounds." Emily believes that ethnic food becomes a site of boundary crossing for outsiders and a powerful tool for contact with different cultures.[30] For Emily, bridging boundaries is not a matter of flattening out distinctions through individual assimilation, but widespread mutual recognition and celebration of diverse ethnic cultures. Indeed, such recognition of ethnic foods challenges the Western self and other duality.[31]

However, while possibly creating nearness through boundary crossing, ethnic food is also a site of struggle.[32] Ethnic food consumption by outsiders is a more palatable way for the mainstream to interact with the exotic other. It allows members of the mainstream to experience and perform a sense of adventure, openness, and cosmopolitanism without requiring them to have deep knowledge and understanding of the culture of the marginalized.[33] In fact, ethnic food consumption by members of the dominant group does not ameliorate racial or ethnic tension. Rather, it can create further difference and distance.[34] Some Korean Americans feel that "their space" is invaded. Sara, a twenty-three-year-old NYU graduate who works in marketing, is ambivalent about the presence of non-Koreans, which she connects to racial issues:

> I think if I see a group of people, honestly, and it's like a mixed group of Koreans and white people and whatever, then I'm like, oh, that looks really nice, they're just having a good time all together trying Korean food. But if it's just a group of [non-Koreans, particularly white] . . . I'm like, oh, that's kind of weird. . . . Not in a restaurant, but for instance, at a club drinking, then I find it off because I know that their motive is . . . it's like an Asian fetish and that really turns me off and that's not cool. . . . Yeah, so I'm very turned off by that.

Sara's interpretation of Koreatown is rooted in how she understands the US racial hierarchy. In most cases, Sara is happy to see her ethnic culture became widespread and recognized by New Yorkers, but as a racially politicized woman of color, Sara distrusts the presence of non-Asians in Koreatown. It is noteworthy that Sara invokes the "Asian fetish," the Western exotification, objectification, hypersexualization, and infantilization of Asian women's bodies.[35] Sara's understanding of white males at Koreatown's bars reflects the frequent danger Asian women face from Orientalism in the Western gaze. For Sara, it might be partially an illusion of a strong belief in multicultural New York, as diversity is often mystified in the realm of consumerism, such as by eating in ethnic restaurants or purchasing ethnic products.[36]

Interestingly enough, while talking to thirty-four Korean nationals during my fieldwork, only a few people recognized or mentioned racial issues in the United States. And those who did acknowledge racial issues did not bring them up when explaining their thoughts and relationships to Koreatown. It may be because they are temporary residents, many of whom plan to return to Korea after finishing school. Or, simply, they have never developed any racial identity in Korea. In fact, a strong belief in racial and ethnic homogeneity as one nation[37]—the increasing number of biracial Koreans and migrant workers and their children notwithstanding—hinders them from recognizing and understanding racial dynamics both in Korea and in the United States, often rendering them colorblind. Rather, the presence of non-Koreans, particularly white people, is a way of confirming their nation's well-being or upward mobility in the global economy. When Kyujin, a thirty-two-year-old graduate student in Massachusetts, says he "felt proud that Koreatown was doing okay," he is projecting Koreatown as an imagined property where the nation and its culture should be given due recognition by non-Korean Others.

If Sara is right, how do we locate these non-Asian consumers, particularly white foodies, on the Koreatown map? Ethnic restaurants offer foodies opportunities to practice and reinforce their status and sociocultural distinction and represent microspaces or ethnosites for intercultural contact with immigrants,[38] where "the foreign become familiar,"[39] while dining out. Are they democratic cultural omnivores who try to extend their scopes to other cultures or agents of culinary cultural capital?[40] Or are they colonial adventurers or culinary colonizers who perpetuate the legacy of empire and exoticize and exploit "Otherness" in the era of neoliberalism,[41] while now embracing a cuisine that was considered to be "abnormal" in the past because it makes them seem more interesting or reinforces conspicuous cosmopolitan?[42] Yet, do these individuals with "a superficial knowledge of the Other's culture" understand the marginalization of the foods of the ethnic others and their struggles when race and ethnicity become commercialized in the marketplace?[43] Is it a fantasy of cosmopolitanism, where "we" belong everywhere?[44]

Koreatown consumers are very diverse in terms of economic status as well as racial and ethnic backgrounds. As discussed in chapter 5, most consumers in Koreatown prior to 2010 were Asians or Asian Americans who shared cultural similarities, along with a small number of individuals who were particularly interested in Korean pop culture. Since then, the consumer base has expanded to non-Asians—mostly K-pop fans (particularly since the pandemic) and foodies. During my interviews, these K-pop fans emphasized that the K-pop community, whether virtual or physical, is friendly to both racial and sexual minorities. A few openly came out to me in interviews, but I did not ask specific gender- or sexuality-related questions unless they voluntarily started talking about it. If non-Korean consumers are racially diverse, how do these minorities perceive and negotiate the "authenticity" of the food and the physical space of Koreatown? I pay particular attention to how these K-pop fans of color who regularly dine and hang out in Koreatown reshape its authenticity, interestingly both responding to and reinforcing their own racial and ethnic identity formation.

Cultural Omnivore or Neocolonial Adventurer?

On a Saturday afternoon in the early-2010s, I was waiting for Pablo, a twenty-one-year-old Mexican American, in front of the Graduate Center on 34th Street and Fifth Avenue in Manhattan, located just two blocks from Koreatown. We met in front of the school, and I suggested that we go into the building to talk since Koreatown would be very crowded, given that it was Saturday afternoon. I had first met Pablo a few years prior, when I started teaching a Korean class at a local community college. He took two classes with me for two consecutive semesters. After I left the position, I emailed my former students to find out if they were willing to participate in my research. Pablo was one of the students who wanted to talk to me about their relationships with Korean culture and Koreatown.

While talking to Pablo, I learned that his father worked for Koreans "in the ghettos of Brooklyn" and "was bad-mouthing about Koreans" because of the working conditions and mistreatment that he received from his employers. However, unlike his father, Pablo seems to have different opinions about Koreans and Korean culture. While he did not have any significant friendships with Koreans, and most of his friends were Latino, he said that he "had to unfortunately break those ties with those Latino peers" and "felt that was a sacrifice." Now he even goes to a Korean church, where he is the only Latino, and has been associated with them about a year and a half.

As discussed earlier, many non-Koreans show their affinity toward Korean culture, Korean food, and Koreatown by juxtaposing Korean culture with their own ethnic culture, while actively searching for similarities between the two. They often express frustration about their own culture, just like many ethnic Koreans do with Korean culture, and feel that they do not entirely fit into their own culture. However, Pablo's expressions about breaking ties and sacrifice sounded extreme to me. Pablo told me he "always felt like an outcast [in Mexican and Latinx communities]" because he is not a stereotypical Mexican who "hangs out, out of school, more like, could be gang-related, gang violence."

However, his understanding of Korean culture and frustration with his own ethnic culture are mainly based on racial stereotypes. He denies being part of his ethnic group because of negative stereotypes of Latinx people like involvement in gang violence. But at the same time, he romanticizes and fetishizes Asian women as ideal partners—a stereotype he shares with many white males. In line with this, Koreatown is more than a place where he can "learn and eat something different rather than just eat what I already know"—it's a place where he can find pretty girls. In fact, during the interview, he talked about Korean girls a lot, making me somewhat uncomfortable. He described two Korean women he got to know in high school—a teacher and a peer—as "pretty," and he thought that one of the girls, the peer, "really had an impact" on him. "It's more of an attraction, I just can't explain it. I feel like I just wanted to chase her but she never really knew me. Because of that, I felt that I am here now, that I have this kind of connection with Korean people," he said.

The conversation that I had with Pablo lingered with me for a while. He might be an extreme case. However, during my fieldwork and even as a language teacher at two nonprofit organizations and a community college in New York City, I was often confused by non-Koreans' unconditional love of and enthusiasm for Korean culture and did not often know how to respond. I often asked myself if it was simply cultural interest or fetishism. Or were some of these Korean culture enthusiasts

Koreaboos?⁴⁵ Should I analyze what I heard from Pablo as being in line with Sara's experiences of white men gazing at Asian women with desire at Koreatown bars? Did Pablo's double identity crisis push him to try to connect to an alternate community, in his case, the Korean community? Would the Korean community, whether Korean nationals or Korean Americans, allow him to claim Korean identity or Korean culture as an outsider? Does he belong here? In other words, who has the rights to claim belonging and authenticity in Koreatown?

Conclusion

See You in Koreatown

A trip, a fantasy voyage.
—Michael Sorkin on Disneyland in 1992, *Variations on a Theme Park*

NYC's K-town isn't what it used to be. . . . Many mom-and-pop business have closed, replaced by restaurants backed or run by *chaebol*, aka "rich class."
—Sam Kim, "NYC's K-Town Isn't What It Used to Be," *Eater*, July 31, 2018

On the *Lee Seo-jin's New York, New York* segment of *Friday Friday Night*, a TV show on the tvN channel in Korea, a well-known Korean actor named Seo-jin Lee recalls his memories from living in New York as a college student at NYU's Stern School of Business in the late 1980s and early '90s. As a middle-aged actor born in the early 1970s, Lee achieved fame as a film and television actor in the late 1990s and early 2000s. However, he has revived his career in recent years through featuring in a series of different variety shows. In his *New York, New York* segment on *Friday Friday Night*, which consisted of ten episodes and aired from January to March 2020, Lee traveled to New York City to revisit some of his old haunts and to observe changes that had occurred since he lived there. He humorously referred to himself as an "Old Yorker" on the show (as opposed to "New" Yorker). In episode 9, "Searching for Hallyu in New York City,"[1] Lee and Young-seok Na—a well-known TV producer as well as producer of his show—visit 32nd Street to relive his memories. Lee appears shocked by the way Koreatown had changed in the intervening three decades.

When they went to dinner at Gammeeok, the oldest restaurant in Koreatown (as of 2020) and the only remaining Korean eating establishment from Lee's New York era, Lee shared how Korean students enjoyed nightlife in his day. He remembers how many young people who missed Korea would gather at the Korean night club New York King, which was only open on weekends, and would party until 2 a.m. They'd then move on to one of the noraebang on 32nd Street for another few hours and round out the night—in the very early morning—with food at Gammeeok, since it was open twenty-four hours.[2] New York King has long since shuttered, and Koryo Video, which he frequented to rent Korean videos, closed many years ago. Even the menu at Gammeeok is different than it used to be. "His time has stood still," the producer Na says, but the space, once full of Korean students and immigrants, has changed. Today Koreatown appears to be the epitome of Hallyu: Some prominent businesses there as of 2024 include Tous Les Jours, the popular Korean bakery chain; bb.q Chicken, a Korean fried chicken franchise that is ubiquitous in Korea as well as Korean business districts in the United States; and Koryo Bookstore, which actually sells more Hallyu-related products than books.

Since the beginning of the twentieth century, ethnic enclaves and ghettos in the United States have most often been described as segregated spaces, providing jobs and accommodations for minority group members and newly arrived immigrants. At the same time, established ethnic enclaves such as Chinatowns, barrios, or Little Italys, despite racial prejudice and discrimination against its members, have lured tourists and local residents in search of new and authentic cultural experiences, from food to entertainment. Ethnic cultures in segregated ethnic enclaves or ghettos in general have been perceived as poor but exotic by the mainstream.

A century later, the landscape of ethnic enclaves has shifted. This book shows how new ethnic enclaves, which I call transclaves, are shaped by transnational flows of capital, people, culture, public policies, and economic investments. By using Manhattan's Koreatown as a case study, this book investigates how this new type of ethnic enclave is located within the contexts of larger economic, institutional, and cultural transformations in these transnational flows between two societies. These dynamics in media, tourism, and economy are shifting in Koreatown faster than ever within the past decade. Koreatown in Manhattan, once overshadowed by the nearby Empire State Building, seems to be finally recognized by tourists and locals alike. The space is no longer a hidden gem that only a few people are aware of. This recognition has transformed Koreatown's landscape. This book, thus, asks how consumers—as transnational actors, in many ways—create and recreate the landscape in return, emphasizing both top-down policies and economic strategies and bottom-up participation of consumers who (re)negotiate Koreatown's urban landscape as a transclave.

A Transclave: An Ethnic Enclave for a Global Market

By critically reviewing Manhattan's Koreatown beyond the traditional ethnic enclave model centered on the ethnic economy and ethnic enclave economy debates in the 1980s and '90s, this book brought new relevance to the topic. Although ethnic enclaves were once an important topic, especially among Chicago sociologists in the first half of the twentieth century, the traditional discourse has fallen out of interest with sociologists in the past three decades. Instead, cultural geographers and urban studies scholars, particularly in European, Canadian, Australian, and, relatively less so, US contexts, have focused on and developed the topic by emphasizing new trends in the global economy. I call for sociologists of various fields, such as urban sociology, immigration, culture, and political economy, to analyze this new global urban change.

Unlike previous perspectives on the ethnic enclave economy that saw it as a space of work or residence heavily relying on a coethnic labor force, the transclave is a hypercommercialized space for leisure and entertainment, not daily living. A transclave is much more ethnically and racially diverse, not limited within coethnic boundaries; its ethnically themed leisure, consumption, and entertainment opportunities are open not only to coethnics, but also to non-coethnic consumers, in what Jerome Krase and Jan Lin call an "ethnic theme park."[3] In transclaves, both transnational corporations and local entities from the sending country, as well as local entrepreneurs and the government in the host country, are actively seeking non-coethnic consumers. They aim to maximize economic profit not only within the enclave but also by promoting the nation and the city as a diverse and multiethnic tourist destination. This understanding of Koreatown as a transclave extends sociological analysis on ethnic enclaves by highlighting the economy based on consumption, leisure, and entertainment opportunities in a global city.

Nation Branding in Sociology

By locating Koreatown within discussions on new ethnic enclaves across the globe, my book introduces discussions of transnational investments by diverse parties ranging from sending states, such as the Korean government and corporations, in order to attract international investors through positive images of the country. Although this strategy does not guarantee instant profits, nation branding draws potential profits through new economic opportunities in tourism, consumption, and cultural content. In this way, the term nation branding (or place branding), originally developed in the fields of marketing, communication, and international relations, needs to be brought to the field of sociology by analyzing the economic and cultural transformation of Korea as a case study.

Investment in nation branding is common, as seen in various case studies since the late 1990s, but investment in a particular space overseas is underresearched. By examining Korea's nation branding project, which has targeted international markets through economic and cultural policies and investments—particularly K-pop and food—I suggest a new research topic for scholarly sociological attention. Rather than analyzing Koreatown as a unique space, this book has tried to locate the space as a case study within wider global trends developed by various nations. For example, the Thai government has devised the Thai Select program to promote the nation's culinary culture overseas.[4] The Department of Export Promotion in Thailand grants certification to Thai restaurants across the globe that offer at least 60 percent "authentic" Thai food on their menus and employ traditional Thai cooking methods developed in Thailand. Yet in New York, investment is not limited to an ethnic enclave but occurs citywide. In fact, although many Thai restaurants are located in the Woodside and Jackson Heights neighborhoods in Queens, the investment is spread widely given the popularity of Thai food across the city.

Likewise, the French government has engaged in promoting French cuisine worldwide. On January 21, 2015, the celebrated chef Alain Ducasse and the Ministry of Foreign Affairs and International Development in France launched the project "Goût de France/Good France," seeking to serve a "French dinner" to the public worldwide. Laurent Fabius, the foreign minister of France, said at the presentation, "The Gastronomic meal of the French has been on the UNESCO World Heritage list since 2010, but it is a heritage that should not simply be contemplated, glorified and savoured; it is a heritage that should be built upon and showcased."[5] Two months later, sixty French embassies and 1,500 restaurants in 160 countries offered 1,500 dinners to the public to celebrate French gastronomy and promote tourism. This annual event was organized by the French Ministry for Europe and Foreign Affairs, partnered with the Collège Culinaire de France.[6] Like the Korean and Thai governments, the French government understands that the nation's culture should not be just celebrated, but promoted, branded, and marketed to encourage maximum revenue.

Home-country governments sometimes work closely with coethnic businesspeople involved in culinary culture in immigrant-receiving countries. This is also evident in the cases of the Goût de France/Good France project's collaboration with local entrepreneurs regarding French cuisine across the globe. This trend is also seen in ethnic enclaves. In some cases, these locals who have already constructed their own community in an ethnic enclave work closely with the sending country's government agencies to promote its nation. In Sydney, local Thai entrepreneurs, the Thai consulate, and the Sydney City Council cooperate to separate Thai Town on Campbell Street from Chinatown, as part of an effort to highlight and thus more effectively market their ethnic culture to locals and tourists.[7] The globalization of Korean food projects explicitly show such transnational public-private partnership, though it does not always work as it is anticipated, creating conflicts between the sending country's government agencies and diasporic entrepreneurs. These examples show that the Korean government's involvement in international projects related to Korean food and investments in Koreatown is not a singular case but rather part of a generalized global trend. This book, thus, opens the door to more sociological research on this topic.

Questions About Koreatown's Authenticity

As Arjun Appadurai argues, in this "ethnoscape," "the homeland is partly invented, existing in the imagination of the deterritorialized group and it can sometimes become so fantastic."[8] The authenticity of enclaves is reinforced by the collective memories and struggles that the specific racial and ethnic minority group shares in urban America, while others insist on their rights to claim its authenticity without understanding its history. In this process, Koreatown is likewise reimagined and reinvented as a space in which to "feel at home" or to have "nostalgia without memory,"[9] while others romanticize a past that they have never experienced and reconstruct the space where "ethnicity becomes spice, seasoning that can liven up the dull dish that is mainstream white culture."[10]

However, among my more than 130 interviewees, only a few recognize that their authentic experience is believed to be real in the marketplace. Adam, a twenty-two-year-old master's student, was born in the United States but was raised in Seoul and England, and came back to the United States for college to study political science at New York University. In his eyes, some fellow Korean Americans believe that visiting Koreatown is one of the vehicles in which they engage in cultural practice. As he puts it, "For them, it's more like engaging in something actively as something they want to like build up . . . Yea in 'their' identity." Adam takes issue with establishing one's own identity in a commercial space, and he tends to distance himself from other Korean Americans. Adam believes that establishing one's own identity in the marketplace might be an illusion. He believes that consuming Korean pop and consumer culture only reflects pseudo-ethnic or convenient, portable, intermittent, and symbolic consumer desire.[11] His perspective is colored by his belief that he knows "the culture" because he grew up in Korea and the rest of his family, including his parents, reside in Korea. Yet, according to Adam, those Korean Americans and non-Koreans who lack strong transnational ties to Korea—through family or root—may be deluded by the marketplace into believing in their experience of ethnic authenticity, though their cultural experience may be inauthentic.

This book, thus, asked questions about what authentic Korean culture is and who has the right to claim Koreatown's authenticity. Like Adam, many Korean nationals often confirm that "we," that is, Korean nationals, define authentic Korean culture—most notably in contrast to Korean immigrants and their children, who cannot claim firsthand understanding of the nation's culture and tastes. "Authenticity" is, therefore, one of the most frequently encountered terms when Korean nationals describe Korean culture, particularly food. Although Korean food in New York is marketed as and believed by Korean Americans and non-Korean New Yorkers to be "authentic Korean food," Korean nationals believe that authentic Korean food is distorted by Korean immigrants and their children.

The conflict over "authenticity" between Korean nationals and Koreatown entrepreneurs, or between Korean nationals and Korean Americans, leads to other questions. There are many racial concerns arising from the presence of non-Korean consumers in what might be considered a space exclusive to Korean nationals and Korean Americans. People of color—particularly Black customers—can feel uncomfortable, sometimes getting what they called "weird looks." Many Black interviewees that I spoke with during my follow-up research shared their own experiences with being othered in Koreatown, while simultaneously acknowledging that the space is changing. Taylor, a twenty-five-year-old Black American, shared that she and her friends had problems at times with some Korean American friends, who sometimes excluded non-Koreans by speaking Korean. "Like most Americans, [they] make you feel weird about liking [Korean culture]. Like constantly reminding you that you're not Korean," she explains. In this case, Koreatown has become a battlefield for claiming cultural authenticity not only between Korean nationals and Korean Americans, but also between ethnic Koreans and non-Koreans.

During my follow-up research, my interviewees spoke of anti-Blackness, colorism, and racism in Korean popular culture and media. Jessica, a Black American, said during our second interview in 2018 that she feels that "[Koreans are] a little bit less surprised when they see people of color walking through" than a few years ago when she first started hanging out in Koreatown. For people of color who consume various aspects of Korean culture, particularly Black and Latinx fans, these experiences are not a fantasy—their excursions in Koreatown are on one hand a fantasy voyage,[12] but they are, on the other, also an encounter with the reality of Korean community or a microcosm of Korean society, colored by racism, and repackaged for consumption in New York's Korean transclave.

The transclave's authenticity currently seems to be defined and claimed by ethnic Koreans and their culture (as it currently exists in the homeland), while its urban identity and authenticity are reconstructed and reinforced by global market forces and reterritorialized in the marketplace through various consumer activities. In such a global marketplace, the promise of authenticity—what is believed to be authentic, genuine, or real—can often be spurious and superficial. The expectations of belonging—whether they are tied to transclave or, on a larger scale, to nation—and notions of national identity across borders can be contingent and conditional in the neoliberal orders, where profits take precedence over anything else.

However, given these neoliberal developments over time, did Koreatown simply lose its soul? In this book, I paid attention to bottom-up engagement among three consumer groups: Korean nationals, Korean Americans, and non-Koreans. Through (re)constructions of Koreatown as a transclave, within new global orders, starting with the global pressure on nation branding strategies after the financial crisis since the 1990s, I also observed active and powerful individual voices and ideas about the authenticity map of Koreatown both in the past and present. Manhattan's Koreatown once offered business opportunities for Jewish merchants, while many Jewish, Italian, and Irish women provided cheap labor for garment factories. The space was once a symbol of urban struggle where poor New Yorkers without homes were able to find temporary shelter and comfort at the welfare hotel in the 1970s and '80s. Indeed, the space has historically been important for marginalized groups such as women, immigrants, and racial minorities, who have made the space more diverse and vibrant.

Rather than simply viewing these individuals as passive recipients of market forces and government policies — both transnationally and domestically— I believe they are active participants who recreate and reconstruct Koreatown's authenticity through their collective histories in the United States, albeit slowly. In addition, they actively negotiate their identities with transnational flows of people, money, politics, and ideas. Some decode and deconstruct the market's deceptive power over consumers, thereby understanding and locating Korean food and Koreatown within the US racial system and critically decoding and decontextualizing the Western gaze toward "the Other." Their voices are often overlooked and disregarded when we only focus on the larger global flows. However, I believe that rather than being entirely eclipsed in the marketplace, these individuals—with their active and sometimes oppositional voices—are surely a part of the ongoing authentication of Koreatown in the Big Apple.

ACKNOWLEDGMENTS

Since the first day I arrived in New York City with my immigration bags in August 2007, my life has evolved with endless help from the countless individuals I have encountered. I am indebted to many people in both the United States, particularly in New York City, and South Korea who have helped me in this long journey.

Most apparently, I am indebted to my 135 research participants, many of whom are my former Korean class students at a local community college and at nonprofit organizations. Though I, a CUNY graduate student, had limited financial means and resources for my project, I was fortunate enough to meet and spend one to two hours with participants—without financial compensation—discussing Korean culture, Koreatown, racial and ethnic identity, discrimination, food, and many other topics. Some of the questions touched on sensitive topics, but many of you were willing to share your thoughts, opinions, and feelings with me. Thank you so much. I strongly believe that this book is an outcome of our collaborations.

My deepest gratitude goes to my wonderfully supportive academic advisor and mentor, Sharon Zukin. This book began to grow in her urban sociology seminar early on in my career as a PhD student and was developed into a manuscript. While completing this book, I feel fortunate enough to have had Sharon as my advisor in my early academic career. Writing is a lonely process, and I wrote my entire first draft in my second language. However, Sharon challenged me to push beyond my boundaries, patiently and thoroughly read my manuscript, and offered me constructive feedback. More importantly, Sharon, a great writer herself, taught me how to write a book. Who would have an advisor who planned ahead of time about your soon-to-be-monograph? The writing group with her other advisees who later became my writing comrades—Aneta Kostrzewa, Jacob Lederman, and Fang Xu—was also something unforgettable. Thank you for reading my chapters and offering constructive feedback throughout almost two years! I also thank my other mentors, Richard Alba, Philp Kasinitz, and Margaret Chin, for advising me how to turn my early draft, full of academic jargon, into a monograph with more real people's stories. While completing the final revisions, I received sad news: Richard passed away in the summer of 2025. As I mourn his passing, I remember and deeply appreciate his dedication to his students—including me.

During my time in graduate school, I was fortunate to make friends in the Department of Sociology who tossed back beers with me at Irish pubs on 35th Street (near the Graduate Center) and ranted with me when I was stuck in writing or stressed by teaching obligations. While juggling many obligations as a graduate student and college instructor, we were able to develop our own sense of community. First, I would like to share my gratitude with four wonderful women sociologists from the Department of Sociology who supported me at every stage of my progress—Bernadette Ludwig, Elizabeth Miller, Jennifer Sloan, and Jessica Sperling Smokoski (in alphabetical order). These friends were there for me whenever I felt lost, discouraged, and depressed about my progress and future while working on my PhD. I still have a beer glass with the message you had inscribed—"Dr. Jinwon Kim, Ph.D."—on my desk. This glass has survived five moves. I should not forget to thank Colleen Eren, who helped and mentored me postgraduation. Colleen, thank you so much for listening to my drama, empathizing with me, and stepping in to go through one of the darkest times of my life as an international faculty member in my previous institution. I believe that my achievement in recent years is indebted to your energy and kindness.

I also wanted to thank my friends, mentors, and colleagues at the Graduate Center who provided support for me as a fellow foreign Asian woman in American academia. Thank you Hosu Kim, Yeong Ran Kim (you are an honorary member!), Meebae Lee, Jung Joon Lee, Hyewon Shin, and Sung Hee Yook. Despite our differences in disciplines, I feel fortunate to have found people—most of whom are now tenured professors in the United States and Korea—who could play the role of "peer mentor" as I navigated the emotional and bureaucratic complexity of higher education in the United States from my early career as a graduate student.

I also wanted to share my gratitude with Jaeeun Kim, Soo Mee Kim, Minjeong Kim, and Myungji Yang outside of CUNY—all fellow sociologists—who have emotionally and practically supported and assisted me in going through the hardest challenges that I encountered in the past few years. Jaeeun, thank you so much for spending numerous times speaking and ranting with me over beers both in New York and in Seoul, over Zoom, or anywhere we meet. Minjeong and Myungji—thank you for offering advice when I did not know how to deal with endless systemic hurdles at work and encouraging me to find an alternative option. Soo Mee, I will not forget the many hours we talked about Asian Americans, Korean Americans, and, of course, K-towns— and coedited a volume! Additionally, to my friends whom I became friends with in college and graduate school in Korea and through the grassroots organization in New York—Young Choi, Minkyung Han, Insoon Heo, Minwoo Jung, Jaehyung Kim, Seonhee Kim, Sunmin Kim, Naeyun Lee, Joohee Nam, Joonwoo Son, Jungsoon Son, Injoo Whang, Hyo Kyung Woo, Sejung Yim, and Jin-mi Yoo, among many others.

While completing this book, I was affiliated with five different institutions. I was fortunate to start my full-time career as a visiting assistant professor at Oberlin College. There, in addition to my department colleagues (special thanks to Daphne John and Greggor Mattson), I had the opportunity to connect with the amazing Koreatown researcher Shelley Lee (through Rick Baldoz), a wonderful editor of an edited volume to which I contributed. Shelley later provided invaluable support during my search for another professional opportunity. I'm so glad we're now close to each other in New England! While working at the two following institutions—Hobart and William Smith Colleges and Hamilton College—I also grew as a teacher and scholar. Working at three institutions on one-year contracts and relocating from one city to another was not easy, but now I find myself thinking about the people I regularly communicated with there.

At CUNY, I was able to meet with diverse groups of CUNY colleagues and friends, who also helped me complete this book project. The Gittell Public Scholar Book Writing Workshop, organized by Heath Brown and Celina Su, offered me opportunities to connect with three amazing scholars in the field of Asian American studies—Angie Y. Chung, Edward Park, and Kyeyoung Park. During the workshop, these three reviewers and mentors, two organizers, and I were in different time zones: Kyeyoung and Edward on PST, Angie, Heath, and Celina on EST, and myself on KST (Korea Standard Time). Though the workshop lasted for over five hours, I never felt disengaged. The three reviewers dedicated themselves to reading and thinking about my manuscript and offering sharp and constructive feedback. Though I stayed up all night, due to the time difference, I was so excited for all the comments and feedback that they offered. I appreciate their time and energy. At New York City College of Technology CUNY, as a tenure-track faculty member, I received substantial support from colleagues within my department (special thanks to Kyle Cuordileone, Randall Hannum, Diana Mincyte, Laureen Park, Peter Parides, and Eric Rodriguez) as well as from those outside it (Soyeon Cho and Euisuk Sung). Thank you all for your heartwarming messages and unwavering support over the past five years, even when I decided to move forward with a new job.

Now I am fortunate to call Smith College my new academic home. The 2023–2024 and 2024–2025 academic years were memorable in many ways in my academic career, and my transition—while completing this book—to the Department of Sociology at Smith College is the most unforgettable moment. I remember academically inspiring and insightful conversations that I had with (then-potential) department colleagues at Smith during my campus visit. Of course, I won't forget the heartwarming moment during my interview when I saw many bright-eyed women and women-identified students. From day one, I wanted to have this job so badly, and I was thrilled to continue my career at Smith a few months later. I am very excited for many more years to come with all of you: Payal Banerjee, Erica Banks, Ginetta Candelario, Leslie King, Timothy Recuber, Nancy Whittier, and Tina Wildhagen—as well as Crystal Fleming (I didn't forget you)! I am also reflecting on colleagues and friends beyond my department and college with whom I have regularly communicated in New England: Irhe Sohn, Chanhee Cho, and Colin MacCormack, as well as colleagues in the Five College Asian/Pacific/American Studies Program. Thank you for your continued support and allyship. I deeply appreciate you for listening to my joys and frustrations—and at times, my rants— over coffee and, of course, beer, as I worked through my experiences and moments of feeling lost.

Throughout the years, I have been invited to present my work at various institutions and conferences as well as workshops. I was invited to present my work at the Korea Society in New York City in 2020, University of Pennsylvania's Korean Studies Colloquium in 2020, American Studies Association of Korea in 2022, Columbia University's Korean Studies Seminar in 2023 (Jenny Wang Medina, thank you for inviting me to be part of this seminar), UCLA's Asian American Studies Center in 2024, and the Politics of Immigration class at Dartmouth College in 2025. Furthermore, the earliest draft of this book was workshopped at the Social Science Research Council's Korean Studies Workshop. Thank you to the organizers, discussants, and audience for offering me constructive feedback.

This project has been funded by grants and fellowships. The follow-up research that I conducted in Seoul and New York City was financially supported by the Powers Grant by Oberlin College in 2016, while the PSC CUNY research grant (Cycle 51, 63067-00 51) supported my book manuscript revision process. This publication was supported by the 2024 Korean Studies Grant Program of the Academy of Korean Studies (AKS-2024-P-016).

I also wanted to show my gratitude toward NYU Press's executive editor and assistant editor in chief, Ilene Kalish, and the Asian American Sociology series editor, Dr. Anthony Christian Ocampo, for encouraging me, supporting my project, and offering advice at every step of this process. Ilene, a brief conversation that I had a few years ago at the conference motivated me to continue this work. I am thrilled to work with you and publish my work at NYU Press. I would also like to express my gratitude to the anonymous reviewers, whose feedback has helped me to further refine my book manuscript. In addition, throughout each writing stage, three people helped me read and copyedit my drafts. Rebekka Gold, Elizabeth Miller, and Thomas Chung—you have saved my life many times!

And last but not the least, many thanks go to my parents—Myongsoo Kim and Myoungsook Park—my younger brother, Yongnam Kim, and my late grandmother. While away from home for the past eighteen years, Mom and Dad, you were always there regardless of how my work was going. Thank you so much for believing in me whether I make any kind of decisions. Yongnam, thank you for taking care of our parents when I am thousands of miles away from home. Though I am shy to share my gratitude, I always appreciate your sacrifice for the family. My grandmother, who migrated from the North to the South during the Korean War, passed away while I was completing graduate school in New York. She was in South Korea without her family, and her husband, my grandfather, had passed away in the late 1980s. I still feel very guilty because I could not be with her during her last days. However, her passing made me reflect on her life and my family history within the context of Korean history and geopolitics in a way I had never considered before, and my mourning became rooted in memories of the food she fed me when I was very young. Little did I know that my grandmother's death would provide such an emotional connection to my current and future research on Korean diaspora in the context of East Asian geopolitics. As a scholar, I believe that it will be a way in which I can carry my grandparents' legacy. I, thus, dedicate this book to my family back home.

APPENDIX

Methodological Notes

MY IDENTITY: RACE, ETHNICITY, AND NATIONALITY

On August 7, 2007, I arrived at John F. Kennedy Airport from Korea. I was met by a friend of mine whom I went to graduate school with in Seoul, and we headed to my temporary accommodations in Queens—what Koreans refer to as a minbakjip, which was like a Korean version of AirBnb back then. This particular guest house was owned by a Korean woman in her sixties or seventies who had immigrated to the United States in the 1970s or the '80s. As soon as I put down my two giant rolling bags (called "immigration bags" among Koreans), my friend, who had arrived in New York a year earlier, took me to Manhattan's K-town. It was in many ways a typical Korean moving day. I opened a cell phone account at a Korean-owned cell phone store, despite not having a permanent address. We ate Chinese noodles at Korean Chinese restaurant (Koreans in Korea commonly have Korean-style Chinese food delivered to their new house or apartment on moving day). Four years earlier, I had lived in a small town in the UK for one year, but New York was so different. In the UK, I had been occasionally warned by other Koreans that I should avoid cooking and eating Korean food because of the unique and pungent smell of this "exotic" ethnic cuisine. Yet, the existence of Koreatown itself was a new experience for me. I was never able to travel to London's Koreatown in New Malden, and I was surprised to see Korean stores with their mix of Korean and English languages. It felt like I was in Seoul—only a very outdated version of it, possibly Seoul in the 1980s, which I only vaguely remembered from my early childhood.

My book project (the one you are reading now) unofficially began that day. I still remember that my friend told me "You will come back soon and spend much time here," while showing me around several Koreatown stores. In turn, during the past eighteen years, I have brought many visiting or newly arrived Korean friends to Koreatown, introducing them to various stores. I sometimes bought treats from Korean bakeries to share with my American friends, while I took others for lunch or dinner there to show my appreciation for favors. I had a dissertation defense party in Koreatown with my advisor and some of her other students—my writing comrades—who had worked with me in a reading group during my early draft writing years. I had a farewell party with my Korean colleagues at CUNY when I was transitioning my position from CUNY to Smith College in 2024. Whether I like this space or not, I still have memories with it.

More importantly, I developed my own relationship to the space, as a cultural place for consumption and entertainment, a place for Korean classes, and, most importantly, a research site. I developed a love-hate relationship with it, and, as my friend had predicted, I ultimately spent a lot of time there, not only because it is only two blocks away from the Graduate Center, where I did my PhD, but also because it reflects my hometown, Seoul, albeit in different ways. As I talked to my Korean consumer interviewees, I learned that my story is part of a larger collective history of our culture. Whether we see what is behind the physical landscape, or believe that we belong here, we all share our past with the space.

My academic interest in Koreatown naturally developed over time. I came to think that the space was interesting enough for a class project in an urban research seminar taught by Professor Sharon Zukin during my second semester at the Graduate Center in 2008. Although I began to read the history of Korean immigration and Koreatown, my observations were limited to the experiences of my fellow so-called FOBs (Fresh off the Boat, a derogatory term for newly arrived immigrants), as consumers, and immigrant entrepreneurs as producers. I strongly believed back then that most consumers in Manhattan's Koreatown were temporary residents, like Korean international students, and Korean staff members at New York or New Jersey branches of Korean corporations.

Coincidentally, an opportunity presented itself in March 2008 while I was working on this project. A friend suggested that I teach Korean classes for her Korean American grassroots organization. The other teachers were enthusiastic about Korean language education and actively engaged in political movements to varying degrees. They believed in the importance of bridging the generational gaps in the Korean community and (re)connecting Korean Americans to their homeland. The Korean classes took place in a small room in Midtown Manhattan, very close to Koreatown. I ended up teaching an intermediate Korean class. Most of my students were second-generation Korean Americans in their 20s and 30s, Korean adoptees, and a smattering of non-Koreans. They wanted to (re)connect to Korea for various reasons. For second-generation Korean Americans, most wanted to learn the language and culture, but hadn't been given much opportunity growing up. They talked about Korean pop culture and food a lot and wanted to be able to communicate with their parents and relatives.

At the same time, I was participating in the organization's meetings, extending my experience and understanding beyond the classroom. The members were progressive Korean Americans—many of whom were 1.5- and later-generation Korean Americans—, and a few Korean nationals. In retrospect, I was never interested in race and ethnicity while living in Korea. At the time, I was part of the mainstream in the Korean racial order, strongly mythologized as a homogeneous society. Until the 1990s, I rarely saw foreigners in Seoul, except for some parts of Yongsan, where the US military base was located, or Hannam-dong, where foreign diplomats lived. Yet after the 1997 financial crisis, the Korean government began to recruit foreign workers from a variety of countries for manufacturing jobs. In addition, many Joseonjok (Korean Chinese, ethnic Koreans with Chinese nationality)[1] were specifically recruited to work in low-paying service jobs. Similarly, in the early 2000s, Korea began to import young foreign brides for old bachelors in the countryside. I intentionally use the word "import" because many people treated these women, mostly from Vietnam, the Philippines, and China, just like products or objects. I resented Korean men who commodified these women's bodies, resented the Korean factory owners who abused and exploited migrant workers, and begrudged Korean citizens who saw them as inferior while treating white Americans and Europeans with deference. But I never thought of these behaviors as reflective of me or something I was part of.

Indeed, as a sociology major in college, I was interested in class issues and urban poverty. I was part of a student group called the Urban Poverty

Research Group, which had been involved in the anti-redevelopment and demolition movement in Seoul until the late 1990s and later offered classes for children in public housing in 2000s. I taught there for over three years in the early 2000s and ultimately wrote my master's thesis on the topic. The NYC organization was, therefore, eye-opening for me. Belonging to the dominant mainstream racial group in Korea, I was ignorant of many racial issues. My Korean American friends educated me on racial issues from the eyes of Asians/Asian Americans, and I began to learn terms like white America, white supremacy, foreignness, model minority, postcolonialism, and the Third World Movement. Through this process, I also became aware of and was able to put a name to some of the unpleasant incidents that I encountered because of my race, ethnicity, and gender in various settings.

However, during my fieldwork, Korean Americans were the most challenging group for me to recruit. Born and raised in Korea, I share many cultural memories with Korean nationals, and it was not hard for me to recruit Korean nationals, as they were willing to help me out, even in random situations. Most of these interviews went well. Then, my network was far more limited with Korean Americans, though I participated in a grassroot organization and taught several Korean classes. Despite my intensive teaching experience and personal networks, I ended up talking with thirty Korean American consumers. Furthermore, I asked them more sensitive and longer questions than Korean nationals, including questions about their experience with racial discrimination and violence. Their average interview time was longer—between one hour and 1.5 hours compared with one hour for Korean nationals; the longest interview lasted two hours. In retrospect, these interviews were very difficult for me. I became very emotionally involved while talking to the Korean American interviewees.

I shared my personal experiences with racialization during interviews, particularly with female interviewees, with whom I shared the experience of being racialized and sexualized in this country. I have encountered people who followed me, referred to me as "cute dumpling" or "China doll," and even touched my body on the street. I also have dealt with people who were well-intentioned but very ignorant in their comments. I used these experiences as an opening for interviewees to talk about their own experiences with racial discrimination and microaggressions.

Typically, I used this story: One day, I was trying to figure out which bus I should take at New York's Port Authority Bus Terminal to get to my friends' house in New Jersey. The express and local bus numbers were complicated, so I asked a white man in line if I was waiting for the right bus. He kindly explained the system to me and advised that I talk with the staff upstairs. I said thank you to him, to which he responded—smiling—"say 'excuse me' when you pass people," indicating his assumption that I lacked the knowledge of American social graces. Despite the fact that I spoke with him in English, this did not count in the face of this man's presumption of my automatically lower status as an Asian woman speaking with an accent. This story resonated with my Korean American interviewees, prompting them to share their own experiences. Yet while I was able to establish rapport using shared experiences with the Korean American participants, it would be misguided to say that I fully understood their struggle.

Nationality also played a role in the interviews. Korean nationals did not mind talking about Koreatown negatively, even downright disparagingly. They were straightforward with me, knowing that I was a Korean national and an international student, and perhaps shared their feelings about Korean immigrants and Koreatown. A few were patriotic and nationalistic, expressing confidence in the ascending popularity of Korean culture and food. While I did not necessarily agree with them, I did not share my thoughts, and masked my reactions.

Conversely, many of the Korean Americans were reluctant to share their thoughts and feelings with me about their experiences with Korea and Korean nationals. As a scholar of Asian American studies and a Korean teacher who shared racial status with them and tried to understand US racial politics, Korean American interviewees openly talked about the discrimination and microaggressions they had faced, which enabled me to collect very interesting data. To overcome the nationality barrier, I often began by criticizing aspects of Korean culture that they did not understand; this sometimes worked, but not always. As a researcher, I often felt that I had limitations when it came to these particular questions due to our different nationalities, cultural backgrounds, and the frustrations each group felt with the other, which was discussed in chapter 4. I likely would have had some different responses if I were Korean American myself.

A BOUNDARY: A TEACHER AND STUDENTS

My project expanded through my teaching at CUNY and nonprofit organizations. I only taught at the nonprofit organization through 2009, but thought that it would be beneficial to continue teaching elsewhere, because I hoped to recruit students for in-depth interviews. So I got a part-time teaching position at a community college in New York City, where a Korean language class was being introduced because of the increasing popularity of Korean pop culture, while continuing to teach sociology classes.

The settings in which I taught were very different. My Korean classes at the community college were very formal. Students took classes both out of general interest and for foreign language requirements. I was older than my students, most of whom were in their early 20s, and was called professor or seonsaengnim ("teacher" in Korean). To avoid ethical issues and IRB protocol violation, and to protect my interviewees, I only asked former students to take part in my research after I left the school in 2011; all the interviews with my former students at the community college were conducted in 2012 or later.

The other two organizations at which I taught were quite different. While I had a few high school and college students in my Korean classes, most were in their twenties, thirties, or occasionally older. This allowed me to build friendships with them; some even asked me to meet outside of class for drinks or coffee, which I occasionally accepted, or to hang out with them as a friend. My role as a teacher did not restrict our relationships with one another, and they could approach me as friends. Unlike my sociology classes, I wanted to avoid being overly "teacherly" or nitpicky in my Korean classes. After I stopped teaching at each respective institution, I asked some students if they would be willing to let me interview them.

Although my former students from the community college talked frankly about their thoughts on Korean culture and Korean people, I often had the impression that they were emphasizing positives. I sometimes tried to incorporate sociocultural and political issues into my class, because my students wanted to learn about Korea, not just the language itself. Yet some students did not want to talk about negative aspects of Korea, even later during interviews. Maybe the hierarchy between myself as the instructor and them as students left them feeling unable to criticize my culture. Or they might have developed fantastical images of Korea through media, as I discussed in chapters 5 and 6. Still others may have seen Korea as they wanted it to be and did not want to look at it critically.

Despite the challenges of collecting these interviews, I know that I was fortunate to meet with these individuals and to hear their stories. They did not mind spending an hour or two with me without any compensation. All the interviews that I conducted were voluntary. I clearly stated that there would be no financial remuneration for participating. Nonetheless, as a gesture of appreciation, I gave them small gifts that I brought from Korea and paid for coffee, tea, and desserts that we had during the interviews.

Instead, I made an effort to build rapport. Although I did intensive fieldwork between 2012 and 2016, and follow-up research between 2016 and 2018 and between 2022 and 2024, I had known many of the participants for years through the organizations and Korean classes. Ultimately, I was able to recruit 135 individuals, without any compensation, in New York City and Seoul. This book is, therefore, the result of my collaboration with these 135 volunteers, who shared their experiences, visions and agendas, and feelings with me.

NOTES

INTRODUCTION

1. All names of interviewees are pseudonyms, unless specified. Public figures, speakers at public events, and individuals covered in the media, such as government officials, chefs, and entrepreneurs are identified by their real names.
2. Some parts of the early draft were revised and published in *City & Community, The International Journal of Cultural Policy, A Companion to Korean American Studies,* and *Koreatowns: Exploring the Economics, Politics, and Identities of Korean Spatial Formations.* However, the material has been largely reorganized, revised, and rewritten in this book. Additionally, twenty-seven new interviews conducted from 2016 to 2024 have been added. These new interviews include three follow-up conversations with key non-Korean informants I originally spoke with in 2012. For the purposes of calculating the total number of interviewees, these three individuals were each counted only once.
3. Kugel 2008.
4. Baldwin 2008.
5. Baldwin 2008.
6. Nye 2004; Centeno, Bandelj, and Wherry 2011.
7. New York City Department of City Planning 2019.
8. Cayla and Eckhardt 2008; Aronczyk 2013; White 2022.
9. Aronczyk 2008, 2013.
10. See Portes and Bach 1985; Sanders and Nee 1987, 1992; Zhou and Logan 1989.
11. Chacko 2003; Laguerre 2010; Shaw 2011; Jinwon Kim 2018; Phillips and Baudinette 2022.
12. Johnston and Baumann 2014; Stock and Schmiz 2019.
13. Quote from American Marketing Association in 1960, cited in Fan 2006.
14. Holt 2004; de Chernatony 2008.
15. Holt 2004, 3–4.
16. Hall and Hubbard 1998.
17. Fan 2006; Jojic 2018; Kavaratzis 2004.
18. Greenberg 2009; Aronczyk 2013; Cleave and Arku 2020.
19. Greenberg 2009.
20. Anholt 1998, 2010, 2011; Aronczyk 2013.
21. Anholt 1998, 2010, 2011; O'Shaughnessy and O'Shaughnessy 2000.
22. Gilboa 2008; Jansen 2008.

23　Jansen 2008; Kaneva and Popescu 2011; Li and Feng 2022; White 2022.
24　Nye 2004; Szondi 2008; Gilboa 2008.
25　Szondi 2008.
26　Nye 2004.
27　Melissen 2005; Szondi 2008.
28　Gilboa 2008.
29　Nye 2004.
30　Aronczyk 2008, 2013; Jansen 2008; Cayla and Eckhardt 2008; Kaneva 2011, 2016; Volcic and Andrejevic 2011; Varga 2013; Jordan 2014; White 2022.
31　Kaneva 2011.
32　Jordan 2014; Varga 2013.
33　Gilboa 2008; Jansen 2008; Navarro 2016; Nguyen and Özçaglar-Toulouse 2021; White 2022.
34　Navarro 2016; White 2022.
35　Aronczyk 2008, 2013.
36　Freely 1998; *Wired* 1998; Jansen 2008.
37　McGray 2002.
38　White 2022, 3; Condry 2009.
39　Dogan and Petkovic 2016.
40　Zhang 2015.
41　Chapple-Sokol 2013; Ichijo and Ranta 2016.
42　Goût de France/Good France 2019.
43　Consulate General of France in New York 2015.
44　DeSoucey 2010; G. Han 2015; Kakim and Park 2020; Kim 2022; Zhang 2015.
45　Kaneva 2016, 175; Volcic and Andrejevic 2011.
46　Statista 2025.
47　The SFA is a membership-based nonprofit trade association since 1952 representing over 3,600 businesses.
48　Specialty Food Association, n.d.
49　Italy-America Chamber of Commerce Southeast, n.d.
50　Benvenuta Italia, n.d.; ItalianFOOD.net 2024.
51　Aronczyk 2008, 44.
52　Volcic and Andrejevic 2011.
53　Prahalad and Ramaswamy 2004.
54　Aronczyk 2008, 54.
55　Varga 2013.
56　Ståhlberg and Bolin 2016.
57　Sklair 2000; Aronczyk 2013, 39.
58　Jordan 2014.
59　Robert E. Park and Ernest W. Burgess were pioneers of this perspective. R. Park 1926; Burgess 1967 [1924], 1928.
60　R. Park 1926, 8–9.
61　R. Park 1926, 9.

62 Wirth 1927. This modern ghetto is differentiated from the Jewish ghettos in medieval society, which were originally rooted in the customs and heritages—religious and secular—of Jews themselves and later compelled by law due to anti-Semitism.
63 Wirth 1927.
64 Marcuse 2002, 212.
65 Wirth 1927, 57.
66 Gans 2008; Massey and Denton 1993; Wacquant 2008.
67 Logan, Zhang, and Alba 2002, 301.
68 Gans 2002, 354; Marcuse 1997.
69 Waldinger 1993; Light et al. 1994.
70 Waters and Jiménez 2005; Donato and Bankston 2008; Durand, Massey, and Capoferro 2005; Fennelly 2008; Marrow 2008.
71 Logan, Zhang, and Alba 2002, 300–301.
72 Illsoo Kim 1981; Boswell and Curtis 1984.
73 Bonacich 1973; Modell 1977; Bonacich and Modell 1980.
74 Light 1984, 201–2; Min and Bozorgmehr 2000.
75 Light et al. 1994, 66.
76 Light et al. 1994.
77 Although the Cuban Refugee Program under the John F. Kennedy administration was designed to relocate Cubans throughout the country, the largest number of Cuban refugees were concentrated in Miami by the early 1970s. Economic capital accumulated in high-wage industrial regions and brought from Cuba allowed for the creation of this immigrant enclave, whose businesses included textiles, leather, furniture, cigar making, construction, and finance, as well as service sectors such as restaurants, supermarkets, clinics, and private schools. Based on the analysis of a longitudinal survey of Cuban male refugees in Miami and Hialeah over two periods—initial interviews in 1973–1974 and follow-ups in 1976–1977—Wilson and Portes argue that immigrants are not restricted to the secondary labor market. See Wilson and Portes 1980.
78 Wilson and Portes 1980; Portes and Bach 1985. According to Wilson and Portes (1980), the dual labor market theory does not capture economic activities observed in immigrant enclaves—particularly in the Cuban enclave in Miami, but also in other ones, such as Japanese and Korean enclaves in other areas.
79 Sanders and Nee 1987, 747, 752, 755. The exchange between Portes and his colleagues and Sanders and Nee continued into the 1990s.
80 Portes 1981, 291.
81 Portes and Jensen 1989, 930.
82 Portes and Bach 1985, 204.
83 Portes and Manning 2008 [1987], 52.
84 Portes and Manning 2008 [1987], 52.
85 Sanders and Nee 1987, 1992.
86 Light et al. 1994.
87 Light et al. 1994.

88 Dae Young Kim 1999.
89 Waldinger 1993; Light et al. 1994.
90 Zhou 1992 [2010]; Chacko 2003; Laguerre 2010; Lin 2011; H. Shin 2018.
91 Portes and Jensen 1989; Logan, Alba, and McNulty 1994, 695; Portes and Manning 2008 [1987].
92 Chacko 2003, 25; Laguerre 2010, 15.
93 Gold 2015.
94 Chacko 2003; Laguerre 2010; Lin 2011.
95 Fong 2010 [1994]; Zhou, Tseng, and Kim 2008; W. Li 1998, 2009; Fittante 2018; Phillips 2021; Liu et al. 2022; Harun and Filion 2022.
96 W. Li 1998, 482.
97 Matsumoto 2018.
98 Aytar and Rath 2012; Kim 2018.
99 West 1990. Strongly influenced by Black Nationalism and the Black Power movements, new ethnic movements, such as yellow power and brown power, and identity politics for disenfranchised groups, such as women and the queer community, became visible in the mainstream discourse. See also Crenshaw 1991; Ogbar 2001.
100 Gans 1979; Halter 2007.
101 Waters 1990, 19.
102 Cui 2015 [1998], 88, cited in Pires and Stanton 2002, 113.
103 Historically, marketers in the United States have recognized the market segmentation of diverse consumer groups, e.g., division according to gender, race and ethnicity, religion, class, age, and nationality; they have devised specific strategies to each group with similar needs (Rossman 1994; Smith and Cooper-Martin 1997) by associating brands with a particular consumer group lifestyles, values, or languages (Aaker, Brumbaugh, and Grier 2000). In recent years, this trend has only intensified, reflecting population changes and increasing purchasing power among racial minority groups in the post-1965 era. For example, Asians are currently the fastest growing racial minority group in the United States. The Asian population is projected to reach 35.8 million by 2060. As a relatively young population, with 35.7 years of median age, the Asian American, Native Hawaiian, and Pacific Islander (AANHPI) groups showcase tremendous purchasing power with $1.3 trillion and a median household income of $104,646 as of 2023 (Nielson 2024). Companies thus allocate advertising and marketing to reflect such changes (Mizrahi 2023; Rossman 1994). See also Cui 2015 [1998]; Pires and Stanton 2002; Halter 2007.
104 Zukin 1995.
105 Greinacher 1998; Lin 1998, 2011; Liu 2009.
106 C. Li 2015.
107 Freeman 1987; Conforti 1996.
108 Cummings 1974, cited in Conforti 1996, 834.
109 Fainstein 2005; Greenberg 2009; Jensen 2007.
110 Hoffman 2003; Aytar and Rath 2012; C. Li 2015.

111 Lin 2011.
112 C. Li 2015.
113 Hoffman 2003.
114 Beverland, Farrelly, and Quester 2010; Newman and Smith 2016, 610.
115 Sharpley 1994, 130, cited in Wang 1999, 351.
116 Boorstin 1961; MacCannell 1973; Cohen 1988; Salamone 1997; Silver 1993; Wang 1999; Zukin 2008, 2009; Johnston and Baumann 2014.
117 Anderson 1990.
118 Collins 2006; Ang 2016; Shaw 2011; Pottie-Sherman 2013.
119 Conforti 1996.
120 Becker 2015.
121 Krase 1997, 105.
122 Boorstin 1961; MacCannell 1973.
123 Boorstin 1961; Wang 1999, 352.
124 MacCannell 1973.
125 Boorstin 1961, 99.
126 Zukin 2008, 727.
127 Halter 2007, 9.
128 Jinwon Kim 2018.
129 Laguerre 2010, 20.
130 Hum 2014. Logan and Zhang (2010) also use global neighborhood.
131 Hum 2014, 6.
132 Chacko 2003.
133 Appadurai 1996, 33.
134 Shaw 2011, 383.
135 See Illsoo Kim 1981; Yun 1997.
136 Illsoo Kim 1981; Light and Bonacich 1991; Claire Jean Kim 2003; Jennifer Lee 2002; Abelmann and Lie 2009; Shelley Sang-Hee Lee 2022. Many Korean entrepreneurs opened small businesses in urban Black American communities. However, cultural differences and racialization of Black Americans later caused a series of Black-Korean conflicts, including unrest in Los Angeles and boycotts and protests in New York.
137 Lin 2011.
138 Koo and Yu 1981; Light and Bonacich 1991.
139 Illsoo Kim 1981.
140 Claiborne 1960.
141 Kyou-Jin Lee 2011.
142 Kyou-Jin Lee 2011.
143 New York Gomtang House, the oldest Korean restaurant in Manhattan's Koreatown, opened on 27th Street in 1979, but moved to 32nd Street in 1982. The restaurant closed on November 1, 2013. Hotel Stanford is owned by Joong-Gap Kwon, who also is an owner of H Mart, an Asian grocery chain, operated by the Hanahreum Group. He started a hotel business in 1986 in Manhattan's Koreatown,

and expanded his business to Panama and Chile. He also began to invest in hotel business in Korea and opened the first hotel in Seoul in 2011. Although it does not necessarily represent Koreanness in terms of interiors, it is well-known to Korean visitors as a Korean hotel with a Korean-speaking staff. T. Jung 2011.

144 Kozol 1988; Gray 1987. In the *New York Times*, in "Streetscape: The Hotel Martinique; Grimy Grande Dame Housing The Homeless Off Herald Sq.," Christopher Gray introduced a history of the Martinique from being a fancy hotel surrounded by PATH, Penn Station, and the flagship stores of Macy's and Gimbels at the turn of the twentieth century to a short-term shelter for homeless families in 1973. During the early twentieth century, theaters left the area and aggregated in Times Square and luxurious stores left for Fifth Avenue. In Gray's *New York Times* piece on the hotel, he states that 436 of New York City's 5,200 homeless families resided at the Martinique as of 1987. The city, together with state and Federal aid, spent about $1,500 a month to keep a family of four at the Martinique, although New York State's housing allowance for welfare families was $270 a month. Gray 1987.

145 Greenberg 2009.

146 According to Grant, the Housing and Urban Development budget decreased by 79 percent from $14 billion in 1983 to $2.7 billion in 1987; New York City witnessed a 300 percent increase in homeless families between 1982 and 1986. Their living conditions were harsh; most of children living in the shelter were underimmunized or nonimmunized and had serious health conditions, such as signs of emotional disturbance, speech delay, and sleep disorders. Grant 1991.

147 Grant 1991.

148 Grant 1991, 78.

149 Weikart 2001.

150 Zukin 1995, 2010; Fainstein, Hoffman, and Judd 2003; Greenberg 2009.

151 Hagen Koo 1991.

152 Deshpandé and Stayman 1994; Ray 2004.

153 Ang 2016, 263.

154 Some had traveled in Korea, while a few were expatriates or planning to teach English in Korea. The racial composition of the classes varied, but about half the students were Asian, either US citizens or temporary residents.

155 *Hallyu*, translated as "Korean Wave," refers to the global popularity of Korean popular culture.

CHAPTER 1. NATION BRANDING

1 Oscars 2020.
2 Moon Jae-in's Cheong Wa Dae 2020.
3 MMA, n.d.
4 Some government organizations changed their names while I was writing this book. In this book, I use the current names of ministries, departments, and institutes as of 2024.

5 Seung-Han Kim 2020; Beaumont-Thomas 2020. Through this law, the oldest members, Jin and Suga, were able to defer their service for another two years. As of August 2025, all seven members of BTS have completed their military duty.
6 H. Chang 1999.
7 Koreans memorialize the Japan-Korea Treaty of 1910, also known as the Japan-Korea Annexation Treaty, as the most humiliating moment in modern Korean history.
8 Shin and Chang 2003; Chang and Shin 2002.
9 Kim Dae-jung (1924–2009) was elected as the eight president of Korea. He was the first opposition leader to win the presidential election in Korea.
10 Byeong-chun Lee 2011.
11 In the past, Korea was a well-known example of intensely and rapidly developing their economy through aggressively executed policy stressing export-oriented and labor-intensive industry driven by chaebol (family-owned business conglomerates) and trade alliances, well-known as an "East Asian development model." The rapid economic growth was executed by strong state intervention through policy reform, becoming more prevalent during the succession of the military regime. The authoritarian Park Chung-hee administration actively controlled the market mechanism through subsidy interventions distorting market prices and the imposition of performance standards on private firms even as economic activity was promoted. See Scitovsky 1985; Pomerleano 1998; K. Chang 1999; Amsden 1989; Krueger and Yoo 2002; Jones and Sakong 1980; Koo and Kim 1992. Furthermore, policymakers encouraged the growth of an export economy through foreign exchange receipts; an export, interest, and tax subsidy; and international loans. Also see Krueger and Yoo 2002; and Collins and Park 1988. Light industry such as clothes, shoes, and wigs had developed in the early 1960s; however, investment in heavy industry gradually increased later in the decade and received a significant boost from the government in the 1970s, resulting in 80 percent of government investment in manufacturing, concentrated in the heavy and chemical industries between 1977 and 1979, according to Haggard and Moon (1990). Chaebol were particularly essential to—and benefited particularly from—this state investment.
12 Byeong-chun Lee 2011; Nye 2004.
13 Aronczyk 2008; Anholt 2011.
14 Geon Park 2007; Park, Jang, and Lee 2007.
15 Shin and Chang 2003, 54–55.
16 Shin and Chang 2003; Byeong-chun Lee 2011.
17 The Korean government devised new policies to boost domestic economic downturn by easing credit card issues. As a result, 80 percent of people in credit delinquent were caused by credit card usages in 2004. Kim 2020; Kang and Ma 2009.
18 Park, Jang, and Lee 2007; Geon Park 2007.
19 Shim and Ha 2017.
20 Sangsoo Kim 1998.

21 Logneun, "Hangukgwangwanggongsa CF - Welkeom tu koria pyeon (1998)," You-Tube video, October 28, 2014, https://www.youtube.com/watch?v=SIcyOrGVLq0 (no longer available).
22 *Kukjung Shinmun* 1998.
23 OECD 2002.
24 The government has incorporated sport-related work into the MCST and changed its name to Ministry of Culture, Sports and Tourism in 2008.
25 OECD 2002.
26 Hallyu can be translated to "The Korean Wave," a term referring to the increasing global popularity of Korean popular culture such as K-pop, K-dramas, and even the Korean language and cuisine.
27 To create a more knowledge-driven economy, the Kim administration devised two broad policies in 1999: Cyber Korea 21 and e-Korea Vision 2006. Cyber Korea 21 (1999–2001) aimed to build an IT infrastructure, particularly a more advanced broadband telecommunications network, on the grounds of achieving productivity and transparency in government, business, and individuals; providing new business opportunities; and exporting telecommunications products and services (Ministry of Information and Communication 1999). E-Korea Vision 2006 (2002–2006) qualitatively advanced on this model by investing in an IT industry, the Kim administration argued, that could not only move Korean society toward more a high-tech society, but, more immediately, create new jobs (Noh 2002). Venture businesses were strategically fostered with government business loans, legislative amendments to encourage stable long-term financing for small-medium size enterprises, and tax benefits; these policies strongly resemble those that enabled Silicon Valley's success (Yang, Joo, and Cho 1998; Kang and Oh 2003). Venture booms from the late 1990s to the early 2000 drove labor market participation of the highly educated unemployed during the crisis (K. Jang 2005) and promoted an image of a technologically advanced nation.
28 Ko et al. 2005; Sujeong Kim 2012.
29 Roh 2000; Yoo and Lee 2001; Hur 2002; E. Han 2005.
30 Dongyeon Lee 2005; Sujeong Kim 2012.
31 "Korea Discount" is a term in the investment and finance worlds that refer to Korean companies and stocks being undervalued compared to other competitors due to low dividend payouts and the dominance of chaebol, large family-owned conglomerates (Lee and Park 2024).
32 Arregle, Beamish, and Hebert 2009.
33 S. Moon 2001.
34 Sun-il Kwon 2002.
35 N. Jung 2002.
36 Kim and Kim 2002.
37 Yeom 2003.
38 Sangkwon Park 2002.

39 Like Kim's "DJnomics"—a combination of President Kim's nickname, DJ (for Daejung) and economics—which argued for the development of both democracy and economic liberalism, the Roh administration sought a balance between economic growth and distribution.
40 Byeongcheon Lee 2003. His policies were later criticized by progressives as neoliberal. Although the Roh administration claimed progressive values, highlighting participation, autonomy, and decentralization of power, his economic policies fell in line with his predecessor's. Park 2009.
41 Kim and Kim 2002; Jeong-soo Park 2009.
42 The Kim administration had announced plans for the improvement of science and technology in six areas: IT (Information Technology), BT (Biotechnology), NT (Nanotechnology), ST (Space Technology), ET (Environment Technology), and CT (Culture Technology).
43 GIA 2007.
44 KAIST is one of the top public research universities, sponsored by public funds.
45 Joyce 2007.
46 Van Ham 2001; Volcic and Andrejevic 2011.
47 Raeyong Park 2003.
48 Hahm 2003.
49 Yongsu Park 2010. According to Yongsu Park (2010), percentages of foreign investment at major businesses have quickly risen. In 2006, foreign shares in stocks of Samsung Electronics, SK Telecom, KT, POSCO, Kookmin Bank, and Shinhan Banks reached more than 50 percent. However, increasing investment by private equity and hedge funds has magnified mergers and acquisitions and led to liquidations, causing numerous layoffs.
50 Aglietta 2000.
51 In-wook Lee 2005. Rather than focusing on the cultural industry itself, the new plan underscored the spread of cultural expression across all strata of society.
52 MCST 2004.
53 H. Moon 2018.
54 KOTRA 2005.
55 *MBC* 2013.
56 H. Lim 2004; Byeongmin Lee 2007.
57 Those agencies include the Committee on Nation Image Improvement; Ministry of Commerce, Industry, and Energy; the Ministry of Culture and Tourism (MCT, now the Ministry of Culture, Sports, and Tourism, MCST); Korea Tourism Organization; Korea Trade-Investment Promotion Agency (KOTRA); and Korea International Cooperation Agency (KOICA).
58 MCST 2007.
59 Voice of America Korean 2007.
60 K. Lim 2012.
61 Chang 2008.

62 Low-carbon green growth is defined by UNEP (United Nations Environment Programme) as industry in which natural resources are sustainable and environmental problems are minimized (OECD 2011a; OECD 2011b; World Bank 2012; Green Growth Knowledge Platform 2013); this was promoted as a new growth engine under the broader nation branding project, a source of economic growth that would also create an environmentally progressive image for the nation.

63 To distinguish himself from the liberal Kim and Roh, Lee Myung-bak projected himself as "the economic president," pledging to restore the economy during the presidential campaign in 2007. His party's slogan for the election, "Lost 10 years," referred to the economic stagnation of the preceding administrations, placing particular blame on Roh's time in office.

64 Their website is no longer available. Instead, Ipsos, a marketing research company, publishes the *Anholt-Ipsos Nation Brands Index*. Ipsos 2023.

65 Taeyeol Kim 2009; Medina 2015.

66 Salmon 2007.

67 *Digital Times* 2009.

68 Joo 2009.

69 Four SERI reports from 2009 to 2012 are available at the KCIS (Korean Culture and Information Service)'s website. See the link: https://www.kocis.go.kr/reference.do.

70 Choe 2009.

71 The union at KBS (Korean Broadcasting System) released a public statement that the company devoted a total of 3,300 minutes to the meeting; even regular programs aired with banners about the G20 (KBS Union 2010).

72 Donghun Lee 2010.

73 Bae 2010.

74 Presidential Archives of Korea, n.d.

75 HSAD 2018.

76 Jeongmin Kang 2015.

77 Taeyoung Kim 2017.

78 Jung, Eun, and Lee 2017.

79 Joohyun Kim 2024. They included the Federation of Korean Industries, Korea Chamber of Commerce and Industry, Korea International Trade Association, Korean Enterprises Federation, and the Korea Federation of Small and Medium Business.

80 Shim 2015.

81 Jung, Eun, and Lee 2017.

82 Jin, Lee, and Saminather 2017; Taeyoung Kim 2017.

83 S. Yoon 2016.

84 MCST 2015.

85 Jeongmo Koo 2016.

86 Ung Lee 2016.

87 MCST 2016.
88 As Korea had received international attention for successfully controlling the pandemic, the Moon administration actively created a series of diplomatic campaigns. Although the administration faced opposition from the opposite party and some members of the public that insisted on international travel bans particularly from China, the Korean government and Korea Centers for Disease Control and Prevention (KCDC) chose an aggressive "trace, test, and treat" approach instead of implementing lockdowns and international travel bans and successfully flattened the curve. Its success story in 2020 swept the international media. In addition, their unique strategies to combat the pandemic were not merely limited to the trace, test, and treat approach. The public trust toward the KCDC, as a response to the director's daily briefings which increased public awareness of the pandemic, and citizens' voluntary cooperation in the government reaction were also major factors, resulting in the establishment of positive images of the nation. See Thompson 2020; and Lee and Kim 2021.
89 "Mask diplomacy" originally refers to China's strategies to ship masks and medical supplies to Europe in order to shift the narratives regarding the COVID-19 pandemic. The Korean government sent medical masks to hospitals in the United States and other countries that were experiencing a shortage of medical supplies. As a part of the seventieth anniversary of the Korean War, the Korean government also shipped masks and care packages to surviving veterans of the Korean War in more than twenty-two countries in order to show that the nation still remembered and respected these veterans seventy years after the Korean War. KTV 2020.
90 Rapkin 2021.
91 MCST 2022.
92 Moon 2021.
93 United Nations 2021a.
94 United Nations 2021a.
95 Lu 2021.
96 United Nations 2021b.
97 KTV 2021.
98 BANGTANTV 2019
99 Baek 2022.
100 Greenberg 2009; Brash 2011.
101 MSS, n.d.
102 Yim 2019; S. Oh 2019. As part of a public-private partnership, thirty-nine companies that were selected in 2019 attended K-Con in Thailand, Dubai Hallyu Expo, World Korean Business Convention, ASEAN–Republic of Korea Commemorative Summit, and Korea Brand Expo in LA in 2019 and 2020 in order to extend overseas markets (S. Oh 2019). Often described as "sales diplomacy" by the media, President Moon and his administration, like their predecessors, made an impor-

tant role to promote products made by small- and medium-sized corporations by devising and developing the umbrella brand, Brand-K.

103 Cheongwadae, which is Korean for "Blue House," was the official residence of the Korean president until 2022. Yoon Suk Yeol, who declared martial law during a televised address on December 3, 2024, was impeached by the National Assembly later that year, and arrested twice in 2025. His impeachment was finalized by the Constitutional Court on April 4, 2025, on charges related to an attempted self-coup. Throughout his presidency, Yoon did not reside at Cheongwadae. However, Lee Jae-myung, who was elected president in 2025 following Yoon's removal from office, has announced plans to relocate the presidential office back to Cheongwadae.

104 Shinmo Yoo 2017.

CHAPTER 2. "TRANSCLAVE"

1 New York City Department of Transportation 2022. The Open Streets program began in May 2020, when the city was suffering from the rapid spread of the COVID-19 virus. With safety concerns, New York State ordered strict indoor gathering limits in March 2020, and one of the industries heavily affected by this policy was the restaurant and bar industry. These car-free streets allowed restaurants and bars to accept their clients outdoors under the state and the city's safety measures.

2 BBC 2020.

3 Recognizing November 22, 2022, as Kimchi Day, N.Y.S. Gen. Assemb. res. no. 574 (adopted February 17, 2022), https://nyassembly.gov.

4 Jaedong Yoo 2022.

5 Expressing Support for the Designation of November 22, 2023, as "Kimchi Day," H.R. 280, 118th Cong., 1st sess. (2023), www.congress.gov.

6 Eunbyul Kim 2022; Eunji Lee 2022.

7 The term *juryusahoi* (mainstream) frequently comes up in the ethnic media, although it is not clearly defined.

8 Ahn 2005.

9 Ahn 2005.

10 Korean Cultural Services New York (now Korean Cultural Center New York) was established in 1979 to promote Korean culture and aesthetics in New York; along with a location in Tokyo, it was one of the first such locations established in an overseas city. The directors of Korean Cultural Center overseas are all government officials, appointed by the Ministry of Culture, Sports and Tourism; the current director engaged in several cultural projects, such as Hallyu and cultural content in the Ministry of Culture, Sports and Tourism. They hold several cultural events, such as arts performances. They also sponsor movie festivals, such as the NYAFF, New York Film Festival, and Tribeca Film Festival in order to introduce Korean movies to New York. For more details, see http://www.koreanculture.org.

11 Ahn 2005.

12 Jinhye Kim 2005.
13 Rockower 2012.
14 Interview with an official, June 2012.
15 MFAFF 2011.
16 Pine and Gilmore 1999; Heldke 2015 [2003].
17 The names have been changed from the Ministry for Food, Agriculture, Forestry and Fisheries (MFAFF) to the Ministry of Agriculture, Food and Rural Affairs (MAFRA) and from the Korean Food Foundation (KFF) to the Korean Food Promotion Institution (KFPI). I have used the current names, MAFRA and KFPI, throughout the manuscript, except in citations, where the original names have been retained to reflect the names at the time of publication.
18 MFAFF 2011.
19 Yang 2011.
20 In my previous work, I referred to this committee as the Eastern United States Korean Cuisine Globalization Committee in order to distinguish it from the committee in the Western United States and their Korean name includes Dongbu, which means Eastern United States or East Coast of the United States. However, in this book, I follow the KCGS USA due to their English translation on their website.
21 Da-seul Kim 2012; Sei-jin Kwon 2012; Hee-eon Koo 2015.
22 J. Choi 2012.
23 Kimchi Chronicles, n.d.
24 Volcic and Andrejevic 2011.
25 News Wire 2011.
26 Tae-jin Park 2011.
27 MFAFF 2011.
28 Sinyoung Kim 2014.
29 Hooni Kim's second restaurant, Hanjan, is now closed. In addition to Danji, he currently operates Little Banchan Shop and Meju, a new Michelin one-star restaurant that opened in 2023, in Long Island City, Queens, across the East River.
30 Wells 2013.
31 Yeongran Lee 2013.
32 Chapple-Sokol 2013.
33 Ichijo and Ranta 2016.
34 Richards 2011.
35 Venkatesh and Meamber 2008, 45; Navarro 2016.
36 Jinwoo Kim 2010.
37 K. Choi 2010.
38 Peterson and Kern 1996; Johnston and Baumann 2014.
39 Krueger and Yoo 2002; Mann 1997; Garrett 1998.
40 The Korean government began to promote tourism and attract foreign tourists in order to revamp the economy after the 1997 economic crisis and in preparation for the 2002 FIFA World Cup. As part of broader efforts, the Korea Tourism Or-

ganization, a government agency, kicked off the project to standardize Romanization of the Korean menu, as individual restaurant owners in Korea had previously used individual transliterations. On December 21, 1998, the Korea Tourism Organization published a guidebook called "Restaurant Menu Romanization Guidebook" and released it in Korea and later overseas. Hyeonsung Yoo 1998. The Romanization effort continued through 2002, the year of the World Cup, not only by the state but also through host city governments, such as those of Jeju and Daejeon. Yonhap News 2002.
41 Hyeonsung Yoo 1998.
42 MFAFF 2009.
43 Heesu Kang 2010.
44 Dishes at some Korean restaurants were translated incorrectly because of homophones without considering meanings. For example, yuk means both "six" and "meat," and hoe means both "times" and "raw fish/meat." Likewise, gomtang was translated as "bear soup" because gom also means "bear."
45 Hoon Kim 2011.
46 I attended this workshop, but the video is also available at the Korean Society's Vimeo channel; see Korea Society 2012.
47 He did not mention the organization's name, but the KFPI and aT center, both under the MFAFF, are the main organizations that deal directly with local entrepreneurs.
48 Ichijo and Ranta 2016; DeSourcey 2010.
49 KCCNY 2022.
50 KCCNY 2022.
51 Michelin Guide 2023. In 2023, two Korean restaurants—bōm and Meju—were added to a list of the Michelin One Star restaurants in New York City. Two Korean restaurants—Atomix and Jungsik—maintained Two Star status; and seven Korean restaurants—Cote, Jeju Noodle Bar, Joomak Banjum, Jua, Kochi, Mari, and Oiji Mi—retained One Star status. In 2024, Jungsik became the first Korean restaurant in the United States to receive three Michelin stars.
52 Diane Kang 2016.
53 Korea Society 2020.
54 Haelim Lee 2018.
55 Wells 2015.
56 *Korea Daily* 2016.
57 Sun-min Lee 2019.
58 Sun-min Lee 2019.
59 Daniel 2019.
60 Korea Society 2012.
61 Korea Society 2012.
62 Diane Kang 2016.
63 Michelin Guide 2019.
64 Michelin Guide 2018.

65 Wells 2018.
66 Korea Society 2020.
67 Sam Kim 2018.
68 Korea Society 2020.
69 Korea Society 2020.
70 Maeil Kyeongje 2019.
71 Flushing is a neighborhood in Queens, New York, with a large Korean residential population and many retail stores, restaurants, bars, coffee shops, and service establishments that cater to Korean consumers.
72 Japhe 2019.
73 Vianna 2019.
74 Korea Society 2020.
75 *News Wire* 2019.
76 Vianna 2019.
77 Vianna 2019.
78 tvN 2020b.
79 Jansen 2008; Volcic and Andrejevic 2011, 606.

CHAPTER 3. RE/MAKING KOREATOWN

1 Barbanel 1988.
2 New Yorkers often shorten the name of "Greenwich Village"—a historically trendy neighborhood in lower Manhattan—to "the Village."
3 Manhattan Koreatown's landscape contrasts with the local business districts in the Koreatowns in Flushing and Bayside and in the suburbs, such as Northern New Jersey and Long Island—so-called ethnoburbs; ethnic businesses have followed this pattern, creating newer Koreatowns across the two states. According to my current research on the Koreatown in Flushing and Bayside, Koreans have moved out or been priced out of downtown Flushing toward eastern Flushing, Bayside, Little Neck, and Long Island, and this pattern has intensified in the past few years. See W. Li 1998; Matsumoto 2018.
4 "Nostalgia" was coined in 1688 by a Swiss doctor, Johannes Hofer, by combining two Greek words: "nostos" (home) and "algia" (longing). As a medical term, it then referred to a medical condition, caused by being away from home. Just like other diseases, this "medical condition" resulting from geographical distance from one's homeland was believed to be eased by leeches, opium, and a journey to the Swiss Alps, in addition to, of course, a return home (Boym 2001; Atia and Davies 2010; Bonnett 2015). However, this term, widely used in medicine, was newly rediscovered and redefined as a modern phenomenon related to the French Revolution and its expansion throughout Europe and beyond (Fritzsche 2001). In the nineteenth century, the rapid pace of modernization and industrialization ignited a yearning for the slow pace of the past (Boym 2001), and nostalgia was rediscovered and redefined as a cultural and literary term (Atia and Davies 2010). Rapid changes in modern society that caused uncertainty

and challenges led people to respond to threats of the present (Vess et al. 2009; Dauncey and Tinker 2015).

5 According to the French historian, Pierre Nora, nostalgia had been institutionally established in *lieux de mémoire* (sites, places, or realms of memory); Nora asserted that these sites of memory could be (1) physical, such as monuments, museums, and statues; (2) symbolic, including ceremonies and pilgrimages; or (3) functional, like associates or dictionaries, evoking emotions about the nation and national identity (Nora 1989; Boym 2001; Legg 2005).

6 Yuval-Davis 2016.
7 Bonnett 2015, 6.
8 Bonnett 2015, 16.
9 Davis 1979; Boym 2001; Duyvendak 2011.
10 Blunt 2003; Ladino 2012; Bonnett 2015; Wilson 2015.
11 Wilson 2015, 484.
12 Both Tiffany and Emily were interviewed by the author in 2012.
13 Kibria 1997.
14 Ko 2018; Chen 2021.
15 Espiritu 1992; Kibria 1997; Tuan 1998; Kurashige 2016.
16 Vincent Chin was a twenty-seven-year-old Chinese American hate crime victim, killed in 1982 in Detroit by two white autoworkers, Ronald Ebens and Michael Nitz, who assumed that Chin was Japanese and had stolen their jobs. Despite the homicide, they did not serve any prison time and were given probation for three years and $3,780 in fines. Clemtson 2002.
17 Huynh 2012; Sue et al. 2016.
18 hooks 2009, 215.
19 Yuval-Davis 2006.
20 Matt 2007; Parla 2009.
21 IIE 2023.
22 International students are only legally allowed to work part-time on campuses or at educationally affiliated institutions, according to Immigration and Customs Enforcement. Despite the fact that PhD students often receive grants and fellowships, most undergraduate and many graduate students pay full tuition, fees, and other living expenses. They are also required to prove evidence of financial support when they apply for a visa. This indicates that many, though not all, international students, particularly undergraduate students, tend to have affluent backgrounds.
23 Class identification in this chapter is subjective; instead of asking about their objective socioeconomic status (i.e., household income, education, and occupation), I asked for respondents' subjective class identification—whether they think their family is working class, middle class, or upper-middle class.
24 Smith and Campbell 2017.
25 Blunt 2003; Ladino 2012; Bonnett 2015.
26 Traditionally, scholars of globalization have looked at how economics, politics, consumer culture, communities, and identity are losing attachment to local

places, or becoming deterritorialized. Tomlinson 1999. The "new metaphors of belonging" refer to people in a globalized world who do not necessarily belong to a certain territory but belong to "a situation" of everyday life encounters. Amin 2005, cited in Antonsich 2010. The deterritorialization, thus, explains how production, consumption, politics, culture, and identities are being detached from local places and losing locality. Misztal 2003, 16.
27 Tomlinson 1999; Hernàndez i Martí 2006, 95; Antonsich 2010.
28 Antonsich 2010.
29 Misztal 2003, 16.
30 Farrar 2011.
31 Anthias 2006, 2008.
32 Bandyopadhyay 2008.
33 Espiritu 1992; Espiritu and Ong 1994; Kibria 1997.
34 Ocejo 2011.
35 Probyn 1996; Askin 2016.
36 Deener 2007, 293.
37 Duyvendak 2011, 62.
38 Probyn 1996; Askin 2016.
39 Rose 1995; Easthope 2004.
40 Kibria 2003; Dhingra 2007.
41 Due to her grandparents' political awareness, Younghee grew up with a greater knowledge of Korean history and politics than most other Korean Americans. Her grandparents spoke Korean to each other, but while they would teach their children some Korean words, they did not push them to learn the language. She and her twin sister use their Korean names.
42 Boym 2001, xiii.
43 Boym 2001, xiii.
44 Tummala-Narra 2009, 239.
45 Ocejo 2011.
46 Rubenstein 2001, 4.
47 Bonnett 2015.
48 Antonsich 2010; Yuval-Davis 2010.
49 Misztal 2003, 11.
50 Hebbert 2005; Halbwachs 1980, 23, cited in Hebbert 2005.
51 Halbwachs 1980; Hebbert 2005.
52 Misztal 2003; Bonnett 2015.
53 Trudeau 2006; Yuval-Davis 2010.
54 Pierce, Martin, and Murphy 2011, 55.

CHAPTER 4. "IT IS MY STREET"
1 Levitt 2009.
2 Sierp and Wüstenberg 2015.
3 Curti 2008.

4   Nora 1989; Hebbert 2005.
5   Hebbert 2005.
6   Farrar 2011.
7   Deener 2007.
8   Gangnam began receiving international attention after K-pop recording artist Psy's song "Gangnam Style," released in 2012, became successful.
9   Meesun Kim 2012.
10 Nora 1989; Legg 2005.
11 Lee Myung-bak is a former Mayor of Seoul (2002–2006) and President of Republic of Korea (2008–2013).
12 Newtro culture refers to a new cultural trend of younger generations looking for old vintage items, from old soju packaging to electronic devices to gentrified neighborhoods with trendy cafés, shops, bars, and restaurants, which used to be industrial neighborhoods, such as Seongsu-dong and Uljiro, resonating with 1960s and '70s Korea or 1920s imperial Japanese-era Seoul. Byungsoo Kim 2019. However, their perception of newtro tends to be very specific, linked to hyperconsumerism, and less likely to change their view on Koreatown.
13 Woorijip is a popular and inexpensive cafeteria-style Korean restaurant in Manhattan's Koreatown.
14 However, in recent years, while Manhattan's Chinatown has declined, Flushing's Chinatown has gained significant popularity among young Chinese people, driven by a massive influx of franchise stores, trendy tea shops, dessert places, and restaurants. In my current research on Asian communities in Queens, I often hear from Chinese interviewees that Flushing has become a new destination for young Chinese.
15 Levitt 2009, 1237.
16 Martin, Martin, and Weil 2006; Naujoks 2010.
17 Martin, Martin, and Weil 2006; Naujoks 2010.
18 Jackson 1999.
19 Zukin 2009.
20 Authenticity is also correlated with class-based consumption. Identifying herself as upper-middle class, Minji often compares her consumption experience in Seoul to that in New York. Seoul is catching up to global trends quickly; when she went back to Seoul during a break from school, she found that luxurious department stores in Gangnam displayed collections of rare items that were often hard to find in New York City. Yet Koreatown did not follow this trend.
21 Trudeau 2006; Yuval-Davis 2006.
22 Trudeau 2006, 434.
23 Hunter, Loughran, and Fine 2018.
24 Angelo and Wachsmuth 2015.
25 Deener 2007.
26 Nientied 2018; Zukin 1995.
27 Deener 2007, 293.

28 Rose 1995, 89; Easthope 2004.
29 Meeting stenography 2010, 11. The inspection of the Administration by the National Assembly was held on October 14, 2010, in the meeting room of the Permanent Mission of the Republic of Korea to the United Nations in New York City.
30 Meeting stenography 2010, 11.
31 The project kicked off in 2003 in Seoul as a part of the urban design projects "Jongro Upgrade" and "Chunggyechun Signboard Improvement" to address concerns that signboards on buildings were illegal, densely crowded and disorganized, and violated the public right to walk. Kyung-a Lee 2007. Then-mayor of Seoul Lee Myung-bak, who later became President in 2008, put great emphasis on urban renewal in central Seoul. Kyung-bin Kim 2004. His successor, Oh Sehoon (2006–2011), underscored the project as part of the "Design Seoul Initiative."
32 Byng 2017.
33 Ashcroft 2003; Bloch and Hirsch 2017.
34 Ritivoi 2002.
35 Valentine and Skelton 2007; Valentine, Sporton, and Nielsen 2008.
36 Ignatieff 1994; Antonsich 2010.
37 Valentine and Skelton 2007.
38 Legg 2005.
39 Jarvis and Bonnett 2013.
40 Deener 2007, 312.
41 Sorkin 1992, 216; T. Yoon 2023.

CHAPTER 5. HALLYU IN KOREATOWN

1 This narrative was reconstructed based on interviews conducted in 2012 with Aria, Taylor, and Hannah.
2 I met Kaylee in the early 2010s, when she was a student in my Korean language class at a community college in New York City. Although she took two of my classes and had shared information about herself, I did not know that her father was Korean Chinese until a formal interview with her, a year after the class ended. My perception of her as Chinese was based on her self-introduction as Chinese or Chinese American and her family name, which could be interpreted as either Chinese or Korean. Her father did not grow up speaking Korean and had no exposure to Korean culture; he was very culturally Chinese. Thus, when asked about her ethnic background, she hesitated but stated that Korea is a part of her background, and she felt this more strongly after spending a few weeks in Korea.
3 Kim and Ryoo 2007; E. Jung 2009; Huang 2011; Kanozia and Ganghariya 2021.
4 Jaeho Kang 2022, 3313.
5 This stage is called Hallyu 2.0. Hallyu 2.0 refers to the new direction of the Korean wave beyond Asia by emphasizing the role of social media and fandom's active engagements in (re)creating the contents. See Lee and Nornes 2015; Jin and Yoon 2016; Song 2020.

6 Ono and Kwon 2013; Oh 2017; McLaren and Jin 2020; King-O'Riain 2021.
7 Jaeho Kang 2022; Lee 2018.
8 Min Joo Lee 2020; Jenkins 1992.
9 Hyunji Lee 2018.
10 Ju 2020.
11 "Stan" is a slang term used on social media to describe obsessive or extremely enthusiastic fans of a particular celebrity, musician, or public figure.
12 ARMY is an acronym for "Adorable Representative M.C. for Youth."
13 Koh 2023. As briefly explained, a fansign is an event where fans have an opportunity to physically meet with their idols to get their autographs on physical vinyl albums or CDs. In many cases, these events are lottery-based for fans who already purchased physical albums. This means that fans who buy more copies of an album or CD have higher chances of winning. Consequently, there are many reports of fans who have many copies of the same album or CD. A hi-touch is an event during a fanmeet or after a concert where fans have opportunities to high-five with each member of the band, while idols stand on the other side of the table and wait for fans to walk for a high-five. These events are often included in top-tier tickets. During the pandemic, labels even organized various online fansign and fanmeet events, where fans could videocall with their idols.
14 Longenecker and Lee 2018.
15 I first learned about Sophie and Isabelle's story through a short Korean documentary about Koreatown in New York, aired by one of Korea's major broadcasting companies. Based on the information about their YouTube channel presented in the program, I reached out to the twins to request an interview in 2012. Due to their locations at the time—Isabelle in Seoul and Sophie in Pennsylvania—they preferred to respond via email rather than participate in individual in-person interviews. I received a single document written in the first-person plural, unless otherwise specified.
16 Kim et al. 2012; Dutch 2019.
17 Iwabuchi 2002, 27. Koichi Iwabuchi argues that the global success of Japanese pop culture, such as manga and anime, are driven from eliminating cultural odor, "cultural features of a country of origin and images or ideas of its national, in most cases stereotyped, way of life are associated positively with a particular product in the consumption process." Iwabuchi 2002, 27.
18 Hyunji Lee 2018; Kim et al. 2012.
19 Marion Schulze explains that K-Dramaland refers to "an imagined world created through the collective activity of writers, directors, actors, and viewers of K-Dramas." Schulze 2013, 378.
20 Jenkins 2006; Dutch 2019.
21 Leeman and Modan 2009.
22 Zukin 1995.
23 "Ramyun" is the Korean pronunciation of the noodle soup dish that most Americans and Japanese refer to as "ramen."

24 Hyunji Lee 2018.
25 Debord 2021 [1967].
26 Sorkin 1992, 208.
27 Sorkin 1992; Gotham 2005.
28 Reijnders et al. 2020.
29 Sorkin 1992, 216.
30 Hannigan 1998, cited in Leeman and Modan 2009.
31 Sorkin 1992, 231.
32 Jinwon Kim 2018.
33 Reijnders 2011; Laing and Crouch 2009; Reijnders et al. 2020.
34 Sorkin 1992, 216.

CHAPTER 6. KOREAN FOOD

1 City of New York Official Instagram 2023. As of July 1, 2024, this particular post has received 468,267 likes and 4,397 comments.
2 @hannabeans, comment on City of New York Official Instagram 2023.
3 @empressngala, comment on City of New York Official Instagram 2023.
4 @azulgris27, comment on City of New York Official Instagram 2023.
5 The National Restaurant Association 2013.
6 Pine and Gilmore 1999; Zukin 2010.
7 Zukin 2010; Johnston and Baumann 2014, 61.
8 Yuhaksaeng refer to Korean students who attend regular schools outside Korea. Generally, language students are not included in this category.
9 During the interview, Laura discussed the constant stream of microaggressions and subtle discrimination she experienced while growing up in a white suburb as one of only a few Asian Americans. She explains "I remember once I was in college, and was at the doctor's office back.... for break. [The nurse] asked me questions like, 'Where do you go to school? What's your major?' And I was like, 'I'm an English major.' Then the nurse was like, 'Pretty soon you will speak better than us.' That was one of the critical moments for me, realizing that [I was different from and not embraced by the white mainstream]." Despite Laura being a native English speaker, she was immediately stereotyped as being a "foreigner" who could not speak English well, because of a racialized appearance that rendered her outside of the category of "American" in the eyes of white Americans.
10 Gabaccia 1998.
11 Goode, Curtis, and Theophano 1984; Alba 1990, 85–93; Lu and Fine 1995, 536; Timothy and Ron 2013.
12 Johnston and Baumann 2014, 81.
13 The Korean translation of authenticity in the urban context is jeongtongseong. My Korean interviewees did not necessarily say the words "authenticity" or "jeongtongseong," but instead, they used terms like "real" and "traditional." However, unlike in the United States, where the terms "authentic" or "authenticity" are widely used in verbal communication by the general public, "jeongtongseong"

is used more frequently in written form in Korea. I decided to use the term "authenticity" because "real" and "tradition" are associated with authenticity. Zukin 2010; Johnston and Baumann 2014. While Korean nationals tended to not actually use the word "authenticity," many Korean Americans and non-Koreans did say "authenticity" during interviews.
14 Johnston and Baumann 2014.
15 Levitt 2009; Martin, Martin, and Weil 2006; Naujoks 2010; Porciani 2019; Ichijo 2020.
16 Jackson 1999.
17 Zukin 2009, 2010.
18 Ray 2004, 81; Mannur 2007; Holak 2014.
19 Flowers and Swan 2012; Xu 2007; Pazo 2016; Alkon and Grosglik 2021.
20 Heldke 2015 [2003]; Arvela 2013; Stano 2016.
21 Lupton 1994.
22 Ziegelman 2010; Cozzi 2015.
23 Peterson and Kern 1996; Johnston and Baumann 2014; De Vries and Reeves 2022.
24 Peterson and Simkus 1992; Peterson and Kern 1996. Richard A. Peterson and Roger M. Kern examine art consumption in general, focusing on music in particular.
25 Johnston and Baumann 2007, 2014; Hyman 2008; Hansen 2008; Matta 2018; Giousmpasoglou, Brown, and Cooper 2020.
26 Johnston and Baumann 2007, 2014; Hansen 2008; Flemmen, Hjellbrekke, and Jarness 2018; Yalvaç and Hazır 2021.
27 Hyman 2008; Mitchell 2010.
28 Hyman 2008.
29 Hollows 2003.
30 Alba and Nee 2003; Bardhi, Ostberg, and Bengtsson 2010; Stano 2016; Montanari 2006.
31 Bardhi, Ostberg, and Bengtsson 2010.
32 Arvela 2013; Turgeon and Pastinelli 2002.
33 Alkon and Grosglik 2021.
34 Turgeon and Pastinelli 2002.
35 Cho 1997; Kwan 1998; Azhar et al. 2021.
36 Jacoby 1994.
37 G. Shin 2006; Seol and Seo 2014.
38 Warde, Martens, and Olsen 1999; Warde and Martens 2000, 2018; Bell 2002; Arvela 2013; Johnston and Baumann 2014.
39 Turgeon and Pastinelli 2002, 251; James 1996.
40 Warde, Martens, and Olsen 1999; Bell 2002; Johnston and Baumann 2014.
41 hooks 2009.
42 Heldke 2015 [2003]; Roberts 2000, cited in Johnston and Baumann 2014.
43 Johnston and Baumann 2014, 90; Arvela 2013, 4; hooks 1992.
44 Heldke 2015 [2003], 48.

45 A Koreaboo refers to a non-Korean who is obsessed with Korean culture and even deny their ethnic culture.

CONCLUSION

1 tvN 2020a.
2 Noraebang is the Korean word for what Americans refer to as "karaoke bars." Noraebang literally translates to "singing room" or "room for singing."
3 Krase 1997, 105; Lin 2011.
4 Department of International Trade Promotion of Thailand, n.d.
5 Atout France, L'Agence de Développement Touristique de la France 2015.
6 Good France n.d.
7 Ang 2016.
8 Appadurai 1996, 49.
9 Appadurai 1996, 30.
10 Ocejo 2011; hooks 1992, 21.
11 Halter 2007.
12 Sorkin 1992.

APPENDIX

1 Joseonjok refers to individuals of Korean ethnicity who are Chinese nationals, that is, born and raised in China. Many *Joseonjok* reside in the Yanbian Autonomous Korean Prefecture in northeastern China, near the North Korean border, and they speak both Korean and Chinese, but with a distinctive accent.

BIBLIOGRAPHY

ENGLISH

Aaker, Jennifer L., Anne M. Brumbaugh, and Sonya A. Grier. 2000. "Nontarget Markets and Viewer Distinctiveness: The Impact of Target Marketing on Advertising Attitudes." *Journal of Consumer Psychology* 9 (3): 127–40.

Abelmann, Nancy, and John Lie. 2009. *Blue Dreams: Korean Americans and the Los Angeles Riots*. Harvard University Press.

Aglietta, Michel. 2000. *A Theory of Capitalist Regulation: The US Experience*. Translated by David Fernbach. Vol. 28. Verso.

Alba, Richard. 1990. *Ethnic Identity: The Transformation of White America*. Yale University Press.

Alba, Richard, and Victor Nee. 2003. *Remaking the American Mainstream: Assimilation and Contemporary Immigration*. Harvard University Press.

Alkon, Alison Hope, and Rafi Grosglik. 2021. "Eating (with) the Other: Race in American Food Television." *Gastronomica: The Journal for Food Studies* 21 (2): 1–13.

Amin, Ash. 2005. "Take the White out of the Union Jack." Paper presented at the Conference on Politics and Ethnicity, Merton College, Oxford, United Kingdom.

Amsden, Alice. 1989. *Asia's Next Giant: South Korea and Late Industrialization*. Oxford University Press.

Anderson, Kay. 1990. "'Chinatown Re-oriented': A Critical Analysis of Recent Redevelopment Schemes in a Melbourne and Sydney Enclave." *Australian Geographical Studies* 28 (2): 137–54.

———. 2018. "Chinatown Dis-oriented: Shifting Standpoints in the Age of China." *Australian Geographer* 49 (1): 133–48.

Ang, Ien. 2016. "At Home in Asia? Sydney's Chinatown and Australia's 'Asian Century.'" *International Journal of Cultural Studies* 19 (3): 257–69.

Angelo, Hillary, and David Wachsmuth. 2015. "Urbanizing Urban Political Ecology: A Critique of Methodological Cityism." *International Journal of Urban and Regional Research* 39(1): 16–27.

Anholt, Simon. 1998. "Nation-Brands of the Twenty-First century." *Journal of Brand Management* 5:395–406.

———. 2010. "Place Image as a Normative Construct; and Some New Ethical Considerations for the Field." *Place Branding and Public Diplomacy* 6 (3): 177–81.

———. 2011. "Beyond the Nation Brand: The Role of Image and Identity in International Relations." In *Brands and Branding Geographies*, edited by Andy Pike, 289–304. Edward Elgar.
Anthias, Floya. 2006. "Belonging in a Globalising and Unequal world: Rethinking Translocations." In *The Situated Politics of Belonging*, edited by Nira Yuval-Davis, Ulrike Vieten, and Kalpana Kannabiran, 17–31. Sage.
———. 2008. "Thinking Through the Lens of Translocational Positionality: An Intersectionality Frame for Understanding Identity and Belonging." *Translocations: Migration and Social Change* 4 (1): 5–20.
Antonsich, Marco. 2010. "Searching for Belonging: An Analytical Framework." *Geography Compass* 4 (6): 644–59.
Appadurai, Arjun. 1996. *Modernity at Large: Cultural Dimensions of Globalization*. Vol. 1. University of Minnesota Press.
Aronczyk, Melissa. 2008. "Living the Brand: Nationality, Globality and the Identity Strategies of Nation Branding Consultants." *International Journal of Communication* 2 (1): 41–65.
———. 2013. *Branding the Nation: The Global Business of National Identity*. Oxford University Press.
Arregle, Jean-Luc, Paul W. Beamish, and Louis Hebert. 2009. "The Regional Dimension of MNEs' Foreign Subsidiary Localization." *Journal of International Business Studies* 40 (1): 86–107.
Arvela, Paula. 2013. "Ethnic Food: The Other in Ourselves." In *Food: Expressions and Impressions*, edited by Don Sanderson and Mira Crouch, 43–56. Brill.
Ashcroft, Bill. 2003. "Language and Race." In *Language Ethnicity and Race Reader*, edited by Roxy Harris and Ben Hampton, 37–54. Psychology Press.
Askins, Kye. 2016. "Emotional Citizenry: Everyday Geographies of Befriending, Belonging and Intercultural Encounter." *Transactions of the Institute of British Geographers* 41 (4): 515–27.
Atia, Nadia, and Jeremy Davies. 2010. "Nostalgia and the Shapes of History." *Memory Studies* 3 (3): 181–86.
Atout France, L'Agence de Développement Touristique de la France. 2015. "Good France (Goût de France) Participating U.S. Restaurants Announced." February 23. https://us.media.france.fr/en/node/2138.
Aytar, Volkan, and Jan Rath. 2012. "Ethnic Neighborhoods as Places of Leisure and Consumption." In *Selling Ethnic Neighborhoods: The Rise of Neighborhoods as Places of Leisure and Consumption*, edited by Volkan Aytar and Jan Rath, 1–15. Routledge.
Azhar, Sameena, Antonia R. G. Alvarez, Anne S. J. Farina, and Susan Klumpner. 2021. "'You're So Exotic Looking': An Intersectional Analysis of Asian American and Pacific Islander Stereotypes." *Affilia* 36 (3): 282–301.
Baldwin, Deborah. 2008. "Exotic Flavor, Beyond Just the Food." *New York Times*, October 17. www.nytimes.com.
Bandyopadhyay, Ranjan. 2008. "Nostalgia, Identity and Tourism: Bollywood in the Indian Diaspora." *Journal of Tourism and Cultural Change* 6 (2): 79–100.

Barbanel, Josh. 1988. "As a Hotel Is Emptied, The Poor Move On." *New York Times*, December 27. www.nytimes.com.
Bardhi, Fleura, Jacob Ostberg, and Anders Bengtsson. 2010. "Negotiating Cultural Boundaries: Food, Travel and Consumer Identities." *Consumption, Markets and Culture* 13 (2): 133–57.
BBC. 2020. "Kimchi Ferments Cultural Feud Between South Korea and China." November 30. www.bbc.com.
Beaumont-Thomas, Ben. 2020. "K-pop Stars BTS Extend Career by Two Years after Military Service Law Change." *The Guardian*, December 1. www.theguardian.com.
Becker, Elisabeth. 2015. "Little of Italy? Assumed Ethnicity in a New York City Neighborhood." *Ethnic and Racial Studies* 38 (1): 109–24.
Bell, David. 2002. "Fragments for a New Urban Culinary Geography." *Journal for the Study of Food and Society* 6 (1): 10–21.
Benvenuta Italia. n.d. "Italy Continues to Lead the Way at the 68th Edition of the Summer Fancy Food Show in New York." Accessed August 1, 2025. www.benvenutaitalia.com.
Beverland, Michael B., Francis Farrelly, and Pascale G. Quester. 2010. "Authentic Subcultural Membership: Antecedents and Consequences of Authenticating Acts and Authoritative Performances." *Psychology & Marketing* 27 (7): 698–716.
Bloch, Alice, and Shirin Hirsch. 2017. "'Second Generation' Refugees and Multilingualism: Identity, Race and Language Transmission." *Ethnic and Racial Studies* 40 (14): 2444–62.
Blunt, Alison. 2003. "Collective Memory and Productive Nostalgia: Anglo-Indian Homemaking at McCluskieganj." *Environment and Planning D: Society and Space* 21 (6): 717–38.
Bonacich, Edna. 1973. "A Theory of Middleman Minorities." *American Sociological Review* 38 (5): 583–94.
Bonacich, Edna, and John Modell. 1980. *The Economic Basis of Ethnic Solidarity: Small Business in the Japanese American Community*. University of California Press.
Bonnett, Alastair. 2015. *The Geography of Nostalgia: Global and Local Perspectives on Modernity and Loss*. Routledge.
Boorstin, Daniel Joseph. 1961. *The Image: A Guide to Pseudo-events in America*. Vintage Books.
Bourdain, Anthony. 2013. *Anthony Bourdain: Parts Unknown*. Season 1, episode 2, "Koreatown, Los Angeles." Aired April 21, 2013, on CNN.
Boswell, Thomas D., and James R. Curtis. 1984. *The Cuban-American Experience. Culture, Images and Perspectives*. Rowman & Allanheld.
Boym, Svetlana. 2001. *The Future of Nostalgia*. Basic Books.
Brash, Julian. 2011. *Bloomberg's New York: Class and Governance in the Luxury City*. University of Georgia Press.
Burgess, Ernest W. 1928. "Residential Segregation in American Cities." *Annals of the American Academy of Political and Social Science* 140 (1): 105–15.
———. 1967 [1924]. *The Growth of the City: An Introduction to a Research Project*. Ardent Media.

Byng, Michelle. 2017. "Transnationalism Among Second-Generation Muslim Americans: Being and Belonging in Their Transnational Social Field." *Social Sciences* 6 (4): 131.

Cayla, Julien, and Giana M. Eckhardt. 2008. "Asian Brands and the Shaping of a Transnational Imagined Community." *Journal of Consumer Research* 35 (2): 216–30.

Centeno, Miguel A., Nina Bandelj, and Frederick Wherry. 2011. "The Political Economy of Cultural Wealth." In *The Cultural Wealth of Nations*, edited by Nina Bandelj and Frederick Wherry, 23–46. Stanford University Press.

Chacko, Elizabeth. 2003. "Ethiopian Ethos and the Making of Ethnic Places in the Washington Metropolitan Area." *Journal of Cultural Geography* 20 (2): 21–42.

Chang, Ha-Joon. 1999. "How to 'Do' a Developmental State: Political, Organizational, and Human Resource Requirements for the Developmental State." In *Constructing a Democratic Developmental State in South Africa—Potentials and Challenges*, edited by Omano Edigheji, 182–99. Human Science Research Council.

Chang, Ha-Joon, and Jang Sup Shin. 2002. "Evaluating the Post-crisis Corporate Restructuring in Korea." *Seoul Journal of Economics* 15 (2): 245–76.

Chang, Kyung-Sup. 1999. "Compressed Modernity and Its Discontents: South Korean Society in Transition." *Economy and society* 28 (1): 30–55.

Chapple-Sokol, Sam. 2013. "Culinary Diplomacy: Breaking Bread to Win Hearts and Minds." *Hague Journal of Diplomacy* 8 (2): 161–83.

Chen, Brian X. 2021. "The Cost of Being an 'Interchangeable Asian.'" *New York Times*, June 10. www.nytimes.com.

Cho, Sumi K. 1997. "Converging Stereotypes in Racialized Sexual Harassment: Where the Model Minority Meets Suzie Wong." *J. Gender, Race and Justice* 1:177–212.

Choe, Sang-hun. 2009. "Korean Leader Pardons Samsung's Ex-Chairman." *New York Times*, December 29. www.nytimes.com.

Claiborne, Craig. 1960. "Food News: Exotic Fare of Koreans." *New York Times*, July 11. www.nytimes.com.

Cleave, Evan, and Godwin Arku. 2020. "Place Branding and Growth Machines: Implications for Spatial Planning and Urban Development." *Journal of Urban Affairs* 44 (7): 949–66.

Clemtson, Lynette. 2002. "A Slaying in 1982 Maintains Its Grip on Asian-Americans." *New York Times*, June 18. www.nytimes.com.

Cohen, Erik. 1988. "Authenticity and Commoditization in Tourism." *Annals of Tourism Research* 15 (3): 371–86.

Collins, Jock. 2006. "Ethnic Diversity and the Ethnic Economy in Cosmopolitan Sydney." In *Landscapes of the Ethnic Economy*, edited by David H. Kaplan, 135–48. Rowman & Littlefield.

Collins, Susan M., and Won Am Park. 1988. *External Debt and Macroeconomic Performance in South Korea*. National Bureau of Economic Research (No. w2596).

Condry, Ian. 2009. "Anime Creativity: Characters and Premises in the Quest for Cool Japan." *Theory, Culture & Society* 26 (2–3): 139–63.

Conforti, Joseph M. 1996. "Ghettos as Tourism Attractions." *Annals of Tourism Research* 23 (4): 830–42.

Consulate General of France in New York. n.d. "Goût de France/Good France." Accessed July 1, 2025. https://newyork.consulfrance.org.

Cool Japan Fund Inc. n.d. "About Cool Japan Fund." Accessed August 1, 2024. www.cj-fund.co.jp.

Cozzi, Annette. 2015. "Now, 'That's Italian': Food, Culture, and the Gendering of Italian-American Identity." *Italian American Review* 5 (2): 75–93.

Crenshaw, Kimberlé. 1991. "Mapping the Margins: Intersectionality, Identity Politics, and Violence against Women of Color." *Stanford Law Review* 43 (6): 1241–99.

Cui, Geng. 2015 [1998]. "Ethical Issues in Ethnic Segmentation and Target Marketing." In *Proceedings of the 1998 Multicultural Marketing Conference*, edited by Jean-Charles Chebat and A. Ben Oumlil, 87–91. Springer.

Cummings, Judith. 1974. "Little Italy Is Love and Mulberry Street Becomes Mall for the Weekend." *New York Times*, December 1. www.nytimes.com.

Curti, Giorgio Hadi. 2008. "From a Wall of Bodies to a Body of Walls: Politics of Affect | Politics of Memory | Politics of War." *Emotion, Space and Society* 1 (2): 106–18.

Daniel, Martha. 2019. "How Vegas High Rollers Prepared This NYC Restaurateur for Fine Dining: On This Episode of Eater's Digest, Simon Kim of Cote Gets Candid About His Path to Two Michelin Stars." *Eater*, October 4. www.eater.com.

Dauncey, Hugh, and Chris Tinker. 2015. "Media, Memory and Nostalgia in Contemporary France: Between Commemoration, Memorialisation, Reflection and Restoration." *Modern & Contemporary France* 23 (2): 135–45.

Davis, Fred. 1979. *Yearning for Yesterday: A Sociology of Nostalgia*. Free Press.

Debord, Guy. 2021 [1967]. *The Society of the Spectacle*. Unredacted Word.

De Chernatony, Leslie. 2008. "Academic Perspective: Adapting Brand Theory to the Context of Nation Branding." In *Nation Branding: Concepts, Issues, Practice*, edited by Keith Dinnie, 14–16. Routledge.

Deener, Andrew. 2007. "Commerce as the Structure and Symbol of Neighborhood Life: Reshaping the Meaning of Community in Venice, California." *City & Community* 6 (4): 291–314.

Department of International Trade Promotion of Thailand. n.d. "Thai SELECT." Accessed August 1, 2025. www.thaiselect.com.

Deshpandé, Rohit, and Douglas M. Stayman. 1994. "A Tale of Two Cities: Distinctiveness Theory and Advertising Effectiveness." *Journal of Marketing Research* 31 (1): 57–64.

DeSoucey, Michaela. 2010. "Gastronationalism: Food Traditions and Authenticity Politics in the European Union." *American Sociological Review* 75 (3): 432–55.

De Vries, Robert, and Aaron Reeves. 2022. "What Does It Mean to Be a Cultural Omnivore? Conflicting Visions of Omnivorousness in Empirical Research." *Sociological Research Online* 27 (2): 292–312.

Dhingra, Pawan. 2007. *Managing Multicultural Lives: Asian American Professionals and the Challenge of Multiple Identities*. Stanford University Press.

Dogan, Evinc, and Goran Petkovic. 2016. "Nation Branding in a Transnational Marketing Context: Serbia's Brand Positioning through Food and Wine." *Transnational Marketing Journal* 4 (2): 84–99.

Donato, Katharine M., and Carl L. Bankston. 2008. "The Origins of Employer Demand for Immigrants in a New Destination: The Salience of Soft Skills in a Volatile Economy." In *New Faces in New Places: The Changing Geography of American Immigration*, edited by Douglas S. Massey, 124–48. Russell Sage Foundation.

Durand, Jorge, Douglas S. Massey, and Chiara Capoferro. 2005. "The New Geography of Mexican Immigration." In *New Destinations: Mexican Immigration in the United States*, edited by Victor Zuniga and Ruben Hernandez-Leon, 1–20. Russell Sage Foundation.

Dutch, Jennifer. 2019. "Consuming K-Drama Cuisine: The Intersection of Fans, Fandom and Food in the Search for a Real Korean Meal." In *The Rise of K-Dramas: Essays on Korean Television and Its Global Consumption*, edited by Jae Yoon Park and Ann-Gee Lee, 6–25. McFarland.

Duyvendak, Jan. 2011. *The Politics of Home: Belonging and Nostalgia in Europe and the United States*. Springer.

Easthope, Hazel. 2004. "A Place Called Home." *Housing, Theory and Society* 21 (3): 128–38.

Espiritu, Yen Le. 1992. *Asian American Panethnicity: Bridging Institutions and Identities*. Temple University Press.

Espiritu, Yen Le, and Paul Ong. 1994. "Class Constraints on Racial Solidarity among Asian Americans." In *The New Asian Immigration in Los Angeles and Global Restructuring*, edited by Paul M. Ong, Edna Bonacich, and Lucie Cheng, 295–321. Temple University Press.

Fainstein, Susan S. 2005. "Planning Theory and the City." *Journal of Planning Education and Research* 25 (2): 121–30.

Fainstein, Susan S., Lily M. Hoffman, and Dennis R. Judd. 2003. "Making Theoretical Sense of Tourism." In *Cities and Visitors: Regulating People, Markets, and City Space*, edited by Lily M. Hoffman, Susan S. Fainstein, and Dennis R. Judd, 239–53. Blackwell Publishing.

Fan, Ying. 2006. "Branding the Nation: What Is Being Branded?" *Journal of Vacation Marketing* 12 (1): 5–14.

Farrar, Margaret E. 2011. "Amnesia, Nostalgia, and the Politics of Place Memory." *Political Research Quarterly* 64 (4): 723–35.

Fennelly, Katherine. 2008. "Prejudice Toward Immigrants in the Midwest." In *New Faces in New Places: The Changing Geography of American Immigration*, edited by Douglas S. Massey, 151–178. Russell Sage Foundation.

Fittante, Daniel. 2018. "The Armenians of Glendale: An Ethnoburb in Los Angeles's San Fernando Valley." *City & Community* 17 (4): 1231–47.

Flemmen, Magne, Johs Hjellbrekke, and Vegard Jarness. 2018. "Class, Culture and Culinary Tastes: Cultural Distinctions and Social Class Divisions in Contemporary Norway." *Sociology* 52 (1): 128–49.

Flowers, Rick, and Elaine Swan. 2012. "Eating the Asian Other?: Pedagogies of Food Multiculturalism in Australia." *PORTAL: Journal of Multidisciplinary International Studies* 9 (2): 1–30.

Fong, Timothy. 2010 [1994]. *The First Suburban Chinatown: The Remaking of Monterey Park, California*. Temple University Press.
Fong, Eric, and Jing Shen. 2011. "Explaining Ethnic Enclave, Ethnic Entrepreneurial and Employment Niches: A Case Study of Chinese in Canadian Immigrant Gateway Cities." *Urban Studies* 48 (8): 1605–33.
Freely, Maureen. 1998. "Scrambled Eggheads." *The Guardian*, June 30. www.politics.guardian.co.uk.
Freeman, Robert C. 1987. "The Development and Maintenance of New York City's Italian-American Neighborhoods." In *The Melting Pot and Beyond: Italian Americans in the Year 2000*, edited by Jerome Krase and William Egelman, 223–37. American Italian Historical Association.
Fritzsche, Peter. 2001. "Specters of History: On Nostalgia, Exile, and Modernity." *American Historical Review* 106 (5): 1587–618.
Gans, Herbert J. 1979. "Symbolic Ethnicity: The Future of Ethnic Groups and Cultures in America." *Ethnic and Racial Studies* 2 (1): 1–20.
———. 2002. "The Sociology of Space: A Use-centered View." *City & Community* 1 (4): 329–39.
———. 2008. "Involuntary Segregation and the Ghetto: Disconnecting Process and Place." *City & Community* 7 (4): 353–57.
Gabaccia, Donna R. 1998. *We Are What We Eat: Ethnic Food and the Making of Americans*. Harvard University Press.
Garrett, Geoffrey. 1998. "Global Markets and National Politics: Collision Course or Virtuous Circle?" *International Organization* 52 (4): 787–824.
Gilboa, Eytan. 2008. "Searching for a Theory of Public Diplomacy." *Annals of the American Academy of Political and Social Science* 61 (1): 55–77.
Giousmpasoglou, Charalampos, Lorraine Brown, and John Cooper. 2020. "The Role of the Celebrity Chef." *International Journal of Hospitality Management* 85:1023–58.
Gold, Steven J. 2015. "Ethnic Enclaves." In *Emerging Trends in the Social and Behavioral Sciences*, edited by Robert Scott and Stephan Kosslyn, 1–18. John Wiley and Sons.
Goode, Judith G., Karen Curtis, and Janet Theophano. 1984. "Meal Formats, Meal Cycles, and Menu Negotiation in the Maintenance of an Italian-American Community." In *Food in the Social Order: Studies of Food and Festivals in Three American Communities*, edited by Mary Douglas, 143–218. Russell Sage Foundation.
Good France. n.d. "Explore the Best of France - Food, Culture, Nature." Accessed August 1, 2025. https://goodfrance.com/.
Gotham, Kevin Fox. 2005. "Theorizing Urban Spectacles." *City* 9 (2): 225–46.
Goût de France/Good France. 2019. *Good France: A Spring Celebration of French Gastronomy*. Press kit for 5th Goût de France/Good France Event, organized by the French Ministry for Europe and Foreign Affairs and Alain Ducasse, March 21, 2019. https://assets.france.fr.
Government of the Republic of Korea. 2017. *A Nation of the People, A Just Republic of Korea, 100 Policy Tasks: Five-Year Plan of the Moon Jae-in Administration*. The Government of the Republic of Korea.

Grant, Roy. 1991. "The Special Needs of Homeless Children: Early Intervention at a Welfare Hotel." *TECSE* 10 (4): 76–91.

Gray, Christopher. 1987. "Streetscape: The Hotel Martinique; Grimy Grande Dame Housing the Homeless Off Herald Sq." *New York Times*, September 27. www.nytimes.com.

Greenberg, Miriam. 2009. *Branding New York: How a City in Crisis Was Sold to the World*. Routledge.

Green Growth Knowledge Platform. 2013. *Moving Towards a Common Approach on Green Growth Indicators: Green Growth Knowledge Platform Scoping Paper*. www.greenpolicyplatform.org.

Greinacher, Udo. 1998. "Ethnic Enclaves: New Urbanism and the Inner City." In *City, Space + Globalization: An International Perspective*, edited by Hemalata C. Dandekar, 126–31. University of Michigan.

Haggard, Stephan, and Chung-in Moon. 1990. "Institutions and Economic Policy: Theory and a Korean Case Study." *World Politics* 42(2): 210–37.

———. 1993. "The State, Politics, and Economic Development in Postwar South Korea." In *State and Society in Contemporary Korea*, edited by Hagen Koo, 51–93. Cornell University Press.

Halbwachs, Maurice. 1980. *The Collective Memory*. Harper & Row.

Hall, Tim, and Phil Hubbard. 1998. *The Entrepreneurial City: Geographies of Politics, Regime, and Representation*. Wiley.

Halter, Marilyn. 2007. *Shopping for Identity: The Marketing of Ethnicity*. Schocken.

Han, Gil-Soo. 2015. "K-Pop Nationalism: Celebrities and Acting Blackface in the Korean Media." *Continuum* 29 (1): 2–16.

Hannigan, John. 1998. *Fantasy City: Pleasure and Profit in the Postmodern Metropolis*. Routledge.

Hansen, Signe. 2008. "Society of the Appetite: Celebrity Chefs Deliver Consumers." *Food, Culture & Society* 11 (1): 49–67.

Harun, Rafael, and Pierre Filion. 2022. "Ethnoburb as a Spatiotemporal Process: Its Implications for Immigrant Settlements." *GeoJournal* 87 (3): 2327–43.

Hebbert, Michael. 2005. "The Street as Locus of Collective Memory." *Environment and Planning D: Society and Space* 23 (4): 581–96.

Heldke, Lisa. 2015 [2003]. *Exotic Appetites: Ruminations of a Food Adventurer*. Routledge.

Hernàndez i Martí, Gil-Manuel. 2006. "The Deterritorialization of Cultural Heritage in a Globalized Modernity." *Journal of Contemporary Culture* 1:91–106.

Hoffman, Lily M. 2003. "The Marketing of Diversity in the Inner City: Tourism and Regulation in Harlem." *International Journal of Urban and Regional Research* 27 (2): 286–99.

Holak, Susan L. 2014. "From Brighton Beach to Blogs: Exploring Food-Related Nostalgia in the Russian Diaspora." *Consumption Markets & Culture* 17 (2): 185–207.

Hollows, Joanne. 2003. "Oliver's Twist Leisure, Labour and Domestic Masculinity in The Naked Chef." *International Journal of Cultural Studies* 6 (2): 229–48.

Holt, Douglas B. 2004. *How Brands Become Icons: The Principles of Cultural Branding*. Harvard Business Press.

hooks, bell. 1992. *Black Looks: Race and Representation*. South End Press.

———. 2009. *Belonging: A Culture of Place*. Routledge.
Huang, Shuling. 2011. "Nation-Branding and Transnational Consumption: Japan-Mania and the Korean Wave in Taiwan." *Media, Culture & Society* 33 (1): 3–18.
Hum, Tarry. 2014. *Making a Global Immigrant Neighborhood: Brooklyn's Sunset Park*. Temple University Press.
Hunter, Marcus Anthony, Kevin Loughran, and Gary Alan Fine. 2018. "Memory Politics: Growth Coalitions, Urban Pasts, and the Creation of 'Historic' Philadelphia." *City & Community* 17 (2): 330–49.
Huynh, Virginia W. 2012. "Ethnic Microaggressions and the Depressive and Somatic Symptoms of Latino and Asian American Adolescents." *Journal of Youth and Adolescence* 41 (7): 831–46.
Hyman, Gwen. 2008. "The Taste of Fame: Chefs, Diners, Celebrity, Class." *Gastronomica* 8 (3): 43–52.
Ichijo, Atsuko, and Ronald Ranta. 2016. *Food, National Identity and Nationalism: From Everyday to Global Politics*. Springer.
Ichijo, Atsuko. 2020. "Food and Nationalism: Gastronationalism Revisited." *Nationalities Papers* 48 (2): 215–23.
Ignatieff, Michael. 1994. *Blood and Belonging: Journeys into the New Nationalism*. Farrar, Straus and Giroux.
Im, Hyug Baeg. 2004. "Faltering Democratic Consolidation in South Korea: Democracy at the End of the 'Three Kims' Era." *Democratization* 11 (5): 179–98.
Institute of International Education (IIE). 2023. "International Students." In *Open Doors: Report on International Educational Exchange*, presentation given November 12, 2023, Washington, DC. https://opendoorsdata.org.
Ipsos. 2023. *The Anholt-Ipsos Nation Brands Index: Press Release – Supplemental Report November 2023*. Ipsos. www.ipsos.com.
ItalianFOOD.net. 2022. "The Best of Italian Food and Beverage on Show in New York." June 13. https://news.italianfood.net.
———. 2024. "Summer Fancy Food 2024: Italian Pavilion unveiled." June 24. https://news.italianfood.net.
Italy-America Chamber of Commerce Southeast. n.d. "About the Project." Accessed August 3, 2025. https://teit.iaccse.com.
Iwabuchi, Koichi. 2002. *Recentering Globalization*. Duke University Press.
Jackson, Peter. 1999. "Commodity Cultures: The Traffic in Things." *Transactions of the Institute of British Geographers* 24 (1): 95–108.
Jacoby, Russell. 1994. "The Myth of Multiculturalism." *New Left Review* 208:121–26.
James, Allison. 1996. "Cooking the Books: Global or Local Identities in Contemporary British Food Cultures?" In *Cross-Cultural Consumption: Global Markets, Local Realities*, edited by David Howes, 77–92. Routledge.
Jansen, Sue Curry. 2008. "Designer Nations: Neo-liberal Nation Branding—Brand Estonia." *Social Identities* 14 (1): 121–42.
Japhe, Brad. 2019. "A Korean Food Hall Comes to Times Square." *Forbes*, September 30. www.forbes.com.

Jarvis, Helen, and Alastair Bonnett. 2013. "Progressive Nostalgia in Novel Living Arrangements: A Counterpoint to Neo-traditional New Urbanism?" *Urban Studies* 50 (11): 2349–70.

Jenkins, Henry. 1992. *Textual Poachers: Television Fans and Participation Culture.* Routledge.

———. 2006. *Fans, Bloggers, and Gamers: Exploring Participatory Culture.* New York University Press.

Jensen, Ole B. 2007. "Culture Stories: Understanding Cultural Urban Branding." *Planning Theory* 6 (3): 211–36.

Jin, Dal Yong, and Kyong Yoon. 2016. "The Social Mediascape of Transnational Korean Pop Culture: Hallyu 2.0 as Spreadable Media Practice." *New Media & Society* 18 (7): 1277–92.

Jin, Hyunjoo, Se Young Lee, Nichola Saminather. 2017. "Chaebol Reform at Forefront of South Korea Presidential Campaign—Again." Reuters, March 27. www.reuters.com.

Jones, Leroy P., and Il Sakong. 1980. *Government, Business, and Entrepreneurship in Economic Development: The Korean Case.* Harvard University.

Johnston, Josée, and Shyon Baumann. 2007. "Democracy Versus Distinction: A Study of Omnivorousness in Gourmet Food Writing." *American Journal of Sociology* 113 (1): 165–204.

———. 2014. *Foodies: Democracy and Distinction in the Gourmet Foodscape.* Routledge.

Jojic, Sonia. 2018. "City Branding and the Tourist Gaze: City Branding for Tourism Development." *European Journal of Social Science Education and Research* 5 (3): 150–160.

Jordan, Paul. 2014. "Nation Branding: A Tool for Nationalism?" *Journal of Baltic Studies* 45 (3): 283–303.

Joyce, Mary. 2007. *The Citizen Journalism Web Site 'OhmyNews' and the 2002 South Korean Presidential Election.* Berkman Center Internet & Society at Harvard University.

Ju, Hyejung. 2020. "Korean TV Drama Viewership on Netflix: Transcultural Affection, Romance, and Identities." *Journal of International and Intercultural Communication* 13 (1): 32–48.

Jung, Eun-Young. 2009. "Transnational Korea: A Critical Assessment of the Korean Wave in Asia and the United States." *Southeast Review of Asian Studies* 31:69–80.

Jung, Kwangho, Jong-Hwan Eun, and Seung-Hee Lee. 2017. "Exploring Competing Perspectives on Government-Driven Entrepreneurial Ecosystems: Lessons from Centres for Creative Economy and Innovation (CCEI) of South Korea." *European Planning Studies* 25 (5): 827–47.

Kakim, Danabayev, and Park Jowon. 2020. "Q-Pop as a Phenomenon to Enhance New Nationalism in Post-Soviet Kazakhstan." *Asia Review* 9 (2): 85–129.

Kaneva, Nadia. 2011. "Nation Branding: Toward an Agenda for Critical Research." *International Journal of Communication* 5:117–41.

———. 2016. "Nation Branding and Commercial Nationalism: Notes for a Materialist Critique." In *Commercial Nationalism: Selling the Nation and Nationalizing the Sell*, edited by Zala Volcic and Mark Andrejevic, 175–93. Palgrave Macmillan.

Kaneva, Nadia, and Delia Popescu. 2011. "National Identity Lite: Nation Branding in Post-communist Romania and Bulgaria." *International Journal of Cultural Studies* 14 (2): 191–207.

Kang, Diane. 2016. "A Fresh Generation of Chefs Is Bringing New Korean Cuisine to the World." *NBC News*, July 5. www.nbcnews.com.

Kang, Jaeho. 2022. "Whither Transnationality? Some Theoretical Challenges in Korean Wave Studies." *International Journal of Communication* 16:3310–28.

Kang, Taesoo, and Guonan Ma. 2009. "Credit Card Lending Distress in Korea in 2003." In *Household Debt: Implications for Monetary Policy and Financial Stability*, 95–106. Bank for International Settlements.

Kanozia, Rubal, and Garima Ganghariya. 2021. "Cultural Proximity and Hybridity: Popularity of Korean Pop Culture in India." *Media Asia* 48 (3): 219–28.

Kavaratzis, Michalis. 2004. "From City Marketing to City Branding: Towards a Theoretical Framework for Developing City Brands." *Place Branding* 1 (1): 58–73.

Kibria, Nazli. 1997. "The Construction of 'Asian American': Reflections on Intermarriage and Ethnic Identity Among Second-generation Chinese and Korean Americans." *Ethnic and Racial Studies* 20 (3): 523–44.

———. 2003. *Becoming Asian American: Second-Generation Chinese and Korean American Identities*. Johns Hopkins University Press.

Kimchi Chronicles. n.d. "Credits." Accessed August 1, 2024. www.kimchichronicles.tv.

Kim, Claire Jean. 2003. *Bitter Fruit: The Politics of Black-Korean Conflict in New York City*. Yale University Press.

Kim, Dae Young. 1999. "Beyond Co-ethnic Solidarity: Mexican and Ecuadorean Employment in Korean-owned Businesses in New York City." *Ethnic and Racial Studies* 22 (3): 581–605.

Kim, Eun Mee, and Jiwon Ryoo. 2007. "South Korean Culture Goes Global: K-Pop and the Korean Wave." *Korean Social Science Journal* 34 (1): 117–52.

Kim, Gooyong. 2017. "Between Hybridity and Hegemony in K-Pop's Global Popularity: A Case of Girls' Generation's American Debut." *International Journal of Communication* 11:2367–86.

Kim, Hani. 2020. "The Sociopolitical Context of the COVID-19 Response in South Korea." *BMJ Global Health*, May 11. https://gh.bmj.com.

Kim, Illsoo. 1981. *New Urban Immigrants: The Korean Community in New York*. Princeton University Press.

Kim, Jinwon. 2018. "Manhattan's Koreatown as a Transclave: The Emergence of a New Ethnic Enclave in a Global City." *City & Community* 17 (1): 276–95.

Kim, Ju Oak. 2021. "BTS as Method: A Counter-hegemonic Culture in the Network Society." *Media, Culture & Society* 43 (6): 1061–77.

Kim, Ron. 2022. "Assemblymember Kim Speaks on Korean Heritage and Welcomes Members of the Korean-American Community during a Press Conference Recognizing Kimchi Day in Albany." New York State Assembly, May 24. https://assembly.state.ny.us.

Kim, Sam. 2018. "NYC's K-Town Isn't What It Used to Be Most Mom-and-Pops Are Gone, and 32nd Street Is Now Dominated by Chains Due to High Rents and Policies in Korea Itself." *Eater New York*, July 31. https://ny.eater.com.

Kim, Seongseop, Miju Kim, Jerome Agrusa, and Aejoo Lee. 2012. "Does a Food-themed TV Drama Affect Perceptions of National Image and Intention to Visit a Country? An Empirical Study of Korea TV Drama." *Journal of Travel & Tourism Marketing* 29 (4): 313–26.

Kim, Taeyoung. 2017. "Creative Economy of the Developmental State: A Case Study of South Korea's Creative Economy Initiatives." *Journal of Arts Management, Law, and Society* 47 (5): 322–32.

Kim, Youna. 2022. "Soft Power and Cultural Nationalism: Globalization of the Korean Wave." In *Media in Asia: Global, Digital, Gendered and Mobile*, edited by Youna Kim, 93–106. Routledge.

King-O'Riain, Rebecca Chiyoko. 2021. "'They Were Having So Much Fun, So Genuinely . . .': K-Pop Fan Online Affect and Corroborated Authenticity." *New Media & Society* 23 (9): 2820–38.

Ko, Lisa. 2018. "Opinion: Harvard and the Myth of the Interchangeable Asian." *New York Times*, October 13. www.nytimes.com.

Koh, Reena. 2023. "Young K-Pop Fans Around the Globe Are Dishing Out Hundreds of Dollars to Fund 90-Second Video Calls with Their Favorite Singers. We Talked to 3 of Them." *Business Insider*, May 20. www.businessinsider.com.

Koo, Hagen. 1991. "Middle Classes, Democratization, and Class Formation." *Theory and Society* 20 (4): 485–509.

Koo, Hagen, and Eun Mee Kim. 1992. "Developmental State and Capital Accumulation in South Korea." In *States and Development in the Asian Pacific Rim*, edited by Richard P. Appelbaum and Jeffrey William Henderson, 121–49. Sage.

Koo, Hagen, and Eui-Young Yu. 1981. *Korean Immigration to the United States: Its Demographic Pattern and Social Implications for Both Societies*. East-West Center.

Korea Daily. 2016. "Korean 'Smoked Mackerel' Ranked in NY Times Top 10 Restaurant Dishes of 2015." January 5. www.koreadailyus.com.

Korea Society. 2012. "An Evening with Hooni Kim, Chef-Owner of Danji." Vimeo video, 1:27:27, October 24. https://vimeo.com/53104292.

———. 2020. "Beyond 32nd Street: Korean Restaurants of the Moment." YouTube video, 37:31, February 27. www.youtube.com/watch?v=ANM_JFNflwc.

Korean Cultural Center New York (KCCNY). 2022. "[Special Online Korean Cuisine Cooking Series] 'Kimjang, Making and Sharing Kimchi with Chef Hooni Kim': Episode #1. 'Baechu Kimchi & Suyuk.'" December 20. www.koreanculture.org.

Kozol, Jonathan. 1988. *Rachel and Her Children: Homeless Families in America*. Crown Publishing Group.

Krase, Jerome. 1997 "The Spatial Semiotics of Little Italies and Italian Americans." In *Industry, Technology, Labor and the Italian American Communities*, edited by Mario Aste, Jerome Krase, Louise Napolitano-Carmen, and Janet E. Worrall, 98–127. American Italian Historical Association.

Krueger, Anne O., and Jungho Yoo. 2002. "Chaebol Capitalism and the Currency-Financial Crisis in Korea." In *Preventing Currency Crises in Emerging Markets*, edited by Sebastian Edwards and Jeffrey A. Frankel, 601–62. University of Chicago Press.

Kugel, Seth. 2008. "From Bi Bim Bop to a Huge Spa." *New York Times*, January 27. www.nytimes.com.

Kurashige, Lon. 2016. *Two Faces of Exclusion: The Untold History of Anti-Asian Racism in the United States*. University of North Carolina Press.

Kwan, Peter. 1998. "Invention, Inversion and Intervention: The Oriental Woman in the World of Suzie Wong, M. Butterfly, and the Adventures of Priscilla, Queen of the Desert." *Asian LJ* 5:99–137.

Ladino, Jennifer K. 2012. *Reclaiming Nostalgia: Longing for Nature in American Literature*. University of Virginia Press.

Laguerre, Michel. 2010. "A Cosmonational Theory of Global Neighborhoods." *Amerasia Journal* 36 (3): xv–xxxiv.

Laing, Jennifer H., and Geoffrey I. Crouch. 2009. "Myth, Adventure and Fantasy at the Frontier: Metaphors and Imagery Behind an Extraordinary Travel Experience." *International Journal of Tourism Research* 11 (2): 127–41.

Lee, Eunji. 2022. "Kimchi Event Held at Capitol Hill to Push for Passing the Resolution to Designate Official Kimchi Day." *Arirang News*, December 6. www.youtube.com/watch?v=NmLYyxloh40.

Lee, Hyunji. 2018. "A 'Real' Fantasy: Hybridity, Korean Drama, and Pop Cosmopolitans." *Media, Culture & Society* 40 (3): 365–80.

Lee, Jennifer. 2002. *Civility in the City: Blacks, Jews, and Koreans in Urban America*. Harvard University Press.

Lee, Jihoon, and Ju-min Park. 2024. "S.Korea Unveils Reform Steps to Tackle 'Korea Discount'; Traders Not Convinced." *Reuters*, February 25. www.reuters.com.

Lee, Min Joo. 2020. "Touring the Land of Romance: Transnational Korean Television Drama Consumption from Online Desires to Offline Intimacy." *Journal of Tourism and Cultural Change* 18 (1): 67–80.

Lee, Sangjoon, and Abé Markus Nornes. 2015. *Hallyu 2.0: The Korean Wave in the Age of Social Media*. University of Michigan Press.

Lee, Seow Ting, and Hun Shik Kim. 2021. "Nation Branding in the COVID-19 Era: South Korea's Pandemic Public Diplomacy." *Place Branding and Public Diplomacy* 17:382–96.

Lee, Shelley Sang-Hee. 2022. *Koreatown, Los Angeles: Immigration, Race, and the American Dream*. Stanford University Press.

Lee, Summer. 2023. "Seoul's Joo Ok Restaurant to Relocate to New York in March." *Michelin Guide*, December 7. https://guide.michelin.com.

Lee, Sun-min. 2019. "A Visit to Korea to Understand Cote's Roots: Restaurateur Simon Kim Reflects on Bringing His Team from the New York Hot Spot to Seoul." *Korea JoongAng Daily*, August 8. https://koreajoongangdaily.joins.com.

Leeman, Jennifer, and Gabriella Modan. 2009. "Commodified Language in Chinatown: A Contextualized Approach to Linguistic Landscape 1." *Journal of sociolinguistics* 13 (3): 332–62.

———. 2010. "Selling the City: Language, Ethnicity and Commodified Space." In *Linguistic Landscape in the City*, edited by Elana Goldberg Shohamy, Eliezer Ben Rafael, and Monica Barni, 182–198. Multilingual Matters.

Legg, Stephen. 2005. "Contesting and Surviving Memory: Space, Nation, and Nostalgia in Les Lieux de Mémoire." *Environment and Planning D: Society and Space* 23 (4): 481–504.

Levitt, Peggy. 2009. "Roots and Routes: Understanding the Lives of the Second Generation Transnationally." *Journal of Ethnic and Migration Studies* 35 (7): 1225–42.

Li, Chuo. 2015. "Commercialism and Identity Politics in New York's Chinatown." *Journal of Urban History* 41 (6): 1–17.

Li, Wei. 1998. "Anatomy of a New Ethnic Settlement: The Chinese Ethnoburb in Los Angeles." *Urban Studies* 35 (3): 479–501.

———. 2009. *Ethnoburb: The New Ethnic Community in Urban America*. University of Hawai'i Press.

Li, Xiufang, and Juan Feng. 2022. "Nation Branding Through the Lens of Soccer: Using a Sports Nation Branding Framework to Explore the Case of China." *European Journal of Cultural Studies* 25 (4): 1118–38.

Light, Ivan. 1984. "Immigrant and Ethnic Enterprise in North America." *Ethnic and Racial Studies* 7 (2): 195–216.

Light, Ivan, and Edna Bonacich. 1991. *Immigrant Entrepreneurs: Koreans in Los Angeles, 1965–1982*. University of California Press.

Light, Ivan, Georges Sabagh, Mehdi Bozorgmehr, Claudia Der-Martirosian. 1994. "Beyond the Ethnic Enclave Economy." *Social Problems* 41 (1): 65–80.

Lin, Jan. 1998. *Reconstructing Chinatown: Ethnic Enclaves and Global Change*. Vol. 2. University of Minnesota Press.

———. 2011. *The Power of Urban Ethnic Places: Cultural Heritage and Community Life*. Routledge.

Liu, Haiming. 2009. "Chop Suey as Imagined Authentic Chinese Food: The Culinary Identity of Chinese Restaurants in the United States." *Journal of Transnational American Studies* 1 (1): 1–24.

Liu, Liangni Sally, Robert Didham, Xiaoan Wu, and Zhihan Wang. 2022. "The Making of an Ethnoburb: Studying Sub-ethnicities of the China-born New Immigrants in Albany, New Zealand." *Integrative Psychological and Behavioral Science* 56:426–58.

Logan, John R., Richard D. Alba, and Thomas L. McNulty. 1994. "Ethnic Economies in Metropolitan Regions: Miami and Beyond." *Social Forces* 72 (3): 691–724.

Logan, John R., Wenquan Zhang, and Richard D. Alba. 2002. "Immigrant Enclaves and Ethnic Communities in New York and Los Angeles." *American Sociological Review* 67 (2): 299–322.

Logan, John R., and Charles Zhang. 2010. "Global Neighborhoods: New Pathways to Diversity and Separation." *American Journal of Sociology* 115(4): 1069–109.

Longenecker, Lisa M., and Jooyoun Lee. 2018. "The Korean Wave in America: Assessing the Status of K-pop and K-drama Between Global and Local." *Situations* 11 (2): 105–27.

Lu, Joanne. 2021. "BTS Spoke at the UNGA. And That's Not the Only Surprise at the U.N. Event." NPR, September 21. www.npr.org.

Lu, Shun, and Gary Alan Fine. 1995. "The Presentation of Ethnic Authenticity: Chinese Food as a Social Accomplishment." *Sociological Quarterly* 36 (3): 535–53.

Lupton, Deborah. 1994. "Food, Memory and Meaning: The Symbolic and Social Nature of Food Events." *Sociological Review* 42 (4): 664–85.

MacCannell, Dean. 1973. "Staged Authenticity: Arrangements of Social Space in Tourist Settings." *American Journal of Sociology* 79 (3): 589–603.

Mann, Michael. 1997. "Has Globalization Ended the Rise and Rise of the Nation-State?" *Review of International Political Economy* 4 (3): 472–96.

Mannur, Anita 2007. "Culinary Nostalgia: Authenticity, Nationalism, and Diaspora." *Melus* 32 (4): 11–31.

Marcuse, Peter. 1997. "The Enclave, the Citadel, and the Ghetto What has Changed in the Post-Fordist US City." *Urban Affairs Review* 33 (2): 228–64.

———. 2002. "The Shifting Meaning of the Black Ghetto in the United States." In *Of States and Cities: The Partitioning of Urban Space*, edited by Peter Marcuse and Ronald van Kempen, 109–42. Oxford University Press.

Marrow, Helen B. 2008. "Hispanic Immigration, Black Population Size, and Intergroup Relations in the Rural and Small-town South." In *New Faces in New Places: The Changing Geography of American Immigration*, edited by Douglas S. Massey, 99–123. Russell Sage Foundation.

Martin, Philip L., Susan Martin, and Patrick Weil. 2006. *Managing Migration. The Promise of Cooperation*. Lexington Books.

Massey, Douglas S., and Nancy A. Denton. 1993. *American Apartheid: Segregation and the Making of the Underclass*. Harvard University Press.

Matsumoto, Noriko. 2018. *Beyond the City and the Bridge: East Asian Immigration in a New Jersey Suburb*. Rutgers University Press.

Matt, Susan J. 2007. "You Can't Go Home Again: Homesickness and Nostalgia in US History." *Journal of American History* 94 (2): 469–97.

Matta, Raúl. 2018. "Celebrity Chefs and the Limits of Playing Politics from the Kitchen." In *Globalized Eating Cultures: Mediation and Mediatization*, edited by Jörg Dürrschmidt and York Kautt, 183–201. Palgrave Macmillan.

McGray, Douglas. 2002. "Japan's Gross National Product of Coolness." *Foreign Policy* 4 (5): 44–54.

McLaren, Courtney, and Dal Yong Jin. 2020. "'You Can't Help but Love Them': BTS, Transcultural." *Korea Journal* 60 (1): 100–127.

Medina, Jenny Wang. 2015. "From Tradition to Brand: The Making of 'Global' Korean Culture in Millennial South Korea." PhD diss., Columbia University.

Melissen, Jan. 2005. "The New Public Diplomacy: Between Theory and Practice." In *The New Public Diplomacy*, edited by Jan Melissen, 3–27. Palgrave Macmillan.

Michelin Guide. 2018. "MICHELIN Guide's Point of View." https://guide.michelin.com.

———. 2019. "The Rise of New Korean Gastronomy: One of the Most Vibrant Food Cultures in the World, a New Generation of Young Chefs Is Leading the Charge in South Korea and Beyond." March 19. https://guide.michelin.com.

———. 2023. "All the 2023 New York MICHELIN Guide Stars." November 7. https://guide.michelin.com.

Min, Pyong Gap, and Mehdi Bozorgmehr. 2000. "Immigrant Entrepreneurship and Business Patterns: A Comparison of Koreans and Iranians in Los Angeles." *International Migration Review* 34 (3): 707–38.

Ministry of SMEs and Startups (MSS). n.d. "What is BrandK?" Accessed July 22, 2025. https://www.brandk.kr/about/brandk.

Misztal, Barbara. 2003. *Theories of Social Remembering*. Open University Press.

Mitchell, Christine M. 2010. "The Rhetoric of Celebrity Cookbooks." *Journal of Popular Culture* 43 (3): 524–39.

Mizrahi, Isaac. 2023. "New Study Shows the Influence of Diverse Consumers (Part 1)." *Forbes*, December 21. www.forbes.com.

Modell, John. 1977. *The Economics and Politics of Racial Accommodation: The Japanese of Los Angeles, 1900–1942*. University of Illinois Press.

Montanari, Massimo. 2006. *Food Is Culture*. New York: Columbia University Press.

Moon Jae-in's Cheong Wa Dae. 2020. "Congratulatory Message from President Moon Jae-in(@moonriver365) on Korean Film 'Parasite' (@ParasiteMovie) Winning Academy Awards." Twitter, February 10. https://twitter.com/TheBlueHouseENG/status/1226768854262509568?s=20.

Moon, Jae-in. 2021. "Address by President Moon Jae-in at 76th Session of United Nations General Assembly." September 21. https://overseas.mofa.go.kr.

National Restaurant Association. 2013. *What's Hot: 2014 Culinary Forecast*. National Restaurant Association.

Naujoks, Daniel. 2010. "Diasporic Identity. Reflections on Transnational Belonging." *Diaspora Studies* 3 (1): 1–21.

Navarro, Betsabé. 2016. "Creative Industries and Britpop: The Marketisation of Culture, Politics and National Identity." *Consumption Markets & Culture* 19 (2): 228–43.

Newman, George E., and Rosanna K. Smith. 2016. "Kinds of Authenticity." *Philosophy Compass* 11 (10): 609–18.

New York City Department of City Planning. 2019. *Zoning Maps*. New York City Department of City Planning. www1.nyc.gov.

New York City Department of Transportation. 2022. *Streets for Recovery: The Economic Benefits of the NYC Open Streets Program*. New York City Department of Transportation. www.nyc.gov.

New York City Government Official Instagram. 2023. "Making kimbap in a NYC lunchroom. #backtoschool." Instagram video, September 8. www.instagram.com/p/Cw76zxKLzYO/.

Nguyen, Arthur, and Nil Özçaglar-Toulouse. 2021. "Nation Branding as a Market-Shaping Strategy: A Study on South Korean Products in Vietnam." *Journal of Business Research* 122:131–44.

Nielson. 2024. *Reaching Asian American Audiences: Understanding Asian Influence and Media Consumption*. The Nielsen Company. www.nielsen.com.

Nientied, Peter. 2018. "Hybrid Urban Identity—The Case of Rotterdam." *Current Urban Studies* 6 (1): 152.
Nora, Pierre. 1989. "Between Memory and History: Les Lieux de Mémoire." *Representations* 26:7–24.
Nye, Joseph S., Jr. 2004. *Soft Power: The Means to Success in World Politics.* PublicAffairs.
Ocejo, Richard E. 2011. "The Early Gentrifier: Weaving a Nostalgia Narrative on the Lower East Side." *City & Community* 10 (3): 285–310.
OECD. 2002. *National Tourism Policy Review: Republic of Korea.* Paris: OECD.
———. 2011a. *Towards Green Growth: Monitoring Progress—OECD Indicators.* Paris: OECD.
———. 2011b. *Towards Green Growth: A Summary for Policy Makers.* Paris: OECD
———. 2012. *National Tourism Policy Review Republic of Korea.* Paris: OECD
Ogbar, Jeffrey O. G. 2001. "Yellow Power: The Formation of Asian-American Nationalism in the Age of Black Power, 1966–1975." *Souls: A Critical Journal of Black Politics, Culture and Society* 3 (3): 29–38.
Oh, David C. 2017. "K-Pop Fans React: Hybridity and the White Celebrity-Fan on YouTube." *International Journal of Communication* 11.
Ono, Kent A., and Jungmin Kwon. 2013. "Re-worlding Culture?: YouTube as a K-Pop Interlocutor." In *The Korean Wave: Korean Media Go Global*, edited by Youna Kim, 199–214. Routledge.
Oscars. 2020. "Parasite wins Best Original Screenplay | 92nd Oscars (2020)." YouTube video, 3:58, March 11. www.youtube.com/watch?v=jrLkc-4uqIQ&list=PLJ8RjvesnvDMZXBtftHY9ebf6XqxUb2RJ&index=7.
O'Shaughnessy, John, and Nicholas Jackson O'Shaughnessy. 2000. "Treating the Nation as a Brand: Some Neglected Issues." *Journal of Macromarketing* 20 (1): 56–64.
Owen, June. 1958. "Food: Korean Dishes; There Are Many Specialties American Cook Can Adapt—Two Recipes." *New York Times*, September 2. www.nytimes.com.
Parla, Ayse. 2009. "Remembering Across the Border: Postsocialist Nostalgia among Turkish Immigrants from Bulgaria." *American Ethnologist* 36 (4): 750–67.
Park, Gil-Sung, Yong Suk Jang, and Hang Young Lee. 2007. "The Interplay Between Globalness and Localness: Korea's Globalization Revisited." *International Journal of Comparative Sociology* 48 (4): 337–53.
Park, Robert E. 1926. "The Urban Community as a Spatial Pattern and a Moral Order." In *The Urban Community: Selected Papers from the Proceedings of the American Sociological Society*, edited by Ernest Burgess, 3–18. University of Chicago Press.
Park, Robert E., and Ernest Watson Burgess. 1921. *Introduction to the Science of Sociology.* University of Chicago Press.
Pazo, Paula Torreiro. 2016. *Diasporic Tastescapes: Intersections of Food and Identity in Asian American Literature.* LIT Verlag Münster.
Peterson, Richard A., and Albert Simkus. 1992. "How Musical Tastes Mark Occupational Status Groups." In *Cultivating Differences: Symbolic Boundaries and the Making of Inequality*, edited by Michele Lamont, 152–86. University of Chicago Press.

Peterson, Richard A., and Roger M. Kern. 1996. "Changing Highbrow Taste: From Snob to Omnivore." *American Sociological Review* 61 (5): 900–907.

Phillips, Bruce A. 2021. "When Transnational Is Local: Jewish Ethnoburbs." *Contemporary Jewry* 41 (4): 793–822.

Phillips, Kathryn, and Thomas Baudinette. 2022. "Shin-Ōkubo as a Feminine 'K-pop Space': Gendering the Geography of Consumption of K-Pop in Japan." *Gender, Place & Culture* 29 (1): 80–103.

Pierce, Joseph, Deborah G. Martin, and James T. Murphy. 2011. "Relational Place-Making: The Networked Politics of Place." *Transactions of the Institute of British Geographers* 36 (1): 54–70.

Pine, B. Joseph, and James H. Gilmore. 1999. *The Experience Economy: Work Is Theatre & Every Business a Stage*. Harvard Business Press.

Pires, Guilherme D., and John Stanton. 2002. "Ethnic Marketing Ethics." *Journal of Business Ethics* 36 (1–2): 111–18.

Pomerleano, Michael. 1998. *The East Asia Crisis and Corporate Finances: The Untold Micro Story*. No. 1990. World Bank Publications.

Porciani, Ilaria. 2019. "Food Heritage and Nationalism in Europe." In *Food Heritage and Nationalism in Europe*, edited by Ilaria Porciani, 3–32. Routledge.

Portes, Alejandro. 1981. "Modes of Structural Incorporation and Present Theories of Labor Immigrations." In *Global Trends in Migration*, edited by Aristide Zolberg, Mary M. Kritz, Charles B. Keely, and Silvano M. Tomasi, 279–97. CMS Press.

Portes, Alejandro, and Robert L. Bach. 1985. *Latin Journey: Cuban and Mexican Immigrants in the United States*. University of California Press.

Portes, Alejandro, and Leif Jensen. 1989. "The Enclave and the Entrants: Patterns of Ethnic Enterprise in Miami before and after Mariel." *American Sociological Review* 54(6): 929–49.

Portes, Alejandro, and Robert Manning. 2008 [1987]. "The Immigrant Enclave: Theory and Empirical Examples." In *Competitive Ethnic Relations*, edited by Susan Olzak and Joane Nagel, 47–68. Academic Press.

Pottie-Sherman, Yolande. 2013. "Vancouver's Chinatown Night Market: Gentrification and the Perception of Chinatown as a Form of Revitalization." *Built Environment* 39 (2): 172–89.

Prahalad, Coimbatore K., and Venkat Ramaswamy. 2004. "Co-creation Experiences: The Next Practice in Value Creation." *Journal of Interactive Marketing* 18 (3): 5–14.

Presidential Archives of Korea. 2024. "Presidential Council on Nation Branding." August 20. http://17koreabrand.pa.go.kr.

Probyn, Elspeth. 1996. *Outside Belongings*. Routledge.

Rapkin, Mickey. 2021. "COVID-19 Couldn't Stop K-Pop's Global Rise." National Geographic, July 7. www.nationalgeographic.com.

Ray, Krishnendu. 2004. *The Migrants Table: Meals and Memories In*. Temple University Press.

Reijnders, Stijn. 2011. *Places of the Imagination: Media, Tourism, Culture*. Ashgate.

Reijnders, Stijn, Abby Waysdorf, Leonieke Bolderman, and Nicky van Es 2020. "Introduction: Locating Imagination in Popular Culture: Place, Tourism, and Belonging." In *Locating Imagination in Popular Culture: Place, Tourism and Belonging*, edited by Nicky van Es, Stijn Reignders, Leoniek Bolderman, and Abby Waysdorf, 1–16. Routledge.

Richards, Greg. 2011. "Creativity and Tourism: The State of the Art." *Annals of Tourism Research* 38 (4): 1225–53.

Ritivoi, Andreea Deciu. 2002. *Yesterday's Self: Nostalgia and the Immigrant Identity*. Rowman & Littlefield.

Roberts, Martin. 2000. "Transnational Geographic: Perspectives on Baraka." In *"New" Exoticisms: Changing Patterns in the Construction of Otherness*, edited by Isabel Santaolalla, 97–114. Brill.

Rockower, Paul S. 2012. "Recipes for Gastrodiplomacy." *Place Branding and Public Diplomacy* 8:235–46.

Rodbard, Matt. 2014. "2014 In Review: Korean Food Had a Ridiculously Big Year in America." Food Republic, December 30. www.foodrepublic.com.

Rose, Gillian. 1995. "Place and Identity: A Sense of Place." In *A Place in the World?: Places, Cultures and Globalization*, edited by Doreen B. Massey and Pat Jess, 87–132. Oxford University Press.

Rossman, Marlene L. 1994. *Multicultural Marketing: Selling to a Diverse America*. Amacom.

Rubenstein, Roberta. 2001. *Home Matters: Longing and Belonging, Nostalgia and Mourning in Women's Fiction*. Palgrave.

Salamone, Frank A. 1997. "Authenticity in Tourism: The San Angel Inns." *Annals of Tourism Research* 24 (2): 305–21.

Salmon, Andrew. 2007. "Cutting the Korean Discount." *Forbes*, May 11. www.forbes.com.

Sanders, Jimy M., and Victor Nee. 1987. "Limits of Ethnic Solidarity in the Enclave Economy." *American Sociological Review* 52 (6): 745–73.

———. 1992. "Problems in Resolving the Enclave Economy Debate." *American Sociological Review* 57 (3): 415–18.

Schulze, Marion. 2013. "Korea vs. K-Dramaland: The Culturalization of K-Dramas by International Fans." *Acta Koreana* 16 (2): 367–97.

Scitovsky, Tibor. 1985. "Economic Development in Taiwan and South Korea: 1965–81." *Food Research Institute Studies* 19 (3): 215–64.

Seol, Dong-hoon, and Jungming Seo. 2014. "Dynamics of Ethnic Nationalism and Hierarchical Nationhood: Korean Nation and Its Othernesss Since the Late 1980s." *Korea Journal* 54 (2): 5–33.

Shaw, Stephen J. 2011. "Marketing Ethnoscapes as Spaces of Consumption: 'Banglatown—London's Curry Capital.'" *Journal of Town & City Management* 1 (4): 381–95.

Sharpley, Richard. 1994. *Tourism, Tourists and Society*. Routledge.

Shin, Gi-Wook. 2006. *Ethnic Nationalism in Korea: Genealogy, Politics, and Legacy.* Stanford University Press.

Shin, HaeRan. 2018. "The Territoriality of Ethnic Enclaves: Dynamics of Transnational Practices and Geopolitical Relations Within and Beyond a Korean Transnational Enclave in New Malden, London." *Annals of the American Association of Geographers* 108 (3): 756–72.

Shin, Jang-Sup, and Ha-Joon Chang. 2003. *Restructuring Korea Inc.* Routledge.

Sierp, Aline, and Jenny Wüstenberg. 2015. "Linking the Local and the Transnational: Rethinking Memory Politics in Europe." *Journal of Contemporary European Studies* 23 (3): 321–29.

Silver, Ira. 1993. "Marketing Authenticity in Third World Countries." *Annals of Tourism Research* 20 (2): 302–18.

Sklair, Leslie. 2000. *The Transnational Capitalist Class.* Wiley-Blackwell.

Smith, Laurajane, and Gary Campbell. 2017. "'Nostalgia for the Future': Memory, Nostalgia and the Politics of Class." *International Journal of Heritage Studies* 23 (7): 612–27.

Smith, N. Craig, and Elizabeth Cooper-Martin. 1997. "Ethics and Target Marketing: The Role of Product Harm and Consumer Vulnerability." *Journal of Marketing* 61 (3): 1–20.

Song, Sooho. 2020. "The Evolution of the Korean Wave: How Is the Third Generation Different from Previous Ones?" *Korea Observer* 51 (1): 125–50.

Sorkin, Michael. 1992. *Variations on a Theme Park: The New American City and the End of Public Space.* Hill and Wang.

Specialty Food Association. n.d. "We Came, We Tasted, We Got Fancy." Accessed July 30, 2024. www.specialtyfood.com.

Ståhlberg, Per, and Göran Bolin. 2016. "Having a Soul or Choosing a Face? Nation Branding, Identity an Cosmopolitan Imagination." *Social Identities* 22 (3): 274–90.

Stano, Simona. 2016. "Lost in Translation: Food, Identity and Otherness." *Semiotica* 2016 (211): 81–104.

Statista. 2025. "Food-Worldwide." Accessed August 5, 2025. www.statista.com.

Stock, Miriam, and Antonie Schmiz. 2019. "Catering Authenticities. Ethnic Food Entrepreneurs as Agents in Berlin's Gentrification." *City, Culture and Society* 18:100285.

Sue, Derald Wing, Jennifer Bucceri, Annie I. Lin, Kevin L. Nadal, and Gina C. Torino. 2016. "Racial Microaggressions and the Asian American Experience." In *Contemporary Asian America*, edited by Min Zhou and Anthony C. Ocampo, 464–88. New York University Press.

Szondi, Gyorgy. 2008. *Public Diplomacy and Nation Branding: Conceptual Similarities and Differences.* Clingendael Institute.

Thrillist. 2018. "Take a Trip to Seoul without Leaving Manhattan." *Thrillist*, October 23. www.thrillist.com.

Thompson, Derek. 2020. "What's Behind South Korea's COVID-19 Exceptionalism?" *The Atlantic*, May 6. www.theatlantic.com.

Timothy, Dallen J., and Amos S. Ron. 2013. "Understanding Heritage Cuisines and Tourism: Identity, Image, Authenticity, and Change." *Journal of Heritage Tourism* 8 (2–3): 99–104.

Tomlinson, John. 1999. *Globalization and Culture*. University of Chicago Press.

Trudeau, Daniel. 2006. "Politics of Belonging in the Construction of Landscapes: Place-Making, Boundary-Drawing and Exclusion." *Cultural Geographies* 13 (3): 421–43.

Tuan, Mia. 1998. *Forever Foreigners or Honorary Whites?: The Asian Ethnic Experience Today*. Rutgers University Press.

Tummala-Narra, Pratyusha. 2009. "The Immigrant's Real and Imagined Return Home." *Psychoanalysis, Culture & Society* 14 (3): 237–52.

Turgeon, Laurier, and Madeleine Pastinelli. 2002. "'Eat the World': Postcolonial Encounters in Quebec City's Ethnic Restaurants." *Journal of American Folklore* 115 (456): 247–68.

United Nations. 2021a. "President Moon Jae-in & BTS at the Sustainable Development Goals Moment." YouTube video, 18:20, September 20. www.youtube.com/watch?v=jzptPcPLCnA.

———. 2021b. "BTS Shine Spotlight on the United Nations as Envoys of the President of the Republic of Korea." YouTube video, 12:22, September 20. www.youtube.com/watch?v=wAXcMD5dOBA.

Valentine, Gill, and Tracey Skelton. 2007. "The Right to Be Heard: Citizenship and Language." *Political Geography* 26 (2): 121–40.

Valentine, Gill, Deborah Sporton, and Katrine Bang Nielsen. 2008. "Language Use on the Move: Sites of Encounter, Identities and Belonging." *Transactions of the Institute of British Geographers* 33 (3): 376–87.

van Ham, Peter. 2001. "The Rise of the Brand State." *Foreign Affairs* 80 (5): 2–6.

Varga, Somogy. 2013. "The Politics of Nation Branding: Collective Identity and Public Sphere in the Neoliberal State." *Philosophy & Social Criticism* 39 (8): 825–45.

Venkatesh, Alladi, and Laurie A. Meamber. 2008. "The Aesthetics of Consumption and the Consumer as an Aesthetic Subject." *Consumption, Markets and Culture* 11 (1): 45–70.

Vess, Matthew, Jamie Arndt, Clay Routledge, Constantine Sedikides, and Tim Wildschut. 2012. "Nostalgia as a Resource for the Self." *Self and Identity* 11 (3): 273–84.

Vianna, Carla. 2019. "Midtown's Big $6M Korean Food Hall Announces Its First Restaurant Vendors." *Eater*, October 17. https://ny.eater.com.

Volcic, Zala, and Mark Andrejevic. 2011. "Nation Branding in the Era of Commercial Nationalism." *International Journal of Communication* 5:598–618.

Wacquant, Loïc. 2008. *Urban Outcasts: A Comparative Sociology of Advanced Marginality*. Polity.

Waldinger, Roger. 1993. "The Ethnic Enclave Debate Revisited." *International Journal of Urban and Regional Research* 17 (3): 444–52.

Wang, Ning. 1999. "Rethinking Authenticity in Tourism Experience." *Annals of Tourism Research* 26 (2): 349–70.

Warde, Alan, Lydia Martens, and Wendy Olsen. 1999. "Consumption and the Problem of Variety: Cultural Omnivorousness, Social Distinction and Dining Out." *Sociology* 33 (1): 105–27.

Warde, Alan, and Lydia Martens. 2000. *Eating Out: Social Differentiation, Consumption and Pleasure.* Cambridge University Press.

———. 2018. "A Sociological Approach to Food Choice: The Case of Eating Out." In *The Nation's Die: The Social Science of Food Choice*, edited by Anne Murcott, 129–44. Routledge.

Waters, Mary C. 1990. *Ethnic Options: Choosing Identities in America.* University of California Press.

Waters, Mary C., and Tomás R. Jiménez. 2005. "Assessing Immigrant Assimilation: New Empirical and Theoretical Challenges." *Annual Review of Sociology* 31:105–25.

Weikart, Lynne A. 2001. "The Giuliani Administration and the New Public Management in New York City." *Urban Affairs Review* 36 (3): 359–81.

Wells, Pete. 2013. "Prized Performers." *New York Times*, December 23. www.nytimes.com.

———. 2014. "In Queens, Kimchi Is Just the Start: Pete Wells Explores Korean Restaurants in Queens." *New York Times*, December 16. www.nytimes.com.

———. 2015. "Restaurant Review: Oiji in the East Village." *New York Times*, August 18. www.nytimes.com.

———. 2018. "At Atomix, a Korean Restaurant Overflowing with Ideas." *New York Times*, October 16. www.nytimes.com.

West, Cornel. 1990. "The New Cultural Politics of Difference." In *Out There: Marginalization and Contemporary Cultures*, edited by Russell Ferguson and Martha Gever, 19–38. MIT Press.

White, Daniel. 2022. *Administering Affect: Pop-Culture Japan and the Politics of Anxiety.* Stanford University Press.

Wilson, Janelle Lynn. 2015. "Here and Now, There and Then: Nostalgia as a Time and Space Phenomenon." *Symbolic Interaction* 38 (4): 478–92.

Wilson, Kenneth L., and Alejandro Portes. 1980. "Immigrant Enclaves: An Analysis of the Labor Market Experiences of Cubans in Miami." *American Journal of Sociology* 86 (2): 295–319.

Wired. 1998. "Rebranding Britannia." October 10. http://archive.wired.com.

Wirth, Louis. 1927. "The Ghetto." *American Journal of Sociology* 33 (1): 57–71.

World Bank. 2012. *Inclusive Green Growth: The Pathway to Sustainable Development.* World Bank.

Xu, Wenying. 2007. *Eating Identities: Reading Food in Asian American Literature.* University of Hawai'i Press.

Yalvaç, N. Simay, and Irmak Karademir Hazır. 2021. "Do Omnivores Perform Class Distinction? A Qualitative Inspection of Culinary Tastes, Boundaries and Cultural Tolerance." *Sociology* 55 (3): 469–86.

Yonhap News. 2021. "Full text of President Moon Jae-in's Speech at U.N. General Assembly." *Yonhap News*, September 22. https://en.yna.co.kr.

Yoon, Sojung. 2016. "New Arts, Tourism Policies for 2016." *KOREA.net*, January 4. www.korea.net.

Yoon, Tae. 2023. "The Ultimate K-Pop Guide to NYC: K-Pop Stores, Dance Lessons, and Cool Korean Hangout Spots Your Favorite Idol Would Approve of." *Thrillist*, November 7. www.thrillist.com.

Yun, In-jin. 1997. *On My Own: Korean Businesses and Race Relations in America*. University of Chicago Press.

Yuval-Davis, Nira. 2006. "Belonging and the Politics of Belonging." *Patterns of Prejudice* 40 (3): 197–214.

———. 2010. "Theorizing Identity: Beyond the 'Us' and 'Them' Dichotomy." *Patterns of Prejudice* 44 (3): 261–80.

———. 2016. "Power, Intersectionality and the Politics of Belonging." In *The Palgrave Handbook of Gender and Development*, edited by Wendy Harcourt, 367–81. Palgrave Macmillan.

Zhang, Juyan. 2015. "The Food of the Worlds: Mapping and Comparing Contemporary Gastrodiplomacy Campaigns." *International Journal of Communication* 9 (2015): 568–91.

Zhou, Min. 1992 [2010]. *Chinatown: The Socioeconomic Potential of an Urban Enclave*. Temple University Press.

Zhou, Min, and John R. Logan. 1989. "Returns on Human Capital in Ethnic Enclaves: New York City's Chinatown." *American Sociological Review* 54 (5): 809–20.

Zhou, Min, Yen-Fen Tseng, and Rebecca Kim. 2008. "Rethinking Residential Assimilation: The Case of a Chinese Ethnoburb in the San Gabriel Valley, California." *Amerasia Journal* 34 (3): 53–83.

Ziegelman, Jane. 2010. *97 Orchard: An Edible History of Five Immigrant Families in One New York Tenement*. Smithsonian.

Zukin, Sharon. 1995. *Culture of Cities*. Blackwell.

———. 2008. "Consuming Authenticity: From Outposts of Difference to Means of Exclusion." *Cultural Studies* 22 (5): 724–48.

———. 2009. "Changing Landscapes of Power: Opulence and the Urge for Authenticity." *International Journal of Urban and Regional Research* 33 (2): 543–53.

———. 2010. *Naked City: The Death and Life of Authentic Urban Places*. Oxford University Press.

KOREAN

Ahn, Junyong. 2005. "Nyuyok hallyu junbi bujok." *Korea Daily*, August 13. www.koreadaily.com.

Bae, Sung-In. 2010. "Jeongsanghoeuiui jeongchigyeongjehak." *Mareukeuseujuui Yeongu* 7 (4): 249–79.

Baek, Jonghyun. 2022. "Danche hwaldong jungdan seoneon BTS, seoulgwangwang hongboneun gyesokanda." *Joongang Ilbo*, July 18. www.joongang.co.kr.

BANGTANTV. 2019. "[EPISODE] BTS (Bangtansonyeondan) @2018 Daehanminguk daejungmunhwayesulsang." YouTube video, 15:08, January 9. www.youtube.com/watch?v=CX-RCQCmo4k.

Bureau of Public Information (Kongbochyo). 1992. *Je 6 gonghwaguksillok—Roh Tae-u daetongnyeong jeongbu 5-nyon 4-gwon*. Kongbochyo.

Chang, Sanghwan. 2008. "Imyeongbak jeongbu haui hanguk ui jeongchi gyeongje: Geulrobeol gyeongje wigiwa imyeongbak jeongbu gyeongje jeongchaek bipan." *Simingwa Segye* 14:265–81.

Choi, Ji-eun. 2012. "<Gimchi keuronikeul> Yesan goemul hansik segyehwa neun bogo baeura." *Korea Economic Daily*, January 8. https://tenasia.hankyung.com.

Choi, Kyungjoon. 2010. "Gimyunok hansikdang? Charari buluiut dopneunge . . ." *OhmyNews*. December 20. www.ohmynews.com.

Digital Times. 2009. "Gukgabeuraendeu ui 22-il baljok: Daegieopjikwon chachul." January 14. www.dt.co.kr.

E-Nation Index. 2020. *2020 Content Industry*. Jipyonuri.

Government Information Agency (GIA). 2007. *Chamyeojeongbu 5nyeon jeongchaek-hongbobaekseo*. Government Information Agency. https://theme.archives.go.kr.

Hahm, Young-hoon. 2003. "Nodaetongnyeong bangmi 3Iljjae. 'Sijangchinhwa gyeongjedaetongnyeong' imijisimgi juryeok." *Digital Times*, May 13. http://news.naver.com.

Han, Eungyeong. 2005. "Hanryuui sobija jigaksang gyeongjejeok pageub hyogwa." *Hangugbangsonghagbo* 19 (3): 325–60.

HSAD. 2018. "Gukgabeuraendeuwiwonhoe X LG- 'Saranghaeyo koria' gwanggo kaempein." YouTube video, 43 seconds, February 13. https://www.youtube.com/watch?v=dCtmhFwaWF8&t=19s.

Hur, Jin. 2002. "Junggukui hanryu hyeonsanggwa hanguk TV deurama suyonge gwanhan yeongu." *Hangugbangsonghagbo* 16 (1): 496–529.

Jang, Kyungsup. 2005. "Urinara munhwa bokji jeongchaekui heureumgwa jeonmang." *Munhwajeongchaeknonchong* 17:225–43.

Jang, Jiho. 2005. "Gimdaejung jeongbuui bencheogieop jiwonjeongchaekui gwanhan gochal." *Hangukhaengjeonghakbo* 39 (3): 21–42.

Joo, Jin. 2009. "[Teukbyeorinteobyu] Eoyundae gukga beuraendeu iwonjang." *Asia Today*, November 11. www.asiatoday.co.kr.

Jung, Namkoo. 2002. "Jeongyeongnyeonui cheryeokhoebok!" *Hankyoreh 21*, June 27. https://h21.hani.co.kr.

Jung, Tae-seon. 2011. "H-mateu gwonjunggap hoejang hangukui hotellieo kiugetda." *E-Daily*, November 11. https://m.edaily.co.kr.

Kang, Dae-Sup, and Gun-Yup Oh. 2003. *Bencheogieopgwa bencheogeumyung*. Jimmundang.

Kang, Heesu. 2010. "Rice Wine? . . . Makgeollireul makgeollira bureuji motadani." *OSEN*, August 9. http://osen.mt.co.kr.

Kang, Hyeran. 2019. "Soando chinhalmeoni sonmat sallyeotdeoni misyullaeng byeol tta." *Joongang Ilbo*, January 5. https://news.koreadaily.com.

Kang, Jeongmin. 2015. "Bakgeunhye daetongnyeongui gongyak ihaeng pyeongga IV: Chwiim hu 2-nyeon, gyeongjeminjuhwa jeongchaekeul jungsimeuro." *Gyeongjegaehyeokripoteu* 2:1–18.

KBS Union. 2010. "G20 Bangsong gwangpung, nugureul wihan geosinga?" *KBS Union*, October 27. www.kbsunion.net.

Kim, Byungsoo. 2019. "Nyuteuro (Newtro) sindeurom." *Maeil Gyeongje*, July 26. www.mk.co.kr.

Kim, Da-seul. 2012. "Hansik segyehwa jiwon yeongbuin yesan daepok sakgam." *Kyunghyang Shinmun*, January 3. www.khan.co.kr.

Kim, Donghee. 2013. "[2013 Jungangilbo eojenda- Hanin gyeongje eopgeureideu] Hanin sanggwoneul gada (1) Manhattan 32 Street." *Korea Daily*, January 1. https://news.koreadaily.com.

Kim, Eunbyul. 2022. "Yeonbanguihoeseo gimchiui nal chukje." *Korea Daily*, December 6. https://news.koreadaily.com.

Kim, Hoon. 2011. "Hansiksegyehwa judohaneun miguk nyuyokdae haninhaksaenghoe." *Yonhap News*, April 11. www.yonhapnews.co.kr.

Kim, Jin-heung, and Young-seok Kim. 2002. "Je2woldeukeobeun ije sijak. Gukmin daechukje seupocheu yukseong gyeongjehyogwa geukdaehwa." *Kukmin Ilbo*, June 24. http://news.naver.com.

Kim, Jinhye. 2005. "Hangunkmunhwawondeung gongdonggihoek 4gae daehyeong ibenteu pyeolchyeo." *Korea Times*, August 30. www.koreatimes.com.

Kim, Jinwoo. 2010. "Gukbi 5oeong deuryeo wen nyuyok hansikdang." *Kyunghyang Shinmun*, December 13. http://news.khan.co.kr.

Kim, Joohyun. 2024. "[10nyeon jeon geunal] 'Mingwanjudo changjogyeongjesidae yeonda' . . . Mingwanhapdong changjogyeongjechujindan chulbeom." *Jeongungmaeil Sinmun*, January 13. www.jeonmae.co.kr.

Kim, Kyung-bin. 2004. "[Areumdaun ganpan] 2. Jongno jeongbineun je2 cheonggyecheon saeop." *Joonang Ilbo*, February 24. www.joongang.co.kr.

Kim, Meesun. 2012. "1950~1960 Nyeondae yeoseongui sobimunhwawa myeongdongui jangsoseonge gwanhan yeongu." *Seoulhakyeongu* 46:59–101.

Kim, Munjo, and Soo-ho Park. 1998. "Hangukui munhwajeongchaek: Hoegowa jeonmang." *Aseayeongu* 41 (2): 297–323.

Kim, Namhee. 2020. "[Geumyungbulsinui yeoksa] 3. Chulhyeolgyeongjaengi bureun 2003 nyeon sinyongkadeu satae." *EBN Saneopgyeongje*, September 26. www.ebn.co.kr.

Kim, Noh-yeol. 2004. "32Ga hanintaun oegugin neunda." *Korea Times*, March 12. http://dc.koreatimes.com.

Kim, Sang-hyup. 2008. "Hankugi yeoreobun seonggongui gyodubo doel geot." *Munhwa Ilbo*, April 17. www.munhwa.com.

Kim, Sangsoo. 1998. "Gimdaejung dangseonja, geummoeugiundong buyucheung dongcham dangbu." *MBC*, January 23. https://imnews.imbc.com.

Kim, Sujeong. 2012. "Dongnamaeseo hallyuui teukseonggwa munhwachwihyangui chogukgajeok heureum." *Bangsonggwa Keomyunikeisyeon* 13 (1): 5–54.

Kim, Seung-Han. 2020. "BTS, man 30sekkaji gundae an gado doenda . . . byeongyeokbeop ilbugaejeongan gongpo." *Maeilkyeongje*, December 22. www.mk.co.kr.

Kim, Sinyoung. 2014. "[Why] 'Nyuyok myeongga 2sedae hansikdang hyeongui binjari meun dongsaengdeul." *Chosun Ilbo*, January 4. http://news.chosun.com.

Kim, Taeyeol. 2009. "[Gyeongje] MB jeonggwon eolgulmadam gukjegomundan." *Weekly Kyunghyang*, April 21. https://weekly.khan.co.kr.

Ko, Jung-Min, Sin-Gyom Kang, Anjae Lee, and Song Ha. 2005. *CEO Information 503: Hallyu jisokkwa kiopui hwalyongbangan.* SERI.

Koo, Hee-eon. 2015. "Segyehwa deoche geollin K-pudeu." *Weekly Dong-A*, February 16. https://weekly.donga.com.

Koo, Jeongmo. 2016. "Bak daetongnyeong "munhwaga sae gyeongje dongnyeok" . . . munhwayunghapbelteu guchuk gangjo." *Yonhap News*, October 24. www.yna.co.kr.

Korean Daily. 2003. "Maenhaeteun hanintaun asian gogaeki hyojanoreut." April 14. https://news.koreadaily.com.

Korea Trade-Investment Promotion Agency (KOTRA). 2005. *Dongbuga hallyuwa munhwasangpumsijang donghyang.* KOTRA.

KTV. 2020. "Chamjeonyongsa maseukeujiwon wallyo . . . hanguk itji aneul geot." *KTV*, June 16. www.korea.kr.

———. 2021. "Miraemunhwateuksa bts jinmyeonmok deureonan bangmulgwan gwallam hwallyaksang! Gimjeongsuk yeosawa hamkkehan nyuyok meteuropollitan bangmulgwan gwallam mit hanguk gongyepum jeondal (feat. RMdo halmal ilke mandeuneun byuneun deom)" YouTube video, 10:14, September 21. www.youtube.com/watch?v=6kjgPUkzszE.

Kukjung Shinmun. 1998. "Je2ui geongukundong, ireoke pyeolchyeojinda, nara giteul dasi seul gukminundong jeongae." August 17. www.korea.kr.

Kwon, Sei-jin. 2012. "Jeongbuyesan 652eokwon tuiphaetjiman seonggwaneun mimi." *Monthly Chosun*, June. http://monthly.chosun.com.

Kwon, Sun-il. 2002. "[2002Woldeukeop][Adyu '2002 seupocheu']<4>Georireul gadeuk meun bulgeun akma." *Dong-A Ilbo*, December 22. www.donga.com.

Lee, Byeongcheon. 2003. "Chamyeojeongbuui gyeongjejeongchaek: Hangukhyeong je3ui gilui nangwan, dongyo, geurigo ganeungseong." *Simingwa Segye* 4:253–72.

Lee, Byeong-chun. 2011. "Oehwanwigi ihu hangugui chukjeokcheje." *Donghyanggwa Jeonmang* 81:9–69.

Lee, Byeongmin. 2007. "Chamyeojeongbu munhwasaneobjeongchaegui pyeonggawa hyanghu jeongchaekbanghyang." *Inmunkontencheu* 9:205–35.

Lee, Donghun. 2010. "Seoul G20 jeongsanghoeuiwa gidaehyogwa." *CEO Information* 772. Samsung Economic Research Institute (SERI).

Lee, Dongyeon. 2005. "Hanryu munhwajabonui hyeongseonggwa munhwaminjogjuui." *Munhwagwahak Tonggwon* 42:175–96.

Lee, Haelim. 2018. "[Ihaerim nyuyok hansikdabansa] Maenhaeteune illeongineun 'Je3ui hansik mulgyeol.'" *Biz Hankoo*, July 13. www.bizhankook.com.

Lee, Hyunsoo. 2020. "Nyuyok maenhaeteun 32beonga hanintaun, haninhoe doumeuro opeun seuteuriteu jijeong." *Jaeoedongpo Shinmun*, August 10. www.dongponews.net.

Lee, In-wook. 2005. "[Busan APEC jeongsanghoeui D–200] 'Choegang IT Korea' segyee simneunda." *Financial News*, May 1. www.bigkinds.or.kr/.

Lee, Jinsoo. 2021. "Nyuyokilwon haninsikdangdeul gujegigeum eolma badanna." *Korea Times*, July 23. http://m.koreatimes.com.

Lee, Kyou-Jin. 2011. "Nyuyong maenhaeteun hangung eumsikjeomui chogi yeoksa: 1960 nyeondae~1970 nyeondaereul jungsimeuro." *Hanguksiksaenghwalmunhwahakoeji* 26 (6): 562–73.

Lee, Kyung-a. 2007. "Ganpan sibeomgarosaeopui hyeonhwanggwa hyanghubanghyang." *OOH Gwanggohakyeongu* 4 (1): 89–108.

Lee, Ung. 2016. "Munhwachangjoyunghapbonbu naenyeon 3wolkkaji pyeji . . . yunghapbelteu jeonmyeongaepyeon(Jonghap)." *Yonhap News*, December 21. www.yna.co.kr/view.

Lee, Yeongran. 2013. "Teurendihan saeop pagodeuldeon jega doenjangsaeop handago haja." *Herald Economy*, January 28. http://biz.heraldcorp.com.

Lim, Haksoon. 2004. "[Teukjip: 21 segi munhwawa munhwasaneope daehan jeonmang] Munhwasaneop yukseongeul wihan jeongbujeongchaekui inyeom." *Sasang Bomho* 60:107–26.

Lim, Kyung-suk. 2012. "Imyeongbak jeongbuui 747 gongyakgwa geu gyeolgwa." *Yeoksawahyeonsil* 86:3–12.

Maeil Kyeongje. 2019. "Hongchuncheonchijeudakgalbi nyuyok maenhaeteuneseo keuge ingi kkeulgo, nyuyok hureosing, raseubegaseuedo jinchul." *Maeil Kyeongje*, December 17. www.mk.co.kr.

MBC. 2013. "Daejanggeumi georeogan gireul ttaraganeun daejanggeum ruteureul gada." October 4. https://imnews.imbc.com.

Military Manpower Administration (MMA). n.d. "Yesul cheyukyowon jedosogae." *Jedosogae*. Accessed May 9, 2022. www.mma.go.kr.

Ministry of Culture, Sports and Tourism (MCST). 2004. *Changuihanguk* [Creative Korea]. Munhwabu.

———. 2005. *Munhwagangguk (C-KOREA) 2010*. Munhwabu.

———. 2007. "Han seutail(HanStyle) yukseong jonghapgyehoek(2007~2011) balpyo." February 15.

———. 2015. "Yungbokap kontencheu meka . . . Munhwachangjoyunghapsenteo gaboni." March 11. www.korea.kr.

———. 2016. "Daehanmingugui saeroun gukgabeuraendeu 'CREATIVE KOREA.'" July 4. www.mcst.go.kr.

———. 2022. "Eon segyejeogin hanryuro kontencheu suchuraek 14jo won dolpa : 2020nyeon gijun kontencheusaneopjosa(2021nyeon silsi) gyeolgwa balpyo." January 24. www.mcst.go.kr.

Ministry for Food, Agriculture, Forestry and Fisheries (MFAFF). 2009. "Nongsikpumbu, hansik menyuui oegugeo pyogian jejang chujin." Press release, April 27. www.korea.kr.

———. 2011. "Nyuyok senteureol pakeuseo hangugeumsik cheheomhaengsa seonghwang." August 17. www.mafra.go.kr.

Ministry of Information and Communication. 1999. *CYBER KOREA 21: An Informatization Vision for Constructing a Creative, Knowledge-Based Nation*. Ministry of Information and Communication of Republic of Korea.

Moon, Hyojin. 2018. "Jeongbubyeol hallyu jeongchaekgwa beopje: Munminjeong-bueseo chotbuljeongbukkaji." In *Hallyuwa munhwajeongchaek: Hallyu 20nyeon hoegowa jeonmang*, edited by the Korean Foundation for International Cultural Exchange, 101–37. Korean Foundation for International Cultural Exchange.

Moon, Seongjin. 2001. "[Woryochodaeseok] Namgungjin munhwagwangwangbu janggwan." *Seoul Gyeongje*, January 27. www.sedaily.com.

National Assembly Secretariat of South Korea. 2010. *2010nyeondo gukjeonggamsa oegyotongsangtongirwiwonhoe hoeuirok*. National Assembly.

National Archives of Korea. n.d. "550eok dalleoui biteul jin gyeongjegukchiui nal: IMF oehwanwigi geukbok." Accessed July 30, 2024. https://theme.archives.go.kr.

News Wire. 2011. "Hansik, nyuyokeodeul jeomsim ipmat sarojapda." April 19. www.newswire.co.kr.

———. 2019. "Hanguk tojong peuraenchaijeu hongchuncheonchijeudakgalbi, nyuyok maenhateun jinchul." *News Wire*, November 12. www.newswire.co.kr.

Noh, Young-kyu. 2002. "E-Korea Vision 2006." *Digital Contents* 5 (108): 42–44.

Oh, Sooyeong. 2019. "[Aju swiun nyuseu Q&A] Gukgadaepyo jungsogieop gongdong sangpyo 'Beuraendeu K'neun mueosingayo?" *Ajugyeongje*, December 24. www.ajunews.com.

Park, Eunkyeong. 2020. "Jungguksik gimchi 'paochai' ISO Inga . . . Jungguk gwanyeongmaeche 'gimchijongjuguk chiyok' jujang." *Kyunghyang Shinmun*, November 29. www.khan.co.kr.

Park, Geon. 2007. "Jibhapgieokui sahoejeok guseonge gwanhan yeongu: Gukchaebosangundonggwa geummoeugiundongeul jungsimeuro: gukchaebosangundonggwa geummoeugiundongeul jungsimeuro." *Munhwawa Sahoe* 2:117–64.

Park, Hyungshin. 2011. "Matjip yeolpungui gamjeongdonghakgwa sahoedonghak." *Sahoewairon* 18:283–314.

Park, Jeong-soo. 2009. "Gyeongjewigi geukbogeul wihan muyeok mit saneopjeongchaek." *Sijanggyeongjeyeongu* 38:45–74.

Park, Jin-hee. 2009. "MB Jeongbuui noksaek gisul gaebal jeongchaek pyeongga." *Hwangyeongsahoehakyeongu ECO* 13 (2): 99–138.

Park, Jin-pyo. 2010. "Ganpangaeseonsaeopui baljeonbanghyange gwanhan yeongu." *OOH Gwanggohakyeongu* 7 (2): 79–105.

Park, Raeyong. 2003. "Nodaetongnyeong bangmi iteuljjae imojeomo." *Kyunghyang Shinmun*, May 13. www.khan.co.kr.

Park, Sangkwon. 2002. "Hanguk woldeukom 4gang haeoe gyeongjejeok hongbo hyogwa 10jowon." *MBC*, July 2. https://imnews.imbc.com.

Park, Tae-jin. 2011. "Mi nyuyokseo hansik cheheom 'koriadei' gaechoe." *E-Today*, August 17. www.etoday.co.kr.

Park, Wonyoung. 2011. "Nyuyokui hansik bum ppudeut." *Korea Times*, September 22. http://ny.koreatimes.com.

Park, Yongsu. 2010. "Chamyeojeongbuui seonggyeok." *Pyeonghwayeongu* 18 (1): 95–118.

Republic of Korea. 2005. "Busan APEC, IT Gangguk imiji segye simneunda." *Daehanminguk Jeongchaekbeuriping*, October 5. www.korea.kr.

Roh, Dong-Ryul. 2000. "Hallyuui jisok ganeungseong mit jeonmang." *Hangukbangsonghakoe semina mit bogoseo*: 117–38.

Shim, Heejung. 2015. "[Munhwasaneop 20junyeon changjogieopeuro geodeupnaneun CJ] CJ 'Seoulchangjogyeongjehyeoksinsenteo'neun." *Seoul Ggyeongje*, August 26. https://m.sedaily.com.

Shim, Saerom and Hyeonok Ha. 2017. "Geum moeugi 351man dongcham, jigeumeun bogi himdeun gongdongche uisikui him." *Joongang Ilbo*, December 4. www.joongang.co.kr.

Sohn, Hyuk-ki. 2005. "Munhwa gwangwang repocheuro 3manbul sidae yeonda." *Daehanminguk Jeongchaekbeuriping*, July 6. www.korea.kr.

tvN. 2020a. "[Iseojinui nyuyoknyuyok]: Seojiniui hakchangsijeol koriataun koseubuteo SNS hatpeul K-jimjilbangkkaji." YouTube video, 17:47, April 2. www.youtube.com/watch?v=eqQizyMcUBs.

———. 2020b. "Jeodo hangugui jabusimeuro yorireul hago sipeosseoyo | Riteulbik hieoro: deo chaellinjeo LITTLE BIG HEROES: THE CHALLENGER EP.178." YouTube video, 10:44, April 20. www.youtube.com/watch?app=desktop&v=uHAyRMYllHc&t=150s.

Voice of America Korean. 2007. "Hanguk gwangwangbeuraendeu, joseunghui sageoneuro migungnae gwanggojungdan." April 20. www.voakorea.com.

Yang, Ho-seon. 2011. "Jeonguncheon hansikjaedan isajang, maenhaeteun peullaegeusip hansikdang seonggonghal geot." *New York Ilbo*, February 4. www.newyorkilbo.com.

Yang, Hyun-bong, Hyun Joo, and Young-sam Cho. 1998. "Jeongchaekyeongu: Hangukbencheogieopui teukseongbunseok mit yukseongbangan." *Bencheogyeongyeongyeongu* 1 (1): 129–53.

Yeom, Seongwon. 2003. "Hangukui gukgaimiji yeongudonghyangui gwanhan yeongu". *Gwanggohagyeongu* 14 (3): 87–117.

Yim, Seong-soo. 2019. "Mun daetongnyeong, taeguk bangkokeseo K-beuraendeuwa hallyu seiljeu." *Kukmin Ilbo*, September 2. http://news.kmib.co.kr.

Yonhap News. 2002. "Woldeukeop daejeonsi eumsikjeomui oegukeopyogi charimpyo baebu." *Yonhap News*, May 15. http://news.naver.com.

Yoo, Hyeonsung. 1998. "Hangukeumsik oegukeo pyogi tongil." *Yonhap News*, December 21. https://n.news.naver.com.

Yoo, Jaedong. 2022. "Mi nyuyokju 'gimchiui nal' mandeun hangukgye uiwon." *Dong-A Ilbo*, May 26. www.donga.com.

Yoo, Jisang. 2013. "[Mannan saram matnan insaeng] Hansik choecho misyullaeng seuta reseutorang oneo syepeu hunikim." *Hankyung Economy Magazine*, September 30. http://magazine.hankyung.com.

Yoo, Sekyung, and Kyung-sook Lee. 2001. "Dongbukasia 3gukui tellebijeon deuramae natanan munhwajeok geunjeopseong." *Hangukeonnonhakbo* 45 (3): 230–67.

Yoo, Shinmo. 2017. "Bakgeunhye jeongbuui saemaeurundong segyehwa eopdeon illo." *Kyunghyang Shinmun*, June 4. https://m.khan.co.kr.

INDEX

Page numbers in italics indicate Figures

Academy Awards, 41–42
Adam (interviewee), 196–97
advertising, 24, 32, 45–52, 83
Aiden (interviewee), 133
ajeossi (middle-aged men), 104–5
Alan (interviewee), 165
Alba, Richard D., 17, 20
Albanian Kosovars, 24
Alex (interviewee), 141–42
Amazon Prime, 153
Americanization, 80, 90
Anderson, Kay, 24
Anholt, Simon, 9, 53–54
Anholt-GfK, 55
AOMG (music label), 146
APEC. *See* Asia-Pacific Economic Cooperation
Appadurai, Arjun, 26, 196
Aria (interviewee), 146–49, 165, 233n1
Arirang (lyrical folk song), 65
Arirang (restaurant), 177
Arirang House (restaurant), 27
Arirang TV (Korean TV network), 88
ARMY ("Adorable Representative M.C. for Youth"), BTS, 41, 154, 234n12
Aronczyk, Melissa, 14
Asia-Europe Meeting (2000), 47
Asian Americans, 105–10, 113, 116–18, 132–33, 149–54, 181–82, 218n103, 235n9
Asian culture, 37, 69, 116
Asian Development Bank, 44

Asia-Pacific Economic Cooperation (APEC) summit (2005), 52
assimilation, 16–17, 19, 108–9, 140, 176, 184–85
aT Center New York, 33, 35, 69, 71–72, 86–89
Atlanta, Georgia, 109, 129–30, 140
Atoboy (restaurant), 90–95, 181
Atomix (restaurant), 90–95, 181
Australia, 24, 32, 44, 193–94
authenticity, 8, 23–24, 92, 138, 166, 172, 181, 194, 232n20, 235n13; cultural, 145; experiences and, 11, 23, 55, 74, 80–81, 125, 163, 168; food and, 11, 14, 37, 194; Korean culture and, 135, 138, 163, 179; Korean food and, 79–80, 87, 89, 92, 97, 135, 169–70, 178–79, 197; Korean franchises and, 138, 145, 174–75; Koreatown and, 125, 168–80, 196–99; pseudo-authenticity and, 24; quasi-authenticity, 24, 161, 164

Bach, Robert L., 19
Baldwin, Deborah, 2
Banglatown, London, 26
bankruptcies, South Korean, 44–45
Barnard College, 113
barrios, 21, 192
Bayside, Queens, 105, 123, 229n3
bb.q Chicken (Korean fried chicken franchise), 79, *174*, 192
Beijing Olympics (2008), 153

269

belonging, 78, 119, 189, 198, 230n26; conditional, 164–65; language and, 140–43; place of, 110; politics of, 142; sense of, 30, 106–9, 112–20, 144–45, 155–56, 165; site of, 112
Ben (interviewee), 176–77, 179
Bergen County, New Jersey, 21
"Beyond 32nd Street" (talk), Korea Society, 95
Big Bang (K-pop boy band), 80, 154
biotechnology, 49–50, 52, 223n42
biracial people, 57, 75, 117, 186
Black Americans, 1–2, 16, 67, 104, 147, 154–55, 158–60, 165, 171, 197, 218n99; Black-Korean conflicts and, 18, 219n136
Bloomberg, Michael, 9
"Blue House" (Cheongwadae), South Korea, 42, 51, 65, 226n103
Bong Joon Ho, 41–43, 60
Bouley, David, 90
Bourdain, Anthony, 166–68
Brand Estonia, 9–10
Brand-K project, 63–64, 225n102
Brandon (interviewee), 182
Brazilian Americans, 161
Brianna (interviewee), 2, 155–56
Brooklyn, New York, 18, 25, 93, 115, 123–24, 179, 187
BTS (Bangtan Sonyeondan), 2, 41–43, 61–64, 69, 150, 153–55, 221n5
budgets, Korean government agency, 86–87, 98, 139
bunsikjip (inexpensive snack restaurants), 174
Bush, George W., 51
businesses, Koreatown, 4, 6–7, 27–28, 30–31, 34, 66, 68–71, 75–81, 83–84, 89, 93, 96, 104–5, 143, 146, 157–58, 219n143, 8384; Kang Suh Heokwan, 27, 79; Koryo Bookstore, 27–28, 142, 149, 192; kyryodang, 96; New York Gomtang House, 27–28, 219n143. *See also specific franchises*

business-friendly nation, 54
business leaders, 51
business sectors, 49, 50, 55
business strategies, 6, 8, 36, 51, 79, 80

Camdessus, Michel, 43
Camila (interviewee), 161, 163–64
Canada, 9, 11, 44, 132
"Candlelight Revolution," South Korea, 60
capital investments, 8–9, 18, 25, 36
CCEI. *See* Center for Creative Economy and Innovation
celebrity chefs, 76–78, 91, 180–81
censorship, South Korean, 47–48
Center for Creative Economy and Innovation (CCEI), South Korea, 58–59
Chacko, Elizabeth, 25–26
chaebol (family-owned business conglomerates), 44, 54–60, 191, 221n11, 222n31
Chang, David, 90, 181
Chang, Ha-Joon, 45
Cheongwadae ("Blue House"), South Korea, 42, 51, 65, 226n103
childhood memories, 91–92, 126, 130, 178–80
Chin, Vincent, 109, 230n16
China, 9, 11–12, 53, 57, 61, 66, 69–70, 76, 88, 111, 150, 225nn88–89
Chinatown, 6, 7, 16, 21, 22, 25, 183
Chinatown, Flushing (Queens), 22, 232n14
Chinatown, Manhattan, 22–23, 32, 115, 132–33, 149–51, 192, 232n14
Chinatown, Melbourne, 24
Chinatown, San Francisco, 25
Chinatown, Sunset Park (Brooklyn), 25
Chinatown, Sydney, 195
Chinese (language), 151
Chinese Americans, 108–10, 132–33, 165, 233n2
Choe, David, 167–68
Choi, Kyung Rim, 85, 96–98
Choi, Roy, 167–68, 181

INDEX | 271

Choi, Soon-sil, 60
Chung, Byung Hwa, 70
Chung, Haecho, 63
Chungmuro (Korea's Hollywood), 42
Chuseok (Korean autumn harvest), 68–69
CIA. *See* Culinary Institute of America
citizenship, 107; Korean, 124, 136–37
city governments, 8–9, 24, 28–29, 32, 168–69, 228n40
CJ E&M (media company), 58–59
CJ Group, 75, 96
Claiborne, Craig, 166–67, 180
Claire (interviewee), 84–85, 98
class, 14, 18–19, 21, 25, 29, 46, 111, 144, 148, 158, 180, 218n103, 230n23, 232n20
code-switching, language and, 143
coethnic labor, 30, 193
Cold War, 10
Collège Culinaire de France, 195
colonialism, 117, 186
colorblindness, 186
colorism, 197
Columbia University, 117–18, 123, 133, 170
comfort food, 158–59, 177, 182
commercialization, 4, 8, 22, 24, 31, 37, 53, 130, 163, 168–69, 171
commodification, 6, 10, 22, 161, 163
commoditization, 24
community, 17, 23, 25, 114, 161, 189; diasporic, 87; imagined, 135; online, 36–37, 122, 149, 153, 155–56, 165; sense of, 117–18, 137, 140, 142, 148–49, 154–55, 164
Connecticut, 131, 134, 154
conservativeness, of Korean immigrants, 134, 144–45
consumer culture, 4, 6, 22, 29–30, 32, 94–95, 126, 138, 175, 196, 230n26
consumerism, 10–11, 15, 112, 126, 185, 232n12
consumers, 6–8, 10–11, 14, 18, 21–22, 29, 48, 53, 88, 136, 150, 193, 196, 198, 218n103; Koreatown, 4, 15, 30–32, 34–37, 74, 76, 78–79, 80–83, 85, 89, 104–5, 123, 129, 142–43, 145, 149, 168–69, 171, 186–87; non-coethnic, 7, 15, 30, 193; non-Korean, 8, 30, 36, 66, 78–79, 82, 85, 90, 139, 149, 152–61, 175, 181, 186–87, 197–98; nostalgia and, 24–25
consumption, 1, 4, 11, 25–26, 76, 81, 94–95, 99, 108, 165, 179, 185, 193–94, 196–98, 208, 230n26, 234n17, 236n24; ethnic, 24, 105, 178, 180, 185; ethnic enclaves and, 19–22, 25–26; of Korean culture, 149–50; of Korean media, 122; Koreatown and, 6–8, 29, 30–31, 71, 113, 115, 161, 164; Seoul-style, 2, 31
"Cool Britannia" (initiative), 10–11
"Cool Japan" (initiative), 10–11
corporations, 12, 22, 30, 58, 64
corporations, Korean, 2, 4, 6–8, 15, 31–32, 36, 49, 67, 71, 74–75, 77, 89, 138, 194; Korean government and, 6, 35, 58–59
corporations l, 2, 9, 30, 99, 193
corruption, political, 44, 60–61, 64, 67, 68, 86, 98
cosmopolitanism, 8, 67, 104–5, 126, 128, 136, 138, 165, 185–86
Cosmos Department Store, 126, 130
COVID-19 pandemic, 109, 155, 164–65, 187; New York City and, 69, 79–80, 226n1; South Korea and, 41–42, 61–64, 66, 225nn88–89, 234n13
"Creative Korea" initiative, South Korea, 49, 52–53, 59–60
Cuban refugees, Cuban immigrants and, 18–20, 217nn77–78
cuisine, French, 11, 82, 92, 180–81, 194–95
cuisine, Japanese, 76, 82, 89, 95, 173, 182
culinary cultures, 75, 174, 184, 194–95
culinary diplomacy, 11
Culinary Institute of America (CIA), 90
cultural content, 2, 11, 32, 44, 48, 52, 59, 61–62, 65, 145, 194
cultural differences, 85, 110, 122–24, 158, 171, 176–77, 219n136
cultural diversity, 24, 119, 183

cultural industries, 10, 43, 47–50, 52–60, 72, 81, 223n52
culture, consumer, 4, 6, 22, 29–32, 94–95, 126, 138, 175, 196
culture, global, 10, 137, 183
culture, Korean, 4, 34, 63, 66–67, 69, 71–72, 78, 81, 86, 94, 104–5, 110, 117–18, 121, 134–37, 145, 148–50, 153, 157–58, 161–65, 181, 183–84, 187–89, 196–98, 233n2; authenticity and, 135, 138, 179; Korean Americans and, 129, 140–42, 178–79; Korean language classes and, 94, 117–18; Korean nationals on, 175; racial fetishization and, 188–89; visits to Seoul and, 161–64
Culture Creation and Convergence Belt initiative, South Korea, 59–60
Cyber Korea 21 (1999), South Korea, 222n27

dalgona (honeycomb candy), 69, 79–80
Danielle (interviewee), 132
Danji (restaurant), 77, 89–90, 93, 181, 227n29
deaths, hate crime–related, 109, 230n16
decentralization, of power, 47, 223n40
Deener, Andrew, 137
democratization, South Korean, 29, 43–44, 47, 57, 60–61, 118, 223n39
Department of City Planning, New York City, 6, 31
Department of Transportation, New York City, 69
deregulation, 44, 51–52
deterritorialization, 112, 196, 230n26
diaspora, 7, 14, 65, 67, 70–71, 76, 87, 99, 134
"Discover Korea's Delicious Secret" campaign, KFPI, 76
discrimination, racial, 26, 116, 171, 192, 235n9
diversity, 8, 23, 73, 82, 104–5, 110, 156, 184–85; cultural, 24, 119, 183; ethnic, 24
doenjang (fermented soybean paste), 89, 172

Dominican Americans, 146, 152, 155, 157–58, 182–83
Don's Bogam (restaurant), 72–73, 96
Drama Fever (streaming service), 153–54
dual labor market theory, 18, 217n78
Ducasse, Alain, 11, 194–95
dwipuri (social gatherings) culture, South Korean, 118–19
Dynamic Korea initiative, South Korea, 48–53, 59–60
"Dynamite" (song), 41–42

East Asian development model, 45, 221n11
East Meets West (TV show), 181
East Village, Manhattan, 90, 93, 107, 181
Eater (website), 1, 68, 93, 96
Ebens, Ronald, 230n16
education, 50, 52, 55, 66, 87, 107–9, 117–19, 132, 170, 176; international students and, 15, 29, 84, 103, 108, 111, 121–23, 125, 144, 161, 169–70, 230n22, 235n8. *See also specific institutions*
e-Korea Vision 2006 (1999–2001), South Korea, 222n27
elementary school, 107, 116, 126, 176
Emily (interviewee), 103, 108–11, 113–16, 176, 178, 184–85
Emma (interviewee), 153–54, 156, 165
Empire State Building, Manhattan, 2, 31–32, 131, 192–93
entrepreneurs, 9, 23, 30–32, 59, 63, 72; Chinese, 150; immigrant, 17–19, 87; local, 32, 67, 82–83, 86–87, 193, 195; Thai, 32, 195; transnational, 15, 71
entrepreneurs, Korean, 7, 32, 36, 67, 139–40, 168, 181, 197, 219n136, 228n47; authenticity and, 181; Korean government and, 35, 75–89, 97–99; Koreatown and, 31, 35, 72, 95, 97, 173; signboards and, 139–40
Eren (interviewee), 114–16
Eric (interviewee), 129–30

Estonia, 9–10
ethnic businesses, 21, 25, 87, 229n3
ethnic communities, 8, 17, 21, 141, 143–44, 172, 176
ethnic consumption, 105, 178
ethnic enclaves, 4, 6–8, 15–31, 115, 133, 141, 149, 192–96, 217nn77–78; ghettos and, 15–17, 217n62; tourism and, 23–24
ethnic identity, 4, 22, 24, 32, 106, 109–10, 115, 117, 177–78, 187
ethnic Koreans, 2, 20, 33, 83, 99, 105, 110, 144, 169, 172–80, 183, 197–98
ethnic neighborhoods, 19, 21, 25, 31
ethnic pride, 23, 92, 121, 184
ethnoburb, 21, 229n3
ethnoscapes, 26, 159, 196
Euh, Yoon-Dae, 55, 57
Eunhye (interviewee), 173
Eunji (interviewee), 124–25, 128
Europe, 14, 16, 17, 24, 41, 76, 217n62
exoticism, 22, 26, 37, 74, 166–67, 176, 185, 186, 192; experience, 159; Korean food and, 82, 172, 180–83
experience economy, 11, 80–81
export economy, South Korean, 27, 48–49, 52–53, 61–63, 71, 89, 221n11

Fabius, Laurent, 195
Facebook, 76, 147, 153, 155
family-owned business conglomerates (chaebol), 44, 54–60, 191, 221n11, 222n31
Fancy Food Shows, SFA, 12
fandom, K-pop, 149, 152–56, 165, 187
fansign events, K-pop, 155, 234n13
Filipino Americans, 151, 162
film industry, Korean, 41–42, 132
filmmaking, Korean, 41–42
financial crisis (1997), South Korea, 4, 6–7, 35–36, 43–46, 48, 54, 64, 66, 198, 222n27, 227n40
fiscal crisis, New York, 9, 28
Five Senses (restaurant), 80

Flagship Korean restaurant project, 74, 82–83
Flatiron District, Manhattan, 90–91, 93, 181
Flushing, Queens, 96, 105, 123, 129–30, 132, 134, 229n3, 229n71, 232n14
FOB. *See* Fresh off the Boat
food, ethnic, 8, 22, 37, 167–68, 170–71, 175–76, 181–85
food, Korean, 13, 32, 36–37, 67, 69, 89–93, 96, 98, 148, 166–69, 171–72, 184–85, 194–95, 197–99; authenticity and, 14, 79–80, 87, 89–91, 92, 97, 153, 169–70, 173–75, 178–79, 187, 197; commercialization of, 37, 168; exoticism and racialization of, 170–72, 180–83, 187–89; globalization of, 33, 35, 68, 73–80, 83–89, 97–98, 184; K-Dramas and, 53, 158–59; Korean Americans and, 97, 110, 115–16, 131–32, 166–67, 170–71, 175–80; Korean government and, 72–75; Korean nationals and, 136, 172–75; nation branding and, 71–89; popularity of, 2, 37, 53, 77, 80, 82, 95, 136, 180; social media and, 166–67, 180. *See also specific dishes*
food and beverage industry, 12, 33, 35, 68
Food Gallery 32 (food court), Koreatown, 79, *80*, 96, 159
Food Network (cable channel), 73, 181
"Food News" (Claiborne), 166–67
Food & Wine magazine, 180
Forbes magazine, 55, 73
Fordham University, 157, 183
foreign debt, South Korean, 44
Foreign Policy (publication), 73
Foreign Travel Liberalization Act (1989), South Korea, 29
franchises, Korean, 4, 31, 36, 67, 71, 79, 96, 105, 125, 138, 157, 164, 174–75, 192
Fresh off the Boat (FOB) (derogatory term), 122, 143, 144

Friday Friday Night (Korean TV show), 191
fusion cuisine, 89, 181

G20 Seoul Summit (2010), 56–57
Gammeeok (restaurant), 169, 192
Gangnam, Seoul, 112, 126, 131, 232n8, 232n20
Garment District, Manhattan, 6, 27
gastrodiplomacy, 11
gastronationalism, 87
gateway cities, 15, 18, 20–22
gaze, 74, 185, 189, 198–99
gender, 30, 66, 109, 188–89
gentrification, 123–24, 232n12
ghettos, 15–17, 21, 24, 125, 128, 187, 192, 217n62
Gisaengchung (film). *See* Parasite
global city index, 73
global culture, 10, 137, 183
global economy, 6, 8–11, 15, 186, 193
globalization, 9, 44, 112, 195, 230n26
globalization, of Korean food, 33, 35, 53, 55, 68, 73–80, 83–89, 97–98, 184
global markets, 6–7, 61, 67, 193, 198
"Global Thai" (initiative), 11
gold, 45–46
"Gold Collection" campaign, South Korea, 45–46
GOT7 (Korean boy band), 155
Gourmet magazine, 180
"Goût de France/Good France" (initiative), 11, 194–95
government, 9–12, 14, 30, 193; city, 24, 35; federal, 28
government, French, 11, 194–95
government, Japanese, 10–11
government, South Korean, 2, 4, 6–8, 42, 44–48, 61, 69–71, 96–99, 139–40, 168, 184, 194–95, 198, 221n17, 226n10, 227n40; budgets, 47, 54, 65, 71, 75, 82, 86–87, 94, 98, 139; impeachments in, 60, 64, 66; investments by, 7, 31, 35–36, 48, 52–53, 59, 67, 71–89, 195, 222n27; Korean Americans and, 70–71; Korean corporations and, 6–7, 31–32, 35–36, 58–59, 67, 87; Korean entrepreneurs and, 7, 35–36, 63, 75–89, 97–99; military junta as, 27, 43, 48, 57, 65, 221n11; on Military Service Act, 42–43; national branding by, 4, 32, 47–63, 66, 72–75, 76–77, 194–95, 225nn88–89; 1997 financial crisis and, 4, 6–7, 35–36, 43–45, 48, 54, 64, 66, 198, 222n27, 227n40; public advertisements sponsored by, 32, 45–46. *See also specific agencies; specific initiatives; specific presidents*
government, Thai, 11–12, 32, 194–95
Grace (interviewee), 121
Grace Street Coffee & Desserts, 79–80, *81*
"The Great Jang Geum" (K-Drama), 53
Greenwich Village, Manhattan, 106, 229n2
grocers, Korean, 18, 26, 115, 179
group identity, 124
Group KFF Inc., 85, 96

H1ghr Music (music label), 146
Hailey (interviewee), 154–56, 158–60, 165
Hallyu ("The Korean Wave"), 36, 48, 53, 57–61, 63–64, 72, 74, 80, 147, 149, 164–65, 191–92, 220n115, 222n26, 226n10, 233n5; in Asian America, 149–51; COVID-19 and, 61–64; new media and, 48, 151–54, 164; sense of belonging and, 164–65
Hanbo (chaebol), 44
hanbok (traditional Korean clothing), 53, 63, 160
"Han Brands" initiative, South Korea, 53, 72
Han Geng, 153
Hanjan (restaurant), 77, 90, 227n29
Han Jin Won, 41–42
Hannah (interviewee), 147–48, 233n1
Hannara Party (People Power Party), South Korea, 82

Hansik (Kim Yoon-ok's cook book), 74–75
hansik (Korean food), 53
hanwoo (Korean beef), 86, 158
Harlem, New York City, 1, 152, 171
hate crimes, 109, 230n16
Hell's Kitchen, Manhattan, 89, 93
Herald Square, Manhattan, 1–2, 31, 106
history, collective, 118, 124, 177, 198
hi-touch events, K-pop, 155, 234n13
H Mart, 75, 131, 159, 182, 219n143
Hofer, Johannes, 229n4
homeland, 14–15, 22, 31, 77, 87, 111–12, 122, 124, 134, 142, 144, 196, 198; nostalgia for, 24–25, 117, 119
homelessness, in New York City, 28, 168, 220n144, 220n146
homemaking, 114; nostalgia and, 36, 99, 105
honeycomb candy (dalgona), 69, 79–80
Hong Chun Cheon (restaurant), 96
Hong Kong, 53, 73, 125, 140, 182
Housing and Urban Development, US, 28, 220n146
Hulu, 153
Hum, Tarry, 25
human capital, 18–20, 77
human rights, 29, 50–51, 61, 110
hypercommercialization, 149, 163, 193
hyperconsumerism, 30–31, 232n12
Hyun (interviewee), 139
Hyundai, 51, 54–56, 59

ICC. *See* International Culinary Center
ICT. *See* Information and Communication Technology
identity, 4, 8, 34, 108, 113, 118, 125, 143, 153, 196; crisis, 140–41, 179, 184, 189; ethnic, 22, 24, 109–10, 115, 117, 177–78; national, 7, 9–10, 26, 44, 49, 112, 184, 198; racial, 109–10, 186; spatial, 114, 124; urban, 124, 137, 168, 198

identity politics, 10, 218n99
imagination, 36–37, 93, 114, 119, 149, 160, 163, 165, 170, 175, 186, 196; collective, 159–60, 163–64, 169
IMF. *See* International Monetary Fund
immigrants, 15–19, 21, 25, 82, 108, 111, 119, 149, 166–67, 186, 217n78; Asian, 151; Chinese, 18–19, 24–25, 150; Cuban, 18–19, 217nn77–78; Italian, 22–23; language barriers and, 26, 76, 123
immigrants, Korean, 4, 30, 31–32, 36, 67, 87, 90, 96, 104, 105, 112, 115, 121–124, 130, 134–36, 138, 157, 168, 171, 173–76, 179; family reunification for, 179; Korean food and, 167; Korean nationals compared to, 175; Koreatown and, 26–27, 104, 168, 175–80; middle-class, 21, 26, 108
Immigration and Nationality Act (1965), US, 4, 15, 17, 22, 26
impeachments, in South Korea, 54, 60, 64, 66, 226n103
India, 9, 12, 111
Information and Communication Technology (ICT), 58–59
information technology (IT), South Korean, 7, 44, 47–49, 52–53, 222n27
infrastructure, 29, 47, 48, 52–53, 58, 66, 83, 85, 222n27
Inha (interviewee), 169–70, 172
Insook (interviewee), 28, 78, 86, 98
Instagram, 31, 153, 166–67, 180, 235n1
Institute for Industrial Policy Studies, 50
Institute of International Education, 111
Interbrand, 10
International Bank for Reconstruction and Development, 44
International Culinary Center (ICC), 90
International Monetary Fund (IMF), 6, 43–45, 48, 54
International Organisation for Standardisation (ISO), 69–70

international students (*yuhaksaeng*),
  15, 29, 108, 111, 121–23, 125, 144, 161,
  169–70, 191–92, 230n22, 235n8; Korean
  nationals as, 29, 111, 121–22, 125; Romanization of Korean food vocabulary
  by, 84
interracial relations, 36, 99
intraethnic conflicts, 36, 123
investments, 6–7, 18–20, 23–24, 55, 59, 66,
  82, 95, 192, 194–95; capital, 8–9, 18, 25,
  36; financial, 10, 58, 71; foreign, 14, 43,
  47–49, 51–52, 63, 223n49; Korean government, 7, 31, 35–36, 44, 67, 71–89; in
  Koreatown, 6–7, 67, 71, 96, 138, 194–95
"I ♥ NY" campaign, 9, 29
Isabelle (interviewee), 146, 156–57, 160,
  164, 183, 234n15
ISO. *See* International Organisation for
  Standardisation
IT. *See* information technology
Italian Americans, 22–23, 27
Iwabuchi, Koichi, 234n17

Jacob (interviewee), 128–29
Jacob Javits Center, Manhattan, 12, *12*, *13*
Jada (interviewee), 165
Jaeho (interviewee), 84
Jaesu (interviewee), 78, 83, 98
James Beard Awards, 86
jang (fermented paste), 89, 97; doenjang,
  89, 172; ganjang, 89; gochujang, 89, 159;
  ssamjang, 77
Japan, 9–12, 44, 53, 95–96, 150; Indepen-
  dence from, 47; Japanese Colonial
  Rule (1910–1945), 45, 117, 232n12
Japanese food, 76, 80, 82, 89, 95, 158, 173,
  182
Japanese pop culture, anime, music, 150,
  154, 158, 234n17
Japan-Korea Annexation Treaty (1910),
  43, 221n7
Jay (interviewee), 140–41
Jenny (interviewee), 113–14

Jensen, Leif, 19
jeongtongseong. *See* authenticity
Jeongwoo (interviewee), 73–74, 88,
  94–95
Jessica (interviewee), 1–2, 160, 197
Jewish people, 16–17, 27, 168, 198, 217n62
Jia (interviewee), 121
Jieun (interviewee), 103, 174–75
Jihye (interviewee), 128, 134, 145
Jinah (interviewee), 136–38
Jinsook (restaurant owner), 28
Jinsun (interviewee), 105
jjapaguri (ram-don), 69, 158
John (interviewee), 131, 134–35
JoongAng Ilbo (newspaper), 91
Joo Ok (restaurant), 68
Joseonjok (ethnic Koreans with Chinese
  citizenship), 237n1
jujaewon (employees of Korean Multina-
  tional Corporations), 122–23
Jungsik (restaurant in New York City),
  89–90, 181, 228n51
Jungsikdang (restaurant in Seoul), 91
juryusahoi (mainstream), 226n7
Juyeon (interviewee), 64–66
JYP Entertainment (music label), 146–48,
  160

KAIST. *See* Korea Advanced Institute of
  Science & Technology
Kakao Talk (Korean messenger app), 111
kalguksu (noodle soup), 84, 177
Kang Suh Restaurant, 27, *79*
karaoke bars (noraebang), 2, 4–5, 79, 94,
  108, 192, 237n2
Kaylee (interviewee), 133, 150–51, 233n2
KBS. *See* Korean Broadcasting System
KCAES. *See* Korea Culture and Arts Edu-
  cation Service
KCCNY. *See* Korean Cultural Center New
  York
KCDC. *See* Korea Centers for Disease
  Control and Prevention

INDEX | 277

KCGC USA. *See* Korean Cuisine Globalization Committee USA
K-Dramaland, 159, 234n19
K-Dramas. *See* Korean dramas
Keller, Thomas, 91–92
KFPI. *See* Korean Food Promotion Institution
KIA (chaebol), 44
Kiana (interviewee), 146
Kim, Brian Sehong, 90, 181
Kim, Chun-jin, 70
Kim, Hooni, 77–78, 85–86, 88, 90, 92–93, 97–98, 181, 227n29
Kim, Hyo-Jae, 139–40
Kim, Ron, 69–70
Kim, Sam, 1, 191
Kim, Simon, 90–92, 94–96, 98
Kim, Young-Mok, 138–40
kimbap (rice roll wrapped with dried seaweed), 80, 166–67, 176
kimchi, 69–70, 88, 157, 170–73, 176, 182
Kimchi Chronicles (documentary series), 75
Kimchi Day, 69–70, 88, 226n3, 226n5
Kim Dae-jung, 41, 43–44, 46–50, 53–54, 58, 64, 221n9, 222n27, 223n39, 223n42
Kimjang (online series), KCCNY, 88
Kim Jung-sook, 62–63
Kim Yoon-ok, 74–75
King Sejong Institute Foundation, 94
Koch, Ed, 28–29
Korea Advanced Institute of Science & Technology (KAIST), 50
Koreaboos, 188–89, 237n45
Korea Brand Index, 56
Korea Centers for Disease Control and Prevention (KCDC), South Korea, 225n88
Korea Creative Content Agency, 65, 94
Korea Culture and Arts Education Service (KCAES), MCST, 64–65
Korea Daily (newspaper), 72, 90
"Korea Discount," 48–49, 55, 222n31
Korea Foundation, 84

"Korea Inc." initiative, South Korea, 54
Korea-Japan World Cup (2002), 47–49
Korean (language), 33–34, 84–85, 94, 117–18, 164–65, 187, 228n44, 231n41, 233n2; church services in, 109–10, 123; K-dramas and, 150–53, 158; Korean Americans and, 140–44; Romanization of, 83–84
Korean Americans, 1–2, 30–34, 69, 82, 146, 150–51, 163, 165, 168, 172, 196–98, 231n41, 235n13; belonging and, 140–43, 165; chefs, 90–96, 181; collective memories and, 99, 113, 119–20; Korean food and, 115–16, 166–67, 170–71, 175–80, 183–87; Korean government and, 70–71; Korean language and, 140–44; in Korean language courses, 33–34, 143–44; Korean nationals and, 36, 118–19, 122, 144, 179–80; Koreatown and, 108–10, 113–19, 128–33, 135–36, 175–80; nostalgia and, 117–20; 1.5-generation, 91, 118–19, 131, 134; racism faced by, 108–9; second-generation, 30, 103–4, 107–10, 113–17, 121, 125, 129, 131, 140–43, 170, 176, 184
Korea National Tourism Organization, 47, 84
Korean autumn harvest (Chuseok), 68–69
Korean barbecue, 91–92, 173, 183
Korean Brand Conference (2002), 50
Korean Broadcasting System (KBS), 45–46, 224n71
Korean Business District, Manhattan, 4, 27, 104, 192
Korean Chinese people (Joseonjok), 233n2, 237n1
Korean communities, 69–71, 109–10, 121–23, 134–36, 144
Korean community, 67, 108, 109, 118, 122, 134, 140, 180, 189, 197
Korean Cuisine Globalization Committee USA (KCGC USA), South Korea, 35, 68–69, 74, 76–77, 86, 96–98, 227n20

278 | INDEX

Korean Cultural Center New York (KCCNY), 33, 35, 72–73, 76–77, 88, 94–95, 266n10
Korean dramas (K-Dramas), 2, 53, 111, 129, 146, 150–54, 157–61
Korean Food Culture Education Program, 88
Korean Food Foundation (KFF), 34, 66. *See also* Korean Food Promotion Institution
Korean Food Promotion Institution (KFPI), South Korea, 66, 73–78, 83–87, 184, 227n17, 228n47
Korean fried chicken, 68, 79, 172, *174*, 175, 192
Korean Harvest and Folklore Festival, Queens, 147
Korean media, 31, 69, 77, 89, 91–92, 111, 122
Koreanness, 59, 91, 114, 163–64, 219n143
Korean Popular Culture and Arts Awards, 63
Korean War (1950–1953), 26, 43, 45, 167, 225n89
"The Korean Wave." *See Hallyu*
Korea Society, New York, 75, 85–86, 90–95
Korea Tourism Organization, 53–54, 84, 94, 223n57, 228n40
Korea Tourism Research Institute, 47
Koreatown (Rodbard), 90
Koreatown, Flushing, Queens, 21, 105, 123, 129–30, 134, 229n3, 229n71
Koreatown, Los Angeles, 20, 97, 129, 167–68, 181
Koreatown, Vancouver, 132
Koreatown (K-Town), Manhattan, 3, 5, 80, *81*, 156, *159*, 162–63, 165, 191, 229n3; authenticity and, 8, 125, 145, 168–80, 196–99; belonging and, 110, 112, 113–17, 119–20, 143–45, 164–65; collective memories and, 105, 106–10, 112, 119, 126; as a commercial district, 6, 31; consumers, 4, 8, 15, 29, 30–31, 78–82, 89, 104–5, 129, 136, 142–43, 145, 148, 168–69, 171, 186–87; consumption and, 6–8, 19, 22, 25, 29–31, 71, 81, 113, 115, 179, 193–94; as an ethnic enclave, 4, 6–8, 26–30; ethnic Koreans on, 105; fantasy and, 117–19, 145, 149, 156–61, 165, 197; fetishism of, 37, 185–89; Food Gallery 32, *80*, 96, *159*; franchises, 4, 31, 36, 71, 79, 96, 105, 125, 138, 157, 164, 174–75, 192; generational divide in, 104; globalization of Korean food project and, 35, 68, 77–80, 83–89, 97–98, 184; Hallyu and, 36, 66, 72, 79–81, 146–49, 156, 165; interracial relations and, 36; intraethnic conflicts in, 36, 123; investments in, 6–7, 67, 71, 96, 138, 194–95; Korean Americans and, 108–10, 113–19, 128–33, 135–36, 175–80; Korean immigrants and, 26–27, 90, 104, 134–35, 144–45, 157, 168, 175–80, 197; Korean nationals and, 29, 33–34, 36–37, 93, 105, 112, 124–26, 128, 130–31, 133–39, 144, 172–75, 179; K-Town-adjacency, 89–96; landscape of, 6; memories of, 103–5; nation branding and, 71–75, 78; new clients in, 180–87; non-Koreans and, 1–2, 37, 69, 83, 104, 112, 137, 139–40, 148–49, 157–65, 171, 180–87; nostalgia and, 106–10, 112, 117–20; quasi-authenticity and, 161, 164; Seoul compared to, 1–2, 6–7, 31, 33, 125–26, 128, 131–32, 135–36, 139, 162–63, 169–70, 178–79; signboards in, *126*, *127*, 128, 138–40; symbolic ownership in, 114–16, 137–43; territorial expansion and, 96–99; in a time lag, 124–28, 134–37; tourism and, 1–2, 105, 149, 168, 192–93; as a transclave, 4, 6–7, 26, 30–35, 67, 71–89, 95, 112, 149, 156, 193–94, 198; zoning and, 6, 31. *See also* businesses, Koreatown; restaurants, Koreatown
Koreatown Association, New York City, 68
Korea University, 55
Koryo Bookstore, 27–28, 142, 149, 192

Koryodang (bakery chain), 96
Koryo Video (rental shop), 192
K-pop, 1–2, 7, 35, 42, 59, 60, 63–64, 65–66, 79, 80, 91, 136, 145, 152–54, 155–56, 160, 180, 194, 222n26, 232n8; fandom, 1, 41, 146–49, 152, 153–156, 165, 187, 233n5; stans, 153, 154, 165, 234n11, 234n13. *See also specific musicians*
Krase, Jerome, 24, 193
K-Town. *See* Koreatown, Manhattan
Ku, Tae Kyung, 90–91, 181
Kwak, Jenny, 95
Kwon, Joong-Gap, 28, 219n143
Kyujin (interviewee), 135, 186

Labour Party, United Kingdom, 10
Laguerre, Michel S., 25
language barriers, 26, 76, 123. *See also* Korean
Latinx people, 20, 25, 152, 165, 187–88, 197; as non-coethnic laborers, 30, 187
Laura (interviewee), 110, 170–72, 175–76, 178–79, 235n9
Lee, Seo-jin, 191–92
Lee Chang-Dong, 52
Lee Jae-myung, 226n103
Lee Myung-bak, 43, 54–57, 60, 65–66, 68, 71, 73–74, 83–84, 86–89, 97–98, 128, 224n63, 232n11, 233n31; globalization efforts of, 78; political scandals under, 61, 64, 86, 98
Levitt, Peggy, 134, 175
LGBTQ community, 155
Li, Wei, 21
liberalization, market, 29, 44–45
"Life Goes On" (song), 41–42
Lim Chang-Yuel, 43
Lin, Jan, 193
Little Banchan Shop (restaurant), 77, 90, 227n29
Little Big Hero (Korean TV show), 88, 97
Little Havana, Miami, 20–21
Little India, Queens, 7, 21

Little Italy, Manhattan, 7, 22–24, 32, 192
LMDC. *See* Lower Manhattan Development Corporation
Logan, John R., 17, 20
London, England, 10, 24, 26, 54, 73, 207
Long Island, New York, 21, 91, 123, 173, 229n3
Long Island City, Queens, 90, 123, 227n29
Los Angeles, California, 15, 18, 20–21, 73, 97, 116, 128–29, 151, 153–54, 162, 167, 181, 219n136, 225n102
"Love Korea" TV campaign, South Korea, 57
Lower Manhattan Development Corporation (LMDC), 23
Lucia (interviewee), 152, 155

Madison (interviewee), 2, 155
MAFRA. *See* Ministry of Agriculture, Food and Rural Affairs
mainstream, US (American mainstream), 71–72, 81, 96, 108, 109, 117, 119, 135, 144–145, 149, 152–154, 156, 167, 176–77, 181, 184–85, 192, 196, 226n7, 235n9; corporations and, 22; food and, 68; industries, streaming services, and platforms, 150, 152–53; markets, marketplace, 22; media, 2, 14, 73, 76, 180
mainstream media, 2, 14, 73, 76, 180
Malaysia, 44, 149–50
marginalization, 28, 109, 113–17, 185–86, 198
marketing, 6, 8–11, 14, 22, 51, 53–54, 56, 58, 74, 81, 87, 157, 179, 185, 194, 218n103, 224n64
marketization, 54, 81
Maryland, 108, 110, 116, 154, 171
"mask diplomacy," COVID-19, 61, 225n89
Matt (interviewee), 116–17
MBC every1 (Korean TV network), 88
McGray, Douglas, 10–11
MCST. *See* Ministry of Culture, Sports, and Tourism

medieval Europe, 16, 217n62
Mei (interviewee), 133
Meju (restaurant), 77, 90, 227n29, 228n51
memories, 65–66, 103–5, 122–23, 131, 137, 157, 163, 167, 171–72, 191, 230n5; childhood, 91–92, 126, 130, 167, 178–80; collective, 15, 36, 99, 103, 105–10, 112–13, 119, 123–24, 126, 145, 196; ethnic culture, 177; ethnic food, 177; home, 120, 177; homeland, 117; Korea, 135, 163; nostalgia and, 57–58, 91–92, 105–10, 116, 123, 164, 170; of Seoul, 125–26, 135, 170
Metropolitan Museum of Art, New York, 62–63
Mexican Americans, 147, 187
Miami, Florida, 18–20, 154, 217nn77–78
Michelin star Korean restaurants, 68, 75, 77, 89, 91–93, 95, 227n29, 228n51
Mi Cin (restaurant), 27, 166–67
microaggressions, 109, 113, 117, 119–20, 171, 210, 235n9
middle-class, 21, 26, 108, 111, 180
Midtown Manhattan, 2, 27–28, 68, 74, 94, 106, 157–58, 209
Mihee (interviewee), 125–26, 130
Mila (interviewee), 152–53, 157–58, 182–83
military duty, Korean, 42–43, 221n5
Ministry for Europe and Foreign Affairs, France, 11, 195
Ministry for Food, Agriculture, Forestry and Fisheries (MFAFF). *See* Ministry of Agriculture, Food and Rural Affairs
Ministry of Agriculture, Food and Rural Affairs (MAFRA), South Korea, 74, 76–78, 82, 84–85, 227n17
Ministry of Commerce, Industry, and Energy, South Korea, 49–50, 223n57
Ministry of Commerce, Thailand, 11
Ministry of Culture, Sports, and Tourism (MCST), South Korea, 42, 47, 49, 50, 52–53, 59–61, 64, 222n24, 223n57, 226n10; KCAES, 64–65

Ministry of Foreign Affairs, Italy, 14
Ministry of Foreign Affairs, South Korea, 49, 84
Ministry of Foreign Affairs and International Development, France, 194–95
Ministry of Information and Communication, South Korea, 52
Ministry of Science, ICT and Future Planning, South Korea, 58
Ministry of SMEs and Startups (MSS), South Korea, 63–64
Minjae (interviewee), 68–71, 78–79, 98
Minji (interviewee), 136–37, 232n20
Miss Korea BBQ (restaurant), 173
modern ghettos, 16, 217n62
modernization, 65, 85, 138, 229n4
Moon Jae-in, 42–43, 60–64, 225n88, 225n102
More Vision (music label), 146
Morning Glory (stationery store), 158
movies, Korean, 2, 7–8, 41–42, 59, 61, 63, 150–51, 184, 226n10
MSS. *See* Ministry of SMEs and Startups
multiculturalism, 8, 22, 24, 37, 52, 57, 73–74, 161, 185
Myeong-dong, Seoul, 126
Myspace, 146

Na, Young-seok, 191–92
Nahee (interviewee), 174
Nam-gung, Jin, 49
National Assembly of the Republic of Korea, 42–43, 50, 60, 82, 138–39, 226n103, 233n29
National Commission for Rebuilding Korea, South Korea, 47
national identity, 7, 9–10, 26, 44, 49, 112, 184, 198
National Intelligence Service, South Korea, 60
nationalism, 11, 45–47, 78, 87, 99; gastro-, 87
national pride, 41–42, 49, 184

INDEX | 281

National Restaurant Association, 168
nationals, Korean, 1–2, 64, 67, 78, 93, 111, 121–23, 135, 164, 186, 196–98; collective memories and, 99, 106–8, 111–12, 119, 123–28; as consumers, 8, 29, 31, 99, 105, 112, 128, 136, 138, 141, 169; Korean Americans and, 36, 118–19, 122, 144, 179–80; Koreatown and, 29, 33–34, 36–37, 93, 105, 112, 124–26, 128, 130–31, 133–39, 144, 172–75, 179–80
nation branding, 4, 6, 32, 44, 46, 50, 54–60, 67, 71–75, 95, 194–195; bottom-up, 7, 14–15, 36, 43, 48–49, 67, 76, 81, 99, 105, 193, 198; food in, 33, 35, 53, 55, 68, 73–80, 83–89, 97–98, 184; Koreatown and, 71–75, 78; policies, 7, 9–10, 14, 48–57, 60–64, 71, 138–40; popular culture, hallyu, and, 7, 10, 11, 47–48, 52–52, 57–60, 61–64, 72, 74, 225n102, 226n10; in the postindustrial world, 8–12, 14–15; public-private partnerships and, 9, 14, 58, 64, 66, 75–89, 195, 225n102; top-down, 7, 35–36, 43, 59, 64–67, 99, 193
Nation Branding Index, 55
nationhood, 10–11, 15, 78, 99, 124, 145
nation-states, 8–9, 11, 35–36, 48, 123
Nee, Victor, 18–20, 217n79
neocolonialism, 186–89
neoliberalism, 22, 43–55, 66–67, 186, 198, 223n40
Netflix, 111, 152–53
New Jersey, 21, 89, 123, 143
New Korean Cuisine, 89–93
new media, 32, 48, 64, 149, 151–54
News Day (newspaper), 73
new transnational generation, 107, 125
Newtro (new retro) culture, 130, 232n12
New Wonjo (restaurant), 173
New York, New York (segment), *Friday Friday Night* (TV show), 191
New York City, New York, 18, 22, 66, 68, 166–67; aT Center New York, 33, 35, 69, 71–72, 86–89; BTS in, 62–63; COV-
ID-19 pandemic in, 69, 79–80, 226n1; Hallyu in, 36, 66, 74, 79–81, 149–50, 155–56, 165, 191; KCCNY, 33, 35, 72–73, 76–77, 88, 94–95, 266n10; Korean government investing in, 6–7, 31, 36, 67, 71, 72–89; Korea Society, 75, 85–86, 90–95; K-pop fandom in, 66, 146–49, 151, 153, 156, 161, 165, 187; non-Asian New Yorkers in, 1–2, 33–34, 76–77, 82, 136, 149, 152–56, 185–87; tourism, 29, 31–32; welfare hotels, 28, 104, 168, 179, 198, 220n144. *See also* Koreatown; *specific departments*; *specific neighborhoods*
New York Gomtang House, 27–28, 219n143
New York King (nightclub), 192
New York Korea Center, 94
New York Times, 2, 27, 73, 77, 93, 167, 180, 220n144
New York Tourism Company, 23
New York University (NYU), 84, 110, 114, 116, 132, 151, 162, 176–77, 184–85, 191, 196; international students at, 103, 106, 108, 123, 125, 136, 191
Nick (interviewee), 184
Nicole (interviewee), 142–43
Nitz, Michael, 230n16
Nixon, Richard, 28
non-Asian New Yorkers, 1–2, 33–34, 76–77, 82, 136, 149, 152–56, 185–87
non-coethnic consumers, 7, 15, 30, 67, 112, 193
non-Korean consumers, 7, 8, 28, 30–31, 32–34, 36–37, 66, 75, 77, 78–79, 82, 85, 87, 90, 94, 104, 121, 123, 135–37, 139–40, 143, 145, 149, 152–161, 163–65, 169, 171, 172, 173, 175, 178, 183, 185–88, 196–198
Nora (interviewee), 151, 162–63
Nora, Pierre, 230n5
noraebang (karaoke bars), 2, 4–5, 79, 94, 108, 192, 237n2
No Reservations (TV show), 167–68
North Carolina, 114–15, 131–32, 136

North Korea, 47, 51, 110
nostalgia, 15, 92, 111–116, 229n4; ethnic food and, 175, 177; home and, 116, 196; homelands and, 24–25, 117, 119; homemaking and, 36, 99, 105; Koreatown and, 106–10, 112, 117–20; memories and, 57–58, 91–92, 105–10, 116, 123, 164, 170; Seoul and, 107, 111–12, 170
"NYC's K-Town Isn't What It Used to Be" (Kim, Sam), 191

Oasis (film), 52
OECD. *See* Organisation for Economic Co-operation and Development
Office of Public Information, South Korea, 46
Ohio, 158
Olympics (1988), Seoul, 29
Olympics (2018), PyeongChang, 56, 60
omnivore, 8, 37, 77, 82, 90, 180, 186–89
1.5-generation Korean Americans, 91, 118–19, 131, 134
online communities, 36–37, 84, 104, 122, 146–49, 155, 165
Open Streets program, New York City, 69, 226n1
Organisation for Economic Co-operation and Development (OECD), 43–44
Orientalism, 185
ossification effects, 134–37, 175
Otherness, the Other, othered and, 140, 160, 176, 186, 197–99
ownership, 120, 135–36, 183–84; symbolic, 114–16, 124, 137–43

Pablo (interviewee), 187–89
Pak Se-ri, 46
Parasite (film), 2, 41, 59–60, 69, 158
Paris Baguette (Korean bakery), 125, 157, 164, 174
Park, Ellia, 93–95
Park, James, 68
Park, Jay (Jae-beom Park), 146–47, 165

Park, Junghyun, 90–91, 93, 181
Park, Robert E., 16, 216n59
Park, Yongsu, 223n49
Park Chan-wook, 60
Park Chung-hee, 57, 65–68, 221n11
Park Geun-hye, 43, 57–60, 64–65
participant observation, 4, 32–35, 89
Parts Unknown (documentary series), 166–68
PCNB. *See* Presidential Council for Nation Branding
Pennsylvania, 116, 131, 156–57, 160, 183, 234n15
people of color, 1–2, 113, 149, 155–56, 187, 197
Poetry (film), 52
political scandals, South Korean, 44, 60–61, 64, 66–67, 68, 86, 98
popular culture, pop culture, 10–11, 22, 234n17
popular culture, pop culture, Korean, 1–2, 7, 32, 48, 53, 67, 71–72, 76, 79–90, 149–52, 158, 161, 164, 178, 182, 187, 197, 220n115, 222n26; during COVID-19, 61–63; Korean food and, 32, 79–80, 135–36, 145, 158, 175, 178, 188; Koreatown and, 148–49; non-Koreans and, 164
Portes, Alejandro, 18–21, 217nn77–78
postindustrial cities, 23, 29
prejudice, racial, 141, 192
Presidential Council for Nation Branding (PCNB), South Korea, 55–57, 66
pride: ethnic, 23, 92, 121, 184; national, 41–42, 49, 184
privatization, market, 44, 50, 52
public diplomacy, 10, 95
public-private partnerships, 9, 14, 23, 58, 63–64, 66, 87, 195, 225n102
Pyeongchang Winter Olympics (2018), 56, 60

racial fetishization, 24, 37, 185, 188–89
racial identity, 109–10, 186
racial issues, 165, 185–86, 197, 210

INDEX | 283

racialization, 113, 117, 119–20, 176, 210, 219n136, 235n9
racial minorities, 15–17, 26, 67, 82, 119–20, 177, 187, 198, 218n103; Koreans Americans as, 110, 113–18, 180
racism, 108–9, 113, 116, 169, 197–98
Radisson Martinique Hotel, Manhattan, 28–29, 168, 220n144
Ram (interviewee), 133
ramyun, 160, 234n23
Reagan, Ronald, 28
Red Apple Boycotts, Brooklyn, 18
religion, 109–10, 123, 156, 165, 177, 218n103
"Restaurant Menu Romanization Guidebook," Korean Tourism Organization, 84
restaurants, Korean, 27, 30–31, 71, 74, 76–77, 80, 84, 87, 89, 91, 97, 103–4, 117, 129–30, 138–39, 141, 143–44, 167, 169, 170, 173, 181, 228n44, 229n71; Arirang House, 27; Michelin star, 68, 75, 77, 89, 91–93, 95, 227n29, 228n51
restaurants, Koreatown, 2, 4, 6–7, 27–28, 30–31, 66, 69, 73, 78–80, 81, 90, 103–5, 116, 125, 129–30, 132–33, 138–39, 141, 143–44, 148, 159, 179, 185–86, 219n143, 226n1, 227n29; Arirang, House, 27, 177; bb.q Chicken, 79, 174, 192; Don's Bogam, 72–73, 96; Food Gallery 32, 79, 80, 96, 159; Gammeeok, 162, 169, 192; Kang Suh, 27; Korean language and, 141–44; Korean nationals on, 138, 169–70, 173–75; memories of, 105, 131–32; New York Gomtang House, 27–28, 219n143; Woorijip, 131–32, 232n13
restaurants, Thai, 11, 89, 194
reterritorialization, 112, 198
revenue, 6, 9, 11, 23, 47, 63, 195; food industry, 11–12, 43; video game, 52–53
Rhee, Eric, 75
Rhythm of the Five Color Luster, 63
Rodbard, Matt, 90
Rodney King incident (1992), Los Angeles, 18

Roh Moo-hyun, 43, 49–54, 58, 61, 64, 72, 223nn39–40, 224n63
Romanization, 83–84, 227n40

Sacramento, California, 25
Saemaul Movement (New Community Movement or New Village Movement), 65
sales diplomacy, 51, 225n102
Sambok (restaurant), 27
Samsung, 51, 52, 55–57, 59–60, 75, 223n49
Sanders, Jimy, 18–20, 217n79
San Francisco, California, 19–20, 25
Sangjin (interviewee), 104–5, 136
Sara (interviewee), 116, 185–86, 189
Schulze, Marion, 234n19
Second-generation Korean Americans, 30, 33, 90, 103, 107–8, 110, 113–17, 121, 125, 129, 131, 134, 140, 142–143, 170, 172, 176, 184; as consumers, 30
segregation, 15–16, 22, 192
self-employment, of immigrants, 17, 19–20, 26
self-identification, 8, 22
Seoul, South Korea, 1, 6, 29, 54, 59, 62–65, 73, 77, 91–92, 96, 121, 131–32, 138–40, 143, 147, 156, 162–64, 170, 173, 177–79, 196, 232n11, 232n12, 232n20, 233n31, 234n15; G20 Seoul Summit, 56–57; Gangnam, 112, 126, 131, 232n8., 232n20; Korean Food Foundation, 34, 73, 227n17; Korean Food Promotion Institution, 66, 73–78, 83–87, 184, 227n17, 228n47; Koreatown compared to, 6–7, 33, 125, 131–32, 162–63, 178; Koreatown entrepreneurs visiting, 31, 77–78, 96–97, 173; memories of, 92, 113, 125–26, 134–35; Metropolitan Government, 35, 51, 125, 128; non-Koreans in, 156–57, 161–64; nostalgia for, 107, 111–12, 170; outdated version of, 128, 136; participant observation in, 32–33; qualitative research in, 32–35, 73, 75, 83, 91–92; -style, 2, 31

Seoul House (restaurant), 27
September 11th Fund, 23
Seunghee (interviewee), 64–65
sexual minorities, 82, 187
SFA. *See* Specialty Food Association
shame, 136, 175
Shaw, Stephen J., 25–26
Shin, Chang-ho, 68
Shin, Jang-Sup, 45
signboards, 138–40, 233n31; in Koreatown, 72, *126, 127*, 128, 138–40
Sklair, Leslie, 14
social gatherings (dwipuri), 118–19
social integration, 44–45, 50, 57
social media, 2, 31, 42, 62, 146, 152–53, 154, 233n5, 234n11, 235n1; Korean food and, 166–67, 180
sociology, 15, 19–21, 30, 193–95
soft power, 4, 6, 10, 50
Sophie (interviewee), 146, 156–57, 160, 183, 234n15
Sorkin, Michael, 161, 191
Sorman, Guy, 50, 55
South Korea, 4, 6–7, 9, 11–12, 26–27, 29, 31, 35–36, 41–67, 69–72, 76–78, 80, 83, 85–88, 91–92, 96–98, 103, 107–8, 110–12, 118, 121–25, 128–30, 134, 138–40, 142, 146–48, 157, 162–64, 173–175, 178–79, 186, 191–92, 196, 219n143, 220n154, 221n5, 221n9, 221n17, 223n51, 227n40, 235n13; biotechnology and, 49–50, 52, 223n42; *Cheongwadae*, 42, 51, 65, 226n103; citizenship and, 124, 136–37; COVID-19 and, 41–42, 61–64, 66, 225nn88–89, 234n13; democratization of, 29, 43–44, 47, 57, 118, 224n39; economic growth and, 50, 54, 57–58, 122, 126, 221n11, 223n39, 224n62; export economy of, 27, 48–49, 52–53, 61–63, 71, 89, 221n11; foreign investment and, 14, 43, 47–49, 51–52, 63, 223n49; heavy industry in, 29, 221n11; ICT, 58–59; IT industry and, 7, 44, 52–53, 222n27; 223n42; "Korea Discount" and, 48–49, 55, 222n31; movies from, 2, 7, 41–42, 48, 59, 61, 63, 150–51, 184, 226n10; neoliberalism and, 22, 43–55, 66–67, 186, 198, 223n40; 1997 financial crisis, 4, 6–7, 35–36, 43–46, 48, 54, 64, 66, 198, 222n27, 227n40; non-Koreans in, 161–64; positive images of, 10, 14, 32, 46, 55, 66, 71, 194, 225n88; public-private partnerships and, 9, 14, 23, 58, 63–64, 66, 87, 195, 225n102; sales diplomacy, 51, 225n102; tourism and, 47, 49, 52–54, 63, 163, 227n40. *See also* culture, Korean; government, South Korean; nation branding; popular culture, Korean; Seoul, South Korea; *specific presidents*
spatial assimilation, 16–17
spatial identity, 114, 124
Specialty Food Association (SFA), 12, *12, 13*, 14, 216n47
Squid Game (series), 2, 69, 79–80, *80*, 152
standardization, 24, 83–85, 92, 128, 138–40, 174–75, 227n40
Statista Market Insights, 11–12
stereotypes, 9, 93, 123–24, 188, 234n17, 235n9
suburbs, 17, 21–23, 129–31, 170, 229n3, 235n9
Summer Fancy Food Shows, SFA, 12, *12, 13*, 14
Sunmee (interviewee), 103–4, 115, 142–43, 178–79
Sunset Park, Brooklyn, 25
Super Junior (K-pop boy band), 153
sweatshop conditions, immigrants facing, 18, 25
Sydney, Australia, 24, 32, 195
symbolic ownership, 114–16, 137–43

Taiwanese Americans, 133
Tasha (interviewee), 171–72
Taste of Korea initiative, 72–73, 78, *79*

Taylor (interviewee), 147–49, 160–61, 165, 182–83, 197, 233n1
Texas, 140
Thai Select program, 11, 194
"32nd Street" (talk), Korea Society, 90–95
Thrillist (website), 1
Tiffany (interviewee), 106–8, 111–12, 125
Tim (interviewee), 129, 132–33, 144
Tokyo, Japan, 54, 73–74, 226n10
The Tonight Show with Jimmy Fallon (TV show), 63
top-down nation branding, 7, 35, 43, 64–67, 99, 193
Totally New Korea initiative, 48
tourism, 4, 7, 8–9, 11, 14, 21–24, 26, 28–29, 105, 192–95; ethnic, 26, 32; New York City, 29, 31–32; in South Korea, 47, 49, 53–54, 63, 163, 227n40
Tourism Development Plan (2002–2011), South Korea, 47
Tourism Vision 21 (1999–2003), South Korea, 47
tourist destinations, 9, 36, 193
Tous Les Jours (Korean bakery chain), 96, 192
Trader Joe's, 167
transclaves, 4, 15, 20–25, 27–29, 36, 99, 144–45, 192–94, 198; Koreatown as a, 6–7, 26, 30–32, 67, 71–89, 95, 149; qualitative research in, 32–35; sense of place in, 112
transnational, 2, 4, 8, 24–25, 27, 29, 37, 71, 81, 87, 91, 107, 113, 119, 125, 149, 164, 195; business, 79; capitalist class, 14; connections, 179; consumption, 76; corporations, 9, 30, 99, 193; culture, 8, 112; enclaves, 30, 192–95; entrepreneurs, 15, 36, 71; factors, 180; flows, 192–93, 198; identities, 113; investments, 55, 72, 125, 194; Koreans, 112; lens, 125; migrants, 14, 76, 112, 144; promotional class, 14; space, 33; ties, 69, 91, 92, 150, 196

transnationalism, 14, 30–31, 71, 92, 107, 111–12, 125, 169, 198–99
transnationality, 31, 111, 120
Tribeca, Manhattan, 89–91, 93, 181, 226n10
Tsai, Ming, 181
tvN (Korean TV network), 88, 97, 191
2PM (Korean boy band), 146–47, 165
Tyler (interviewee), 149–50, 164

UN. *See* United Nations
UNESCO. *See* United Nations Educational, Scientific and Cultural Organization
United Kingdom, 10, 44
United Nations (UN), 61–62, 72–74
United Nations Educational, Scientific and Cultural Organization (UNESCO), 14, 65, 88, 195
United States (US), 4, 8, 14, 17, 21, 22, 26, 28, 30, 35–36, 44, 51, 67, 70, 76, 87–89, 91–92, 97–98, 103, 106–7, 111–14, 117–18, 122, 124–25, 129, 131, 134, 138, 140, 145, 149, 151–53, 155–56, 161, 167–68, 172–74, 177, 179–80, 186, 192, 196, 198, 225n89; citizenship, 107; culinary scene, 82, 91–92, 161, 180, 228n51; culinary schools, 90; mainstream, 71–72, 81, 96, 108–9, 135, 144–45, 150, 153–54, 176–77, 184; racial hierarchy, 114, 177, 185; Roh visiting, 51. *See also specific cities, states*
University of Chicago, 15–20
upper-class, 46
upper-middle class, 46, 126, 203n23, 232n20
upward mobility, 21, 27, 186
urban identity, 124, 137, 168, 198
urban imaginary, 114, 119
urban planning, 23, 28
urban policies, 4, 23, 128, 140
urban studies, 15, 20–21, 193
US. *See* United States

vaccines, COVID-19, 62
Variations on a Theme Park (Sorkin), 191
video games, 7, 52–53
Vietnam, 53, 89, 183, 209
Visa Waiver Program, US, 111
Visit Korea Year 2001, 47
Vongerichten, Jean-Georges, 75, 91–92
Vongerichten, Marja, 75

wages, 18, 25, 28–29
welfare hotels, Manhattan, 28, 104, 168, 179, 198, 220n144
Wells, Pete, 93
whiteness, 114, 165
wholesalers, Korean, 4, 18, 26–27, 30, 95, 104, 157
Wilson, Kenneth L., 217nn77–78
Wine Spectator (magazine), 73
Wirth, Louis, 16, 217n62

Woo, Jinyoung, 72
Woorijip (restaurant), 131–32, 232n13
working-class, 25, 111, 144, 148
World War II, 180

Yang, Il-sun, 77
Yeojin (interviewee), 125
Yeongji (interviewee), 88–89
Yeun (interviewee), 121
Yim, Jungsik, 89–91, 181
Yoojin (interviewee), 135, 137, 183
Yoon Suk Yeol, 226n103
Younghee (interviewee), 117–19, 231n41
YouTube, 31, 111, 152–53, 158, 234n15
yuhaksaeng. *See* international students

Zhang, Wenquan, 17, 20
zoning, Koreatown, 6, 31
Zoppas, Matteo, 14

ABOUT THE AUTHOR

JINWON KIM is Assistant Professor of Sociology at Smith College, where she researches and teaches urban sociology, Asian American communities, race and ethnicity, immigration, transnationalism, and consumerism. Born and raised in Seoul, South Korea, she studied and taught sociology in New York City before moving to Northampton, MA. She is now acclimating to a quiet small-town lifestyle in the Pioneer Valley. She earned her PhD and MPhil in sociology from the Graduate Center, City University of New York, in New York and her MA in sociology from Seoul National University and BA in urban sociology from the University of Seoul, both in South Korea.

www.ingramcontent.com/pod-product-compliance
Lightning Source LLC
Chambersburg PA
CBHW020452300426

44174CB00032B/323